Low Level Aggression

D1633922

First steps

on the ladder to violence

Arnold P. Goldstein

Research Press
2612 North Mattis Avenue Champaign, Illinois 61822
www.researchpress.com

Copies of this book may be ordered from the publisher at the
address given on the title page.

Cover design by Linda Brown, Positive I.D. Graphic Design, Inc.
Composition by Jeff Helgesen
Printed by McNaughton & Gunn, Inc.

ISBN 0-87822-423-8

Library of Congress Catalog Number 99-73652

With warm appreciation to . . .

Ann Wendel
Russ Pence
Karen Steiner
Gail Salyards
Dennis Wiziecki
Suzanne Wagner
Sherry Lord

. . . special friends and skilled collaborators in taking the word from idea to page.

Contents

Figures & Tables

FIGURES

TABLES

CHAPTER ONE

Introduction

Aggression is primarily learned behavior. It is taught at home, at school, on the street, in the mass media, and elsewhere. It is learned via processes no different from the learning of any other behaviors, positive or negative. By trial and error, one attempts alternative means for dealing with a situation, and hurting others proves to be the alternative that "works." Or, in contrast to such direct learning, one sees others, especially others one respects, using aggression successfully, and by means of vicarious or imitative learning, one's own competence in how and when to aggress is enhanced. Because of differences in hormonal structure or temperament, people are not equally predisposed to learn and employ aggressive behaviors. It nonetheless seems well established that, indeed, it is learning that largely accounts for the acquisition of aggressive means of responding to one's world. Psychologists, however, typically distinguish between learning a behavior (i.e., acquisition) and actually carrying it out (i.e., performance). Once one knows how to share, confront, cooperate, ignore, or aggress, the choice to do so is largely a matter of past rewards or punishments for such behavior and one's appraisal of the likelihood that the behavior will be rewarded or reinforced if used now.

The core purpose of this book revolves around this key consequence of reinforced performance for the continued, and especially escalated, use of the rewarded behavior. If a young student curses a teacher and, in so doing, believes he has gained stature in his classmates' eyes, continued cursing becomes all the more probable. If a late adolescent deals with jealousy by smacking his girlfriend when he sees her talking to another boy, her subsequent obedience to his wishes makes further smacking more likely when, in his view, she has transgressed in other ways. So, too, for the adult who bullies in the workplace, the daughter or son who abuses or neglects an aged parent, the husband and wife who scream at each other, and the parent who disciplines with harsh spankings. Unfortunately, it is not only the continued use of cursing, smacking, bullying, abuse, neglect, or screaming that is made more likely by the behavior's perceived success; it is also its escalation to progressively more serious and more injurious forms of aggression.

This book is very much about escalation. My central belief, a belief increasingly finding at least initial empirical support, is that we as a society have far too often ignored the very manifestations of low-level aggression that, when rewarded, grow (often rapidly) into those several forms of often intractable high-level aggression that are currently receiving a great deal of society's attention. Thus, our media, our politicians, and our social and behavioral scientists focus broadly and in depth on murder, rape, assault, gangs, guns, and other forms and correlates of serious aggression but largely ignore their aggressive precursors—such as vandalism, bullying, harassment, threats, insults, and incivilities. "Catch it low to prevent it high" is a prescription that I and others have increasingly begun to apply, evaluate, and promote. I will promote it heavily throughout this book.

DEFINITIONS OF LOW-LEVEL AGGRESSION

In the research and applied literature on the subject, aggression is commonly defined as intentional physical or psychological injury to another person. On the face of it, then, providing a companion definition for low-level aggression may appear simple. Perhaps it should be defined as intentional physical or psychological injury that is only mildly injurious to another person—or moderately so. And indeed, as we shall see, consensus of a sort can be reached among researchers at least as to what constitutes "mild" or "moderate" injury. Yet serious definitional questions immediately arise. Whose perspective—the perpetrator's, the target's, a third-party observer's—should be called upon to provide such seriousness or severity ratings or rankings? Shall we take the perpetrator's view and define the behavior along a scale of expressive intensity, or the target victim's and seek a measure of injuriousness or harm done? If we opt for a harm-based definition, how shall injury or harm to the target be measured and when and, again, by whom? And what of frequency or repetitiveness? Does a steady diet of cutting insults from a parent constitute higher level aggression than occasional hard smacks to the face? Though ultimately low-level aggression must be defined subjectively, must be defined by its target, and is incident specific, a number of definitional approximations are appropriate.

Across-Incidents Chronology

The tracing of aggression pathways is one contributory approach to the task of defining low-level aggression because, generally, less harmful (in the target's perspective) or less intense (in the perpetrator's perspective) aggressive behaviors precede more harmful and/or intense expressions. (Such a sequence, although typical, is by no means invariant. One can imagine, for example, an incident in which a perpetrator first shoots a target person and only *then* curses the victim.)

Loeber et al. (1993) have identified three common developmental pathways from "less serious manifestations" to "more serious manifestations" followed by a large percentage of the boys studied as they progressed from disruptiveness to delinquency. Figure 1.1 depicts the behavioral sequence characterizing each pathway (Loeber & Hay, 1994).

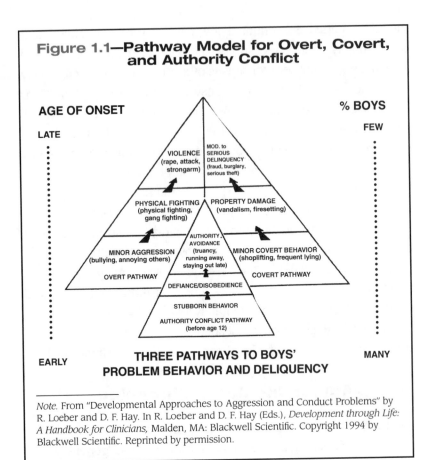

Figure 1.1—Pathway Model for Overt, Covert, and Authority Conflict

AGE OF ONSET

% BOYS

LATE

FEW

VIOLENCE
(rape, attack,
strongarm)

MOD. to
SERIOUS
DELINQUENCY
(fraud, burglary,
serious theft)

PHYSICAL FIGHTING
(physical fighting,
gang fighting)

PROPERTY DAMAGE
(vandalism, firesetting)

AUTHORITY
AVOIDANCE
(truancy,
running away,
staying out late)

MINOR AGGRESSION
(bullying, annoying others)

MINOR COVERT BEHAVIOR
(shoplifting, frequent lying)

OVERT PATHWAY

COVERT PATHWAY

DEFIANCE/DISOBEDIENCE

STUBBORN BEHAVIOR

AUTHORITY CONFLICT PATHWAY
(before age 12)

EARLY

**THREE PATHWAYS TO BOYS'
PROBLEM BEHAVIOR AND DELINQUENCY**

MANY

Note. From "Developmental Approaches to Aggression and Conduct Problems" by R. Loeber and D. F. Hay. In R. Loeber and D. F. Hay (Eds.), *Development through Life: A Handbook for Clinicians,* Malden, MA: Blackwell Scientific. Copyright 1994 by Blackwell Scientific. Reprinted by permission.

The Authority Conflict Pathway is the earliest in terms of age. It begins with stubborn behavior; proceeds to defiance, such as refusal and disobedience; and culminates in authority avoidance, as concretized by truancy and running away from home. The Covert Pathway starts with frequent lying, shoplifting, and other "minor covert behaviors"; moves on to property damage, such as vandalism or firesetting; and culminates in moderate to serious covert delinquency, such as fraud or burglary. The Overt Pathway commences with minor overt behaviors, such as annoying others or bullying; proceeds to individual or gang physical fighting; and reaches its extremity in assault, rape, or other violent behavior.

Other pathway models have been offered to depict common routes of escalation from minor to serious levels of aggression or delinquency (Farrington, 1991; LeBlanc, 1996; Moffitt, 1993; Nagin, Farrington, & Moffit, 1995). The timing (age of onset) of aggressive acts, their variety, their rate of escalation, and their chronicity are each proposed to relate to their eventual level of seriousness.

Within-Incidents Chronology

We may further concretize low-level aggression, again by examining the sequencing of behavior, but in this instance within the temporal confines of single aggressive incidents. To start such an effort by noting incident beginnings, Table 1.1 lists, in order of frequency, opening moves made by perpetrators toward targets in violent incidents occurring in school settings (National Institute of Justice, 1997).

Consistent with my urging of a catch-it-low strategy is these authors' proposal:

> Reducing the occurrence of opening moves appears to be the most promising approach to preventing escalation to violence. . . . One of the most frequent opening moves is offensive touching. The design of school-based violence prevention programs could include policies and practices that strongly discourage this type of behavior, however minor some of its expressions may appear. The study findings reveal many instances in which these opening moves escalate to fierce combats, suggesting that efforts to reduce this behavior will reduce serious violent incidents. (pp. 5, 7)

When such policies and practices are not in place—or exist but fail—aggressive opening moves are often followed by an escalating sequence some have termed "character contests." These are retaliatory progressions of verbal and eventually physical attempts to harm, to save face, and ultimately to defeat one's antagonist.

Table 1.1—Opening Moves in Violent Incidents among Students

Unprovoked offensive touching: throws, pushes, grabs, shoves, slaps, kicks, or hits

Possessions: interferes with something owned or being used

Request to do something

Backbiting: someone says something bad about another person to someone else and this gets back to the person

Play: verbal teasing (playful "put downs") or rough physical play

Insults: not meant to be playful

Crimes

Accusations of wrongdoing

Defense of others

Challenges: physical or nonverbal gestures

Threats of physical harm

Advances to boyfriend or girlfriend of actor

Told authority figure about bad behavior of actor

Other actions perceived as offensive

Note. From National Institute of Justice, *Research in Brief,* October 1997, Washington, DC: Author.

Figure 1.2 depicts this sequence as it might evolve from an opening move of backbiting or insulting gossip or rumor mongering (Office of Juvenile Justice and Delinquency Prevention, 1997).

Felson (1978) has studied such character contests in his work on aggression as impression management. He comments:

> An insult . . . places the target into an unfavorable situational identity by making the person appear weak, incompetent and cowardly. A successful counterattack is one effective way of nullifying the imputed negative identity by showing one's strength, competence, and courage. . . . Given the sacredness and vulnerability of the self, the ambiguous line between disagreement and disparagement,

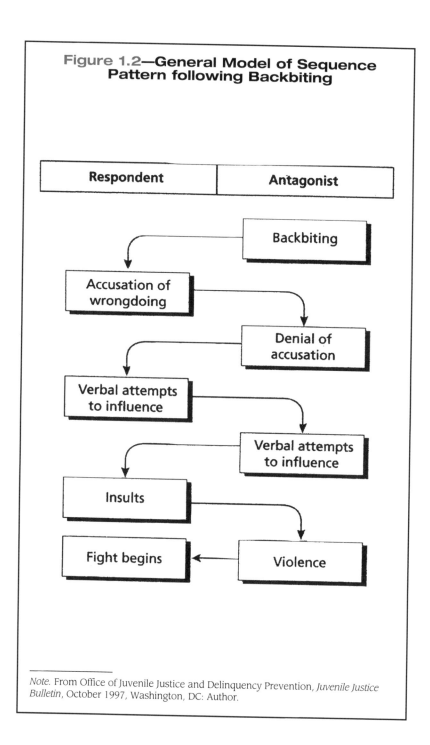

Figure 1.2—General Model of Sequence Pattern following Backbiting

| Respondent | Antagonist |

- Backbiting
- Accusation of wrongdoing
- Denial of accusation
- Verbal attempts to influence
- Verbal attempts to influence
- Insults
- Violence
- Fight begins

Note. From Office of Juvenile Justice and Delinquency Prevention, *Juvenile Justice Bulletin*, October 1997, Washington, DC: Author.

and the tendency for perceived attack to result in counter-attack, small arguments readily escalate through a recip-rocal process into aggressive encounters. (pp. 207, 211)

A character contest may escalate not only to an exchange of blows but, as Luckenbill (1977) observes, also to an exchange of bullets. Such a lethal progression, he suggests, proceeds through a five-stage sequence. In its opening stage, person A says or does something that person B believes may be an insult, one threaten-ing his "honor and face." Or, alternatively, A refuses to comply with a request by B that B believes is legitimate. In the second stage, B decides that A's move is indeed an attempt by A to insult B. B then, in stage three, responds to A with an expression of anger and con-tempt, a response seeking to recapture the honor and face lost as a result of A's opening move. In stage four, the parties agree—by what they do and what they do not do—that their dispute will be settled by violent means. Person A, also motivated to avoid a loss of honor and face, continues expressing the original (opening) in-sult, may escalate the insult, and/or may make a provocative physical gesture toward B. The process culminates in stage five, in which one or both persons make lethal moves.

Though Athens (1985) has challenged the pervasiveness of character contests, other researchers have described this very same process of escalation of aggression as resulting from disin-hibition (J. H. Goldstein, Davis, & Herman, 1975), amplification (Berkowitz, Lepinski, & Angulo, 1969), positive feedback (Marsh, Rosser, & Harre, 1978), interaction sequencing (Raush, 1965), af-fronts (Tuppern & Gaitan, 1989), and posturing (Grossman, 1995). Findings in support of such a progression of aggression, however explained, are provided later in this chapter.

Ratings and Rankings

The earliest examination of scaled ratings of the seriousness of an-tisocial behavior was conducted by Thurstone (1927), in his attempt to demonstrate that scaling techniques already employed in the arena of psychophysical judgments could also be applied to social continua. It was Sellin and Wolfgang (1964), however, who made the most extensive effort to construct a seriousness-based ordering of offense descriptions. In doing so, they systematically varied the dollar amount associated with each offense, the extent of personal injury, and the type of weapon employed as the ingredients determining rated seriousness. As Gottfredson, Young, and Laufer (1980) later demonstrated, it was not the simple additivity of these ingredients that determined perceived seriousness, but their interaction.

Warr (1989) reported a national survey on fear of crime and found that the degree of citizen fear was a joint product of the seriousness of each given crime and the likelihood of its happening. Murder is very serious but statistically quite unlikely. Receiving an obscene phone call is rather likely, but it was ranked as the least serious of the sixteen crimes listed in the survey. Of this combination of seriousness and likelihood, which crime was feared most? Having someone break into one's home while one is away. Ranked second: being raped. Ranked third: being hit by a drunk driver while driving one's car. This fear-of-crime survey, I believe, may hold an important implication for the effort to define more fully low-level aggression. From the perspective of the target—which, as noted earlier, is the perspective assumed here—the likelihood of a given act of aggression may well be a significant contributor to its rated level of seriousness.

Forgas, Brown, and Menyhart (1980) also found probability of occurrence to exert a significant influence upon seriousness ratings, along with the perceived justifiability of the act and the degree to which the act was sanctioned or not sanctioned by those in authority.

Alternatively, the seriousness level of an aggressive act may be judged on the joint basis of its wrongfulness and its harmfulness. Thomas and Bilchik (1985) observe:

Felonies are more serious than misdemeanors, and misdemeanors more serious than infractions. Among sins, the mortal variety is more serious than the venial. At first glance, the meaning of the phrase seriousness of violations may seem quite straightforward. However, studies suggest that people's judgments of seriousness can be based either on an act's moral impropriety (wrongfulness) or on the extent of harm it causes (harmfulness). And for some people, seriousness can involve some combination of wrongfulness and harmfulness. . . . Individuals who apply a moral-impropriety criterion in comparing grand theft with petty theft will judge the two equally serious because theft of any amount of money is wrong. In contrast, those who apply a harmfulness standard will judge grand theft the more serious because it causes greater damage to the victim. (p. 453)

In a seriousness rating study conducted by O'Connell and Whelan (1996), raters were asked to judge the seriousness of the offenses shown in Table 1.2 and apparently, as Thomas and Bilchik (1985) assert, did so on the basis of a joint reflection of harmfulness and wrongfulness.

In order of increasing seriousness, the rating results obtained by O'Connell and Whelan (1996) were as follows. Five clusters of ratings emerged. The lowest in seriousness, the authors note, are crimes held by some to be "victimless," namely dealing in soft drugs and consensual underage sex. Crimes in the next cluster, dole fraud and fraud on business, do have victims, but the victim "is either diffuse or is an impersonal institution, so that the impact on any particular individual is diluted" (p. 308). In the third cluster (corrupt police, fraud on public), the researchers note, the victim is a more concentrated, less diffuse group of people harmed by the offense. The final two clusters (burglary, mugging, assault on

Table 1.2—Criminal Offenses and Their Descriptions

Description given to respondent	Abbreviation
1. The offender attacks a victim with a knife and the victim dies.	Murder
2. The offender breaks into a person's house and steals property worth £30.	Burglary
3. The offender dishonestly obtains social welfare benefits to the value of £30.	Dole fraud
4. The offender sells marijuana to an adult.	Marijuana sale
5. The offender assaults a Garda (police) officer with his fists. The Garda officer is injured and sent to hospital.	Garda assault
6. The offender, a 14-year-old boy, has sexual intercourse with a 14-year-old girl with her consent.	Underage sex
7. The offender sets up a bogus company and through it, fraudulently obtains £3,000 from a big manufacturer.	Fraud on business
8. The offender, using physical force, robs a victim of £75. The victim is injured but not sent to a hospital.	Mugging
9. The offender sets up a bogus mail-order company and through it fraudulently obtains £1,500 from a number of private individuals.	Fraud on public
10. The offender, a Garda (police) officer, who discovers a burglary in a shop, steals £30 worth of goods from the store.	Corrupt Garda

Note. From "Taking Wrongs Seriously" by M. O'Connell and A. Whelan, 1996, *British Journal of Criminology, 36,* p. 304. Copyright 1996 by Oxford University Press. Reprinted by permission.

police, murder) show increasing levels of individualized violation and personal harmfulness. In judging seriousness, the authors conclude:

Our interpretation would suggest that people think mainly of degree of badness of the offending conduct and of the offender who commits it, but also, to a lesser extent, try to estimate the impact on the victim when considering seriousness of an offense. (p. 309)

Goldstein, Palumbo, Striepling, and Voutsinas (1995) took a complementary approach to defining aggression levels. Their national survey of teachers in the United States yielded a pool of 1,000 descriptions of in-school aggressive incidents along with the details of how each incident was resolved. Via what may best be described as an intuitive cluster analysis, these investigators grouped the 1,000 incident reports into 13 categories arrayed from low-level through moderate-level to high-level aggression, as depicted in Table 1.3.

Consistent with this book's core approach to aggression control and reduction is the statement of Goldstein et al. (1995):

Any act of aggression can escalate quickly into a serious situation. In fact, it is only possible to judge the level of severity of an aggressive incident in the specific context in which it occurs. What we can say, however, is that poor management of aggression at the lower levels facilitates its high level expression. Conversely, the teacher skilled at maintaining compliance or thwarting student disruptiveness is, we believe, considerably less likely to be faced with vandalistic, out-of-control, or armed students. "Catch it low to prevent it high" is a productive intervention strategy. (pp. 19–20)

Cron (1998) sought to apply the Goldstein et al. (1995) incident categories to her compilation of 1,200 descriptions by school bus drivers of on-the-bus student aggression and other antisocial behaviors. Consistent with the person-environment transactional theme I will reiterate throughout this book, Cron found the Goldstein et al. schoolhouse-based clusters to be not a sufficiently good

---

Table 1.3—Schoolhouse Incident Categories

1. Horseplay
2. Rules violation
3. Disruptiveness
4. Refusal
5. Cursing
6. Bullying
7. Sexual harassment
8. Physical threats
9. Vandalism
10. Out-of-control behavior
11. Fights
12. Attacks on teachers
13. Group aggression

Note. Reprinted from *Break It Up: A Teacher's Guide to Managing Student Aggression* (p. 19) by A. P. Goldstein, J. Palumbo, S. Striepling, and A. M. Voutsinas, 1995, Champaign, IL: Research Press. Copyright 1995 by the authors.

---

fit to her incident data and thus prepared a more setting-appropriate, school-bus-relevant array of incident categories, as indicated in Table 1.4.

In a manner reflecting the catch-it-low spirit and intentions of this book, Cron (1998) makes this observation:

> In his book, *Young Men and Fire,* Norman Maclean describes a forest fire in which thirteen smoke jumpers died. Maclean states that ". . . reality almost anywhere having inherent in it the principle that little things suddenly . . . can become big as hell, the ordinary can suddenly become monstrous. . . . Since this principle comes about as close to being universal as a principle can, you might have thought that someone in the early history and training of the smoke jumper would have realized that some-

Table 1.4—School Bus Incident Categories

Low level
>   Littering, eating, drinking
>
>   Excessive noise
>
>   Rules violation
>
>   Out of seat
>
>   Disturbing others

Medium level
>   Profanity
>   Refusal to obey driver
>   Arm/head/body out window
>   Smoking
>   Throwing objects

High level
>   Destruction of property
>   Pushing/tripping/attacking others
>   Discriminatory language (including sexual harassment)
>   Attack on driver
>   Weapons
>   Group attack

Note. From *Driving Me Crazy: School Transportation and Student Discipline* by T. Cron, 1998, Santa Fe, NM: Goin' Mobile. Copyright 1998 by Trina Cron. Reprinted by permission.

thing like the Mann Gulch fire would happen before long. But no one seems to have sensed this first principle because of a second principle inherent in the nature of man, namely, that generally a first principle can't be seen until it has been written up as a tragedy and becomes a second principle." This is a story about the first principle staying the first principle, about keeping the ordinary from becoming monstrous. I want to tell this story so the [school bus] industry, school administrators, and the public will see the potential for fire before there is smoke. (p. 5)

A final rating approach to defining seriousness combines the national survey of crime seriousness ratings conducted by Wolfgang, Figlio, Tracy, and Singer (1985) and the reflections of Kelling and Coles (1996) upon the survey results as they bear upon low-level crime and aggression in particular. The survey yielded ratings in which the most severely rated crimes were the planting of a bomb in a public building, resulting in the death of 20 persons, followed by the forcible rape and murder of a woman. Rated at the "least severe" extreme, in descending order, were a noisy person disturbing the neighborhood, a group hanging around a neighborhood after being told by police to disband, a drunk in public, a 16-year-old breaking curfew and (as the least severe infraction rated) a person under 16 playing hooky from school.

Kelling and Coles (1996) assert that those very infractions rated least serious in Wolfgang et al.'s (1985) national survey are judged and experienced by many citizens and communities as the most serious.*

> Criminal behavior is meaningful to all of us not merely because it involves an act of violence against a person or property. Any act becomes more serious if the setting in which it is carried out heightens the act's intensity, the resulting fear, and propensity for damaging the community as a whole. (p. 30)

In their view, five qualities of the context in which (rated) low-level disorderly behavior occurs can, individually and collectively, transform such behavior into an (experienced) high-level, serious act. These elements are time (when it occurs), place (where it occurs), previous orderly or disorderly behavior by the perpetrator, the condition of the target person(s), and the specific disorderly act itself.

---

* The quotations on this and following pages have been reprinted with the permission of The Free Press, an imprint of Simon and Schuster, Inc., from *FIXING BROKEN WINDOWS: RESTORING ORDER AND REDUCING CRIME IN OUR COMMUNITIES* by George L. Kelling and Catherine M. Coles. Copyright © 1996 by George L. Kelling and Catherine M. Coles.

Boisterous backyard noise emitted by a group of neighbors on a Saturday evening and interfering with sleep at 10:30 P.M. is experienced as a much less serious disorder than noise from unknown others at the same decibel level at 3 A.M. on a Tuesday, especially when the same disorderliness has occurred on 3 other workdays in the past 2 weeks.

What, then, is low-level aggression? We have examined its diverse operational definitions in aggression seriousness research conducted both across and within incidents and employing either rating or ranking methodologies. Although this body of research does yield a general consensus regarding which particular behaviors are deemed to be "low level," a consensus that has guided the selection of behaviors to be examined in the remainder of this book, we must quickly acknowledge that judgments about the level of intensity of an aggressive act must remain very much within the perception of its target: Different people will experience the same aggressive act quite differently. For example, Sparks, Genn, and Dodd (1977) found that given acts of aggression are perceived to be increasingly serious with increasing age of the rater. Victims of aggressive behavior rate such behavior as more serious than do its perpetrators (Idisis, 1996; Wolf, Moav, & Silfen, 1991). M. A. Walker (1978) reported that men rate violent offenses more seriously than women do, and persons of higher social class perceive violent offenses as significantly more serious than do raters from lower social class backgrounds. The reverse social class finding concerning property offenses emerged in work by Sparks et al. (1977). Consistent differences among ethnic groups in aggression seriousness ratings have also been reported (Figlio, 1975; Lubel, Wolf, & Krausz, 1992; Rossi, Waite, Bose, & Berk, 1974). Rose and Prell (1955) found that women tended to rate child beaters, bigamists, forgers, and drunk drivers as significantly more serious offenders than do men. Levi and Jones (1985) report that although ordinary citizens and police officers assigned similar rankings of crime seriousness, the citizens gave most offenses higher absolute ratings than did the police. Finally, and perhaps not surprisingly, prison inmates who have committed certain crimes rate those crimes as less serious than do either inmates who have not perpetrated the offenses in question or prison staff (Sechrest, 1969).

Though some research reports no effect of age, sex, or income on crime seriousness ratings (Cullen, Clark, & Polanzi, 1982), the thrust of the studies just reviewed is toward considerable individual variation in such ratings. Thus, although a broad operational consensus is reachable regarding which behavior may be categorized as "low level," what constitutes low-level aggression in any given incident must nonetheless be defined via the subjective experience of the person to whom it is directed.

THE ESCALATION OF LOW-LEVEL AGGRESSION: RESEARCH FINDINGS

Insults, threats, teasing, and even many forms of bullying, harassment, and abuse are often merely unpleasant, annoying, or aversive—and not seriously injurious. In this book I am less concerned with these several incarnations of low-level aggression in their own right, but I focus upon them because of their not infrequent high-level-aggressive sequelae. In the previous sections, I described pathway models and aggressive incident chronologies, asserting that such escalation was a common phenomenon. In this section, I wish to survey several arenas of research that support this assertion.

Laboratory Research

An initial series of investigations conducted by J. H. Goldstein and colleagues consistently found what these researchers termed a "trials effect" (J. H. Goldstein et al., 1975; J. H. Goldstein, Davis, Kermis, & Cohn, 1981). As several others have also reported, studies using the Buss (1961) aggression machine find that both experimental and control participants regularly increase, in both intensity and duration, the level of shock they believe they are administering to another person as the study's trials proceed. Examining alternative explanations for this consistent escalation result, J. H. Goldstein and colleagues found evidence in support of a process of disinhibition. As the researchers state, "Once punishment is administered, it becomes increasingly easy to administer more intense punishment, regardless of the behavior of the learner [target]"(J. H. Goldstein et al., 1975, p. 167). Others have suggested that pain cues from the victim may be able to break into this process and halt the escalation by the aggressor, although under some circumstances, such feedback has served as reinforcement for pain infliction and caused it to escalate further, not diminish (Suedfeld, 1990; Zimbardo, 1969).

Taylor, Shuntich, and Greenberg (1979) had their research participants engage in a short series of aggressive interactions in the form of competitive encounters in which, as just described, more intense shocks were seemingly administered. The researchers then examined each participant's behavior in a subsequent session, one in which the other party did not behave in a provocative manner. In this session too, however, participants continued to behave in a highly aggressive manner, a finding the researchers explained both as a trials or practice effect and as a response to anticipated counteraggression in the face of one's own aggressive provocation.

Yet another mechanism that apparently facilitates escalation in this paradigm is what Freedman and Fraser (1966) have termed the "foot-in-the-door" phenomenon. Willingness to engage in high levels of diverse negative behaviors has reliably been shown to be made more likely by prior compliance with requests to participate in low levels of such behaviors. Extending this effect to the realm of aggression, Gilbert (1981) made this observation:

Milgram's (1963) incremental shock procedure for quantifying obedience may be partly responsible for the high levels of obedience obtained. The innocuous beginning of the shock sequence (low voltage, no negative feedback) may elicit compliance before the frightening implications of the procedure are clear, and the gradual escalation in shock intensity may deprive subjects of a qualitative breakpoint needed to justify changing obedience to disobedience. (p. 690)

In addition to disinhibition with practice, anticipated retaliation, and foot-in-the-door, a fourth explanation for the escalation of aggression rests on the concept of deindividuation. A construct first introduced by Festinger, Pepitone, and Newcombe (1952), deindividuation is the circumstance in which individuals, usually in groups, experience diminished self-awareness and self-regulation, lessened inner restraint, and heightened freedom to engage in aggressive or other deviant behaviors. Examples of deindividuation can be found in mob behavior, in group bullying, in gang violence, and in the thug-like behavior of fans at soccer or other athletic events. It is a process engendered by high levels of emotional arousal, by diffusion of personal responsibility, and by the anonymity of single persons in collectives. Its expression in aggressive behavior is further facilitated by modeling and contagion influences. Jaffe and Yinon (1979) and Jaffe, Shapir, and Yinon (1981) studied this phenomenon in a laboratory context and indeed found consistent outcomes when comparing individual- and group-administered aggression, as measured by the pace and intensity of (apparent) shock administered. On both escalation criteria, persons in groups significantly exceeded individuals acting alone. This finding offers strong support for the role of deindividuation in the escalation of aggression, especially group aggression.

Earlier in this chapter, I examined the character contest as one common progression from low-level to intense aggression. Harris, Gergen, and Lannamann (1986) have provided useful empirical support for this phenomenon in their study of what they term "aggression rituals." Participating raters were asked to judge a series of case studies of persons interacting, describing as they did so the possible reactions of the parties on a range of behaviors from conciliation to aggression. Their findings bear directly on the aggression escalation process.

> Of equal interest in the present study was the progressive restriction of options as the behavioral sequence unfolded. At the outset of the interchange, respondents judged aggression and conciliation almost equally probable and desirable. In this early state the actors thus possessed a considerable latitude of action. Yet, as the interchange proceeded this latitude was systematically reduced. Aggressive options became increasingly probable and desirable, and conciliation a perceived impossibility. Most dramatically, progressive constriction was simultaneous with increments in the seriousness of the aggressive actions. At the outset, one is unsure what ritual or pattern is to be played out. With increased amounts of aggressive interchange, one realizes "the name of the game" and plays accordingly. Physical violence, then, may become a "natural" next step within the ritual, and it may often be a virtual necessity for the actor to take this step. (p. 263)

Whether and why escalation occurs is largely a function of the appraisals and behaviors of the parties involved, but it is also a function of the physical and social context in which the character contest takes place. I have examined aggression and its growth as a "person-environment duet" elsewhere, in an exploration of the ecology of aggression (Goldstein, 1994). The likelihood of its escalation, to be sure, is influenced by qualities of the persons involved—impulsiveness (Halperin et al., 1995), level of self-esteem (Kernis, Granneman, & Barclay, 1989), cognitive biases (Dodge & Frame, 1982), temperamental difficulties (Kingston & Prior, 1995), school and family bonding (O'Donnell, Hawkins, & Abbott, 1995), values (B. McCarthy, 1994), dominance needs (Weisfeld, 1994), and more. However, these several "person" qualities take on their escalation potency as they interact in duet fashion with the qualities of the setting in which the event is based. Some of these qualities are physical. In schools, aggression and its escalation are more likely on the playground, in the (boys') bathrooms, in the cafeteria, and in the hallways between classes than in the classroom or in other venues (Goldstein & Conoley, 1997). In the home, the bedroom is the deadliest room, the kitchen next most dangerous, followed by the living room and other sites, with the safest room in the house being the bathroom (Gelles, 1972). Stores are most vulnerable to becoming violent crime sites when they are (a) close to major transportation routes, (b) on streets with little vehicular traffic, (c) next to vacant lots, and (d) in areas with few other stores or commercial activity (Duffalo, 1976). Alcohol intoxication, a person quality, certainly has been shown to prime character contests and fuel their escalation (Pernanen, 1991), but the degree of such escalation has also been demonstrated to be a result of qualities of the bar or other drinking establishment itself (Felson, Baccaglini, & Gmelch, 1986; Leather & Lawrence, 1995). Neighborhoods, too, do much to determine whether or not aggression is likely and its escalation frequent. Later in this chapter I will examine neighborhood features in greater depth, especially the presence of incivilities, because it is in this domain that the spirit of "catch it low" largely began.

The social environment plays an equally significant role in the escalation process. The group deindividuation example I have already discussed. Audience effects have been shown to matter a great deal, especially for character contests (Borden, 1975; Cratty, 1981). Perhaps most important, however, regarding the social ecology component of the person-environment duet is the behavior of the target person. Floyd (1985) is correct in asserting that "victimization needs to be understood in terms of the reciprocal behaviors in a relationship between an aggressor and a victim" (p. 9). As I will make concrete in my chapter 3 examination of bullying, it is the behavior of *both* the bully and the whipping boy that may make the bullying, if not begin, continue and at times escalate. Here, as with victims of rape, assault, murder, or other forms of aggression, one must be especially careful not to *blame* the target for his or her own victimization even while seeking to identify the target's contribution to the incident.

Laboratory study of the aggression escalation process is modest in amount, interesting in result, and pregnant in potential. I strongly encourage its continuance and expansion.

Delinquency Research

Much of the aggression escalation research involving children and youth has focused on the behavioral precursors to adolescent delinquency and adult crime, that is, on criminal pathways. Notwithstanding the important proviso that "adult criminality seems to be always preceded by childhood misconduct, but most conduct-disordered children do not become antisocial or criminal adults" (Sampson & Laub, 1993, p. 2), a substantial portion of such youth proceed fully during their lives along an escalating Authority Conflict, Covert, or Overt Pathway of aggression.

As Ford (personal communication, June 13, 1998) has observed, there are instances in the developmental psychopathology literature in which the terms *pathway* and *trajectory* are used interchangeably, though they are in fact similar-appearing but quite different processes. A trajectory is a route or course whose defining characteristics (duration, velocity, and especially destination) are essentially determined at the outset. The thrown object and the fired bullet are examples of such predestination at the instant of departure. A pathway, in contrast, takes on its defining characteristics not only at its inception but also over the full span of its route. A walk in the woods, for example, while typically possessing an initial direction, speed, and planned destination, finds these defining qualities altered in small and/or large ways by terrain, obstacles, precipitation, temperature, wind, and other route features as the walk progresses. The developmental evolution of aggression reflects a pathway, not a trajectory model. As others have noted, aggression is a "situated transaction" (Fagan & Wilkinson, 1998), a "contextual event" (Toch, 1986), a "person-environment duet" (Goldstein, 1994) whose direction, intensity, form, and target are shaped both by its initial (often low-level) character and by subsequent, along-its-pathway interpersonal and physical influences. More is represented here than either a semantic quibble or a theoretical distinction. The course of the thrown object or the fired bullet is not easily altered or stopped once the action is begun; the walk in the woods is substantially more amenable to significant in-progress alteration.

Thus, research tracing youths' progression along the three pathways posited by Loeber and Hay (1994) shows that although there are various exceptions—crossing pathways, starting in the middle of a pathway, progressing on two pathways simultaneously, concomitantly perpetrating both more and less serious crimes within one pathway—a great many youths do indeed follow one or another of the pathways quite as described. Loeber and Stouthamer-Loeber (1998) observe, significantly, that the model's fit is best when a distinction is made between youths whose antisocial behaviors are transient events (i.e., "experimenters") and those for whom aggression and criminal behavior continue over an extended period (i.e., "persisters"). It is these latter youths whom these investigators, as well as Elliott (1994), have shown most clearly to follow the pathways. Loeber and Stouthamer-Loeber conclude:

> In summary, the prediction of serious outcomes such as violence can best be conceptualized according to a model in which steps toward violence are specified. That is, few

individuals begin a full-blown violent career. Instead, they "ease" into it through minor offenses, and the earlier these begin, the more likely the individual will eventually show more examples of violent behavior. (p. 250)

Related escalation outcomes have been reported by a number of investigators, whether youth aggression was rated by parents (Mitchell & Rosa, 1979), teachers (Roff & Wirt, 1984), or peers (Viemero, 1996). In each investigation, childhood aggression emerged as an antecedent of later frequency of often considerably more severe adolescent and adult criminal offending. LeBlanc (1990), on the basis of his own findings, describes this sequence well:

We find that there are five stages in the development of offending and that they form a sequence. They are, in order, emergence, exploration, explosion, conflagration, and outburst. At first, usually between age 8 and 10, the delinquent activities are homogeneous and benign, al- most always expressed in the form of petty larceny; this is the stage of emergence. This period is followed, gener- ally between ages 10 and 12, by a diversification and es- calation of the offenses, essentially comprising shoplifting and vandalism; this stage is one of exploration. Later, at about age 13, there is a substantial increase in the variety and seriousness of the crimes; and four new types of crime develop—common theft, public disorder, burglary, and personal theft; this is the stage of explosion. . . . Around age 15, variety and seriousness increase further as four more types of crime are added—drug trafficking, motor vehicle theft, armed robbery, and personal attack; this is the stage of conflagration. [There is] also a fifth stage which occurs only during adulthood; it is a progress toward more sophisticated or more violent forms of crim- inal behavior; it is called outburst. (pp. 11–12)

Tracking a large sample of youth from their adolescent years into adulthood, Stattin and Magnusson (1989) found that compared to youngsters who were low or average on aggression, high-aggressive youth were as adults (a) involved in more serious crimes, (b) involved in more frequent crimes, and (c) particularly more likely to commit confrontive and destructive offenses.

Focusing on school-based predictors, Hamalainen and Pulkkinen (1996) found adult serious crime at age 27 to be accurately forecast by age 8 aggressive (verbal and physical) and norm-breaking (disobedience, truancy) behavior. Many investigators have shown that aggression is a remarkably stable behavior over the life span. It is clear, however, that for a great many perpetrators, what is stable is the presence of aggression in their lives. In contrast, the intensity or seriousness of such behavior is far from stable; it shows substantial and predictable escalation of intensity.

The role of reinforced performance is central to the escalation process. Patterson (1992), writing of the progressively more intense conflict levels displayed in the parent-child pairs he studied, comments:

> According to the coercion model, an increase in amplitudes is likely to prove functional (i.e., the other person is apt to withdraw from the exchange). In the short run the person who withdraws reduces the pain he or she experiences; in the long run, however, he or she has increased the risk that the other person will use high-amplitude coercive behaviors in future bouts. The reciprocal escalation is thought to be most likely if the "power" is relatively equal for both parties.

> Other forms of antisocial behavior may escalate because they produce positive reinforcing outcomes, or they are reinforcing because they produce a means of avoiding unpleasant experiences. Skipping school is more reinforcing than simply being tardy. Stealing a car is more re-

inforcing than stealing a T-shirt. The longer a child is in the coercive process and the higher his rate of performance, the greater the risk for engaging in more severe forms of antisocial acts. It is hypothesized that all boys who remain in a coercive process are moving steadily toward greater severity of antisocial acts. (p. 73)

Later chapters will provide additional examples of the manner in which escalation of yet other forms of low-level aggression yields reward to the perpetrator and thus spurs the escalation process.

Incivility Research

The escalation of aggression and kindred behaviors has also been well demonstrated in field studies that focus on the consequences of physical and social incivilities. Further, beginning evidence has emerged in this arena in clear support of a catch-it-low intervention strategy. Physical incivilities are concrete ecological features that serve as both reflections of and impetus for neighborhood disuse, disdain, decay, and deterioration. They include trash and litter; graffiti; abandoned or burned-out stores, houses, and automobiles; dirt; vacant lots; broken windows and streetlights; ill-kept buildings; vandalism of diverse sorts; and similar expressions of a cycle of decline. Physical incivilities are accompanied by social incivilities, in an often dramatic display of person-environment reciprocal influence. Social incivilities may include increased presence of aggressive gangs, drug users, prostitutes, "skid row" alcoholics, and bench or street sleepers; increased presence of drug purveyors; increased crime by offenders and increased fear of crime by neighborhood residents; and increased panhandling, harassment, chronic loitering, gambling, and drinking. In addition to "incivility" (Hunter, 1978), these physical and social neighborhood characteristics have been labeled "prelude to trouble" (Skolnick & Bailey, 1986), "urban unease" (J. Q.Wilson, 1986), "non-normal appearances" (Goffman, 1971), "early signs of danger" (Stinchcombe et al., 1980), "cues to danger" (Skogan, 1990) "signs of crime" (Skogan & Maxfield, 1981), and "soft crimes" (Reiss, 1985). Gates and Rohe (1987) and Skogan and Maxfield (1981) have reported that neighborhood incivility level appears to be a correlate of such sociodemographic indices as race, income, neighborhood cohesion, prior victimization, and neighborhood crime level. Higher levels of incivility are reported by African Americans and Latinos, people with low income levels, people criminally victimized previously, and people living in high-crime neighborhoods and in neighborhoods with less cohesion or sense of control. Another correlate of incivility is more incivility (Lewis & Salem, 1986), in what appears to be a contagious downward-spiraling process. La-Grange, Ferraro, and Supanic's (1992) interview survey of 1,100 persons in widely distributed neighborhoods revealed a strong association between the level of both physical and social incivility on the one hand, and both the perception of risk and the fear of victimization on the other. This latter finding replicates earlier demonstrations of the incivility-fear association (Rohe & Burby, 1988; Taylor & Hall, 1986).

Does the level of incivility relate to, and perhaps actually help cause, the level of neighborhood crime? Taylor and Gottfredson (1986) reported a correlation of .63 between incivilities and crime rates, though both appeared on further analysis to grow from the neighborhood's sociodemographic characteristics. J. Q. Wilson and Kelling (1982) hold that incivility does in fact progress to serious levels of crime and disorder. As Skogan (1990) notes:

> According to Wilson and Kelling, disorder undermines
> the process by which communities ordinarily maintain
> social control. Where disorder problems are frequent and
> no one takes responsibility for unruly behavior in public
> places, the sense of "territoriality" among residents
> shrinks to include only their own households; mean-
> while, untended property is fair game for plunder or de-

struction. Further, a neighborhood's reputation for toler-
ating disorder invites outside troublemakers. Criminals
are attracted to such areas because they offer opportunities for crime. Where disorder is common and surveillance capacities are minimal, criminals will feel their
chances of being identified are low, and may be confident
that no one will intervene in their affairs. (p. 10)

Skogan (1990) describes a parallel sequence of decline from
disorder to serious crime. Its components are citizen withdrawal
from community involvement, heightened fear, outmigration of
families and inmigration of unattached and transient individuals,
diminished sense of mutual responsibility, and weakened informal
social control. At its incivilities' nadir,

uncollected litter blows in the wind. In cold weather, men
gather around fires in trash cans. Unattached males, the
homeless, and the aimless live in seedy residential hotels
and flophouses. Abandoned buildings serve as "shooting
galleries." . . . Vacant lots are filled with rubble. Residential and commercial buildings stand scarred by arson.
(pp. 13–14)

Skogan's own investigation in this domain gathered information
regarding incivilities and their consequences from an average of
325 people in each of 40 different neighborhoods in the United
States. In his appropriately titled report, *Disorder and Decline,* he
found strong evidence that perceived crime, fear of crime, and actual level of crime victimization were each a function of neighborhood physical and social incivility.

Others have observed similar aggression-escalating consequences of disorder and incivility in school settings. J. Q. Wilson
and Petersilia (1995), for example, describe graffiti on school walls,
debris in corridors, and students coming to school late and wan-
dering the halls as the foundation upon which more serious violence rests.

[Low-level] disorder invites youngsters to test further and further the limits of acceptable behavior. One connection between the inability of school authorities to maintain order and an increasing rate of violence is that, among students with little faith in the usefulness of the education they are supposed to be getting, challenging rules is part of the fun. When they succeed in littering or writing on walls, they feel encouraged to challenge other, more sacred rules, like the prohibition against assaulting fellow students and even teachers. (p. 149)

Incivility does relate to crime and violence, and it is likely to do so in a cause-and-effect manner. The mediating processes connecting the two may be contagion (Lewis & Salem, 1986), an array of sociodemographic neighborhood characteristics (Taylor & Gottfredson, 1986), a diminished sense of control (Janowitz, 1975), neighborhood residents' sense of "unworthiness" (Rainwater, 1966), and/or the reduced interactions and surveillance associated with the perception of the neighborhood as first an inhospitable and, later, a dangerous place (Skogan, 1990). Whatever its mediation of crime, incivility appears to be a significant ecological characteristic of many problem neighborhoods and thus is worthy of further inquiry and examination, with regard to both cause and intervention.

A major step forward in both planning and evaluating a city-wide "catch it low to prevent it high" incivility intervention program was reported by Kelling and Coles (1996) in their aptly titled book, *Fixing Broken Windows.* They comment:

We used the image of broken windows to explain how neighborhoods might decay into disorder and even crime if no one attends faithfully to their maintenance. If a factory or office window is broken, passersby observing it will conclude that no one cares or no one is in charge. In time, a few will begin throwing rocks to break more windows. Soon all the windows will be broken, and now passersby will think that, not only is no one in charge of the building, no one is in charge of the street on which it faces. Only the young, the criminal, or the foolhardy have any business on an unprotected avenue, and so more and more citizens will abandon the street to those they assume prowl it. Small disorders lead to larger and larger ones, and perhaps even to crime.

A rights-oriented legal tradition does not easily deal with this problem. The judge finds it hard to believe that one broken window is all that important or that the police should be empowered to exert their authority on people who might break more windows. The judge sees a snapshot of the street at one moment; the public, by contrast, sees a motion picture of the street slowly, inexorably decaying. (p. xv)

The crime problem does not begin with a serious, or "index" crime. Conceiving of it and addressing it as such, as has occurred for thirty years in national debates about crime, leads to bad public policy, poor legal thinking and practice, and distorted criminal justice practices and priorities. (p. 5)

As these researchers began to implement the fixing-broken-windows strategy on New York City's streets and in its subways, it was not only traditional criminal justice's exclusive focus on high-level or index crimes that proved to be an obstacle.

It raised questions within the realms of public policy, criminal justice, policing, and constitutional law (specifically, legal projections for individual rights). . . . Most police considered themselves too busy responding to calls for service and dealing with serious crime to give attention to disorder. Similarly, for many civil libertarians efforts to reduce disorder would impermissibly violate constitutional projections for the fundamental liberties of individuals who had committed no "criminal" act. In particular, advocates for the mentally ill, the homeless, and minority groups expressed outrage over what they perceived to be an attack on the poor and disadvantaged. (Kelling & Coles, 1996, pp. 21–22)

Yet, in spite of these several levels of resistance, implementation of the policy persisted. Graffiti were removed from almost all trains within 2 hours, or trains were kept out of service until clean. A similar energetic stance was taken toward aggressive begging and panhandling, farebeating in the subways, obstructing of pedestrian traffic on sidewalks, drinking of alcohol in public, defacing of public property, littering, and other forms of low-level infraction. Though the evidence lacks control group comparisons and in other ways suffers from the looseness of most real-life field evaluations, the broken windows efforts appear to have produced substantial positive outcomes, yielding reductions in both low-level infractions and considerably more serious offenses. Thus, Kelling and Coles (1996) assert,

there is growing evidence to suggest that police attention to "quality-of-life" issues and low-level crimes, making use of tactics significantly at variance with 911 policing, may have a significant impact in lowering incidence rates of index crimes. For example, in New York City, as of June 30, 1995, the rate of reported murders by handgun was down 40.7 percent from the previous year, largely attributable, according to federal and local officials, to "quality-of-life" enforcement by the police. (p. 100)

In part this positive outcome appears to have grown from the manner in which many perpetrators engage in both low-level and high-level crimes.

During the early days of the farebeating effort, police discovered that a high percentage of those arrested for farebeating either were carrying illegal weapons or had warrants outstanding for their arrest on felony charges, many for crimes committed in the subway. . . . Perhaps nothing so convinced the police about the linkages among disorder, farebeating, and robberies as the finding time and time again, that many farebeaters were robbers as well and offenders guilty of "disorderly acts." Consequently, when action was taken against farebeaters, serious crime dropped. (p. 134)

Just as searching farebeaters in the subway yielded weapons and sent a message through the TPD that fighting disorder was effective as a means of addressing crime generally, so similar accounts are making their way throughout the NYPD: a person arrested for urinating in a park, when questioned about other problems, gave police information that resulted in the confiscation of a small cache of weapons; a motorcyclist cited for not wearing a helmet, on closer inspection was carrying a nine-millimeter handgun . . . a vendor selling hot merchandise, after being questioned, led police to a fence specializing in stolen weapons. These stories made concrete the importance of dealing with minor problems in order to forestall major problems. Just as every farebeater was not a felon, not every petty criminal is a serious criminal; yet enough are, or have information about others who are, that contact with petty offenders alerts all criminals to the vigilance of the police and gives police legitimate access to information about more serious problems. (p. 146)

I have quoted from *Fixing Broken Windows* at length because it serves as the touchstone research effort in framing what I hope will become a broadly employed intervention strategy to confront human aggression in its many and diverse expressions. Kelling and Coles (1996) comment in conclusion:

> Four elements of the Broken Windows strategy explain its impact on crime reduction. First, dealing with disorder and low-level offenders both informs police about, and puts them into contact with, those who have also committed index crimes, including the hard-core "6 percent" of youthful offenders. Second, the high visibility of police actions and the concentration of police in areas characterized by high levels of disorder protect "good kids," while sending a message to "wannabes" and those guilty of committing marginal crimes that their actions will no longer be tolerated. . . . Third, citizens themselves begin to assert control over public spaces by upholding neighborhood standards for behavior, and ultimately move onto center stage in the ongoing processes of maintaining order and preventing crime. Finally, as problems of disorder and crime become the responsibility not merely of the police but of the entire community, including agencies and institutions outside but linked to it, all mobilize to address them in an integrated fashion. Through this broadly based effort, a vast array of resources can be marshaled, and through problem solving, targeted at specific crime problems. (pp. 242–243)

In addition to laboratory, delinquency, and incivilities investigations, other venues and other expressions of aggression and related behaviors have been part of the research arena for the study of escalation. Ill-tempered, high-tantrum preschoolers are quite likely to become (even more) ill-tempered adults (Caspi, Elder, & Bem, 1987). And, as noted previously in a clear demonstration in the home context of the power of reinforced performance, Patterson (1992) has also shown that escalation of aggression by both parent and child progresses as they reciprocally reinforce each other for doing so.

In close adult relationships, Wilmot (1987) has investigated what he terms the "regressive spiral" of escalating interpersonal conflict. Gottman (1982) has described the reciprocation of negative affect in cross-complaining couples. In approximately half of the married couples studied by Woffordt, Mihalic, and Menard (1994), early relationship pushing, grabbing, shoving, and slapping had grown over a 3-year interval to hitting, biting, kicking, or other acts of high-level aggression. The escalation of aggression has similarly been shown to occur in the children's classroom (Wehby, Symons, & Shores, 1995), the college residence hall (Palmer, 1996), the workplace (Labig, 1995), and the old-age home (Decalmer & Glendenning, 1997). It is a broadly located, frequently occurring, reliable phenomenon.

As I noted at the chapter's beginning, a major force that drives the escalation process is the reinforced performance of low-level aggression. Graziano (1994) asks, "Why study subabusive violence?" His answer is central to this book's theme:

> Several researchers argue that the easy and widespread acceptance of corporal punishment as being appropriate—even necessary—in child rearing provides a stable foundation of attitudes, beliefs, and reinforced practices on which rest the abusive levels. Graziano (1989) argues that becoming a child abuser entails a learning process involving a sequence of escalation from subabuse to abusive treatment of children. In that model, repeated incidents of socially acceptable and commonly modeled corporal punishment provide reinforced practice and learning in its application. A repertoire of learned punishments is thus readily developed by the parent. Then, under certain conditions of pressure, stress, and patterns of negative reinforcement in parent-child interactions,

the previously learned behavior can escalate to abusive levels. In that process, it was suggested, not only behavior is shaped, but so too are the perceptions of the parent. Thus through escalation parents come not only to act abusively but to perceive their own abusive behavior as acceptable and "proper," and they can maintain their self-perceptions as good parents who have acted correctly and responsibly. This entire systematic learning process in which behavior and beliefs move up the violence continuum was labeled escalation. (p. 415)

THE PLAN OF THIS BOOK

I have sought to set the stage in this chapter. The several existing definitions of low-level aggression and their bases have been described, as has my working definition as operationally concretized by the topics selected for inclusion in the chapters to follow. Low-level aggression, although far from unimportant in its own right, assumes its chief significance via its tendency when rewarded to escalate to higher and more seriously injurious forms of interpersonal violence. The remainder of this book explores the many forms of low-level aggression for purposes of encouraging an escalation-minimizing response strategy. In schools in the United States today, for example, there is growing adoption of a zero-tolerance intervention stance: "You bring a weapon to school. No questions asked. You are expelled for a year. No appeal considered." We need, I believe, an equally rigorous, zero-tolerance approach to low-level infractions. Sanctions or punishments when such behaviors occur need not be severe, but they do need to be perceived by their recipients as unpleasant and to be administered in a consistent manner: "Ann, we are going out to the playground. I'm sorry, but you know the rules of this class. Because you said those curse words, you have to stay here this period and work on these exercises. You'll be staying in Mr. Green's room. Hope you can join us tomorrow."

I have long believed that one of the most important socializing lessons that parents or teachers can impart to children is that both compliance and noncompliance with rule demands have consequences. Follow the rules of life, be it in the home, the classroom, the street, or elsewhere, and positive consequences are likely to follow. Violate those rules, and the consequences will likely be negative. When they are not—when, to the contrary, low-level infractions are rewarded—the escalation process is launched. It is thus in the spirit of and toward the goal of "catch it low to prevent it high" that I now proceed to a full description of the diverse forms of verbal, physical, criminal, and minimal maltreatment. I will describe their several forms of expression, research bearing upon their causes and consequences, and, when available, detailed information on successful interventions for their control and reduction.

CHAPTER TWO

Verbal Maltreatment

VERBAL ABUSE

The effects of verbally aggressive messages in interpersonal communication provide sufficient and compelling justification for studying verbal aggression in order to gain control over its occurrence. . . . The most fundamental effect is self-concept damage. . . . Such damage can be even more harmful and long lasting than the results of physical aggression. . . . For instance, the self-concept damage done by teasing a child about an aspect of physical appearance can endure for a lifetime and exert an enormous impact on the amount of unhappiness experienced. All of the following effects stem, to some degree, from self-concept damage. . . . Some are more temporal in nature: hurt feelings, anger, irritation, embarrassment, discouragement. Others pertain more to interpersonal relations: relationship deterioration and relationship termination. Despite the seriousness of these effects, the more grave from both a personal and societal perspective, is that verbal aggression sometimes escalates into physical violence. (Infante & Wigley, 1986, pp. 61–62)

Verbal abuse has been defined as behavior that seeks to communicate to others that they are bad, possess negative qualities, or are not meeting some internal or external standard (T. A. Kinney, 1994). Infante, Riddle, Horwath, and Tumlin (1992) describe it as actions that attempt to attack the self-concepts of other people in order to inflict psychological pain. What specific statements concretize these definitions? What are the words that hurt? According to Marshall (1994), they are words that seek to control, corrupt, degrade, denigrate, dominate, embarrass, exploit, induce fear or anxiety, humiliate, induce guilt, induce powerlessness, create jealousy, punish, reject, sabotage, threaten, or isolate. Epstein and Krakower (1974) created a set of 71 potentially verbally abusive statements that might be directed at a male target, then had a large sample of raters judge the statements on a 7-point scale ranging from "not hostile" to "extremely hostile." Table 2.1 presents these scaled statements and their mean hostility ratings by male, female, and combined raters.

Epstein and Krakower's (1974) verbal aggression statement pool is a useful beginning both for operationally defining the construct and for providing stimulus items of use for further research in this domain. A logical next step is to take such item pools, useful but unwieldy, and via cluster-analytic means create category systems that demonstrably allocate abusive statements into meaningful groupings. Four researchers and their collaborators performed this valuable service (Infante, Sabourin, Rudd, & Shannon, 1990; T. A. Kinney, 1994; Mosher & Proenza, 1969; Vangelisti, 1994). Following is a presentation of these category outcomes.

Infante et al. (1990) conducted their effort in the context of family violence research. Cluster analysis revealed 10 types of verbally abusive messages: character attacks, competence attacks, background attacks ("You're just like your father, a loser"), physical appearance attacks, maledictions ("You'll never amount to anything"), teasing, ridicule, threats, swearing, and nonverbal emblems (derogatory faces, derogatory gestures). Infante et al.'s cluster-analytic efforts have proven useful not only in organizing this domain of low-level aggression but also in designing remedial

Table 2.1—Items of Verbal Aggression Scale with Mean Hostility for Male Raters, Female Raters, and All Raters

Item	86 male raters	100 female raters	186 raters
He seems to be troubled by something.	1.57	1.20	1.39
He must feel uneasy at times.	1.55	1.50	1.52
He's undecided about some issues.	1.62	1.45	1.53
He seems uncomfortable in this room.	1.59	1.50	1.54
He's probably moody sometimes.	1.87	1.24	1.56
He has a rather sad expression.	1.85	1.57	1.70
He is sometimes unhappy with his life.	1.89	1.56	1.73
If unhappy, he'd go off by himself.	2.15	1.36	1.76
He dislikes uncertain situations.	1.83	1.70	1.76
He seems to be a little anxious.	2.02	1.53	1.78
He doesn't seem overly optimistic.	1.90	1.90	1.90
He's not entirely satisfied with himself.	2.07	1.76	1.90
He rarely reads the newspaper.	2.00	1.91	1.96
His mind seems to be wandering.	1.97	2.05	2.01
Some of his remarks are ambiguous.	2.23	1.89	2.06
Sometimes he's a little too cautious.	2.13	2.02	2.08
I find him hard to understand.	2.47	2.07	2.27
He seems to be unsure of himself.	2.49	2.04	2.27
The world just passes him by.	2.32	2.29	2.30
He doesn't smile very much.	2.66	2.18	2.42
He'd be difficult to get to know.	2.57	2.51	2.54
He's not totally honest with himself.	2.68	2.53	2.61
His voice has no life to it.	2.47	2.79	2.64
He doesn't think very logically.	3.06	2.58	2.83
He seems to lack originality.	2.89	2.85	2.87
His vocabulary is somewhat limited.	2.85	2.96	2.91
I'm not sure we'd get along too well.	3.30	2.58	2.95
He seems very apathetic about life.	3.03	3.24	3.14
He's as timid as a scared little animal.	3.33	3.07	3.19
He seems totally unsure of life.	3.06	3.33	3.20
He must have difficulty relating to others.	3.60	3.02	3.32
He seems to have no sense of humor.	3.53	3.13	3.34
He seems to be overly dependent.	3.45	3.36	3.40
He can't look you straight in the eye.	3.40	3.47	3.44
He'd let people walk all over him.	3.38	3.56	3.47
He's probably very unsociable.	3.22	3.71	3.48

Table 2.1—(continued)

Item	86 male raters	100 female raters	186 raters
His ideas are a bit simple-minded.	3.65	3.35	3.49
He has a sloppy appearance.	3.45	3.64	3.54
He'd do anything that was fashionable.	3.79	3.56	3.67
He just seems to follow the crowd.	3.85	3.56	3.71
He's strictly a conforming type.	3.91	3.56	3.74
He has a mediocre personality.	3.65	3.83	3.75
His voice is very annoying.	3.67	4.00	3.85
He doesn't think for himself.	4.00	3.83	3.91
He's as helpless as a child.	4.10	3.87	3.98
He must not have much self-respect.	4.13	3.91	4.02
He appears to be socially inept.	3.99	4.37	4.19
It's hard to believe he has any friends.	4.06	4.33	4.20
He has a very shallow personality.	4.19	4.36	4.27
He has many unpleasant mannerisms.	4.36	4.42	4.39
He is a very cold individual.	4.09	4.76	4.41
He's insensitive to others' needs.	4.33	4.84	4.60
He seems to be terribly insincere.	4.51	4.78	4.64
His manners are coarse and uncouth.	4.81	4.78	4.79
You couldn't count on this guy.	4.64	4.93	4.80
He comes across as a clod.	4.85	4.84	4.84
I'd bet he's a real coward.	4.79	4.92	4.86
He really is an inarticulate bore.	4.70	5.13	4.91
He looks puny and impotent.	4.66	5.27	4.96
He's really pretty obnoxious.	4.81	5.16	4.98
It's clear he has no guts.	5.09	5.19	5.14
He's a totally maladjusted person.	5.23	5.18	5.21
Personally, I wouldn't trust him.	4.93	5.46	5.22
As a male, he's a real jellyfish.	4.96	5.58	5.26
He looks like a real degenerate.	5.26	5.49	5.38
He sounds like a real phony.	5.38	5.40	5.39
He'd make a pretty lousy friend.	5.45	5.53	5.49
This person is an obvious hypocrite.	5.37	5.68	5.54
As a human being, he's a real loser.	5.33	5.86	5.61
People like him are useless.	5.77	6.00	5.88
He doesn't deserve to be alive.	6.66	6.60	6.63

Note. Reproduced with permission of the authors and publisher from: Epstein, N., and Krakower, S. A measure of verbal aggression. *Perceptual and Motor Skills,* 1974, 39, 218–219. © Perceptual and Motor Skills 1974.

efforts to train people in competent and nondamaging coping responses to such aggression.

T. A. Kinney's (1994) typology, which builds upon the work of Infante et al. (1990), is depicted in Table 2.2. Kinney drops the teasing, ridicule, threat, swearing, and nonverbal emblem categories, seeing these more as message delivery means than as message types. Kinney asserts that message content is but one of three components of the strategy used by verbally abusive persons. To better understand and respond to such attack behavior, one must attend not only to the target of the communication (i.e., the preceding cluster analysis) but also to its form and force. Its form may be teasing, threat, ridicule, or other means intended to harm, control, or demean. Its force is largely determined by voice characteristics such as pitch and volume and accompanying gestures and posturing as well as the intensity of the particular words chosen. Kinney illustrates:

> For example, the message "You're an idiot!!" would be considered strong if it were delivered in a loud, dominant tone, and would be intensified if it contained an expletive. On the other hand, the message "If you do not understand, please ask one of us to explain it to you" would be considered weak if delivered in a subdued and calm manner, and because the message contains a politeness marker (please). (p. 201)

Kinney has demonstrated the utility of his category system via both reliability research, showing that raters can consistently classify arrays of verbally abusive messages employing this system, and predictive validity studies, relating the typology to recipient distress levels (e.g., as predicted, greater recipient distress is experienced when the abusive message's target is a stable rather than transient characteristic of the message recipient).

Central importance of message delivery force to perception of level of aggression is underscored further by Mosher and Proen-

Table 2.2—Kinney Verbal Abuse Clusters

Group membership attacks

Items

1. "He acts like such a male." (involuntary)
2. "This is a very good paper for you being a football player. Who wrote it for you?" (voluntary)
3. "You're a racist."
4. "He's a Japanese. He must be studying economics or engineering."

Motivational attacks

Items

1. "You are so lazy. You never do your fair share of work around the house."
2. "My God, you are lazy."
3. "Man, you're a lazy pig. All you do is sleep and eat. Whenever we go on vacation you're always sleeping. Some things never change."

Preparedness attacks

Items

1. "You're so spoiled, you're such a baby. Why don't you grow up?" (immaturity)
2. "Hey, could you get your dishes cleaned and out of the sink?" (avoidance of duty)
3. "Why are you so damn blind in these types of situations? Wake up and look around you." (lack of planning)
4. "I can't believe you don't know what you are going to do after you graduate." (lack of planning)

Awareness attacks

Items

1. "I hate you. You're pathetic. You think you are so great, but you're not." (socially ineffective)
2. "How long is it going to be before you get that stick out of your a___?" (personally ineffective)

Characteristics attacks

Items

1. "You fat son-of-a-b_____!" (appearance)
2. "You're so dumb, I can't believe you didn't know that." (intelligence)
3. "I'm sick of you staring at my boyfriend. If you don't knock it off, I'll beat the crap out of you." (annoying action)
4. "You're incompetent." (ability)

Relational attacks

Items

1. "I forgot the typewriter because of you. You are so self-centered, all you think about is yourself!" (self-centeredness)
2. "I'm sick of doing all the work on this project. Don't you care about this project or your grade? What is wrong with you?" (professional responsibility)
3. "I'm sick of you never being around when we need you." (involvement)
4. "I don't understand why you can't help me. I thought I could rely on you, of all people. I guess I know who my real and true friends are!" (reciprocation)

Note. From "An Inductively Derived Typology of Verbal Aggression and Its Association to Distress" by T. A. Kinney, 1994, *Human Communication Research, 21,* 183–122. Copyright 1994 by Sage Publications, Inc. Reprinted by permission of Sage Publications, Inc.

za's (1969) verbal aggression intensity categories: criticism, stereotypic derogation, severe derogation, stream of profanity, and threat of physical attack. Greenberg's (1976) sentence rating results using this category approach are reflected in Table 2.3.

The fourth cluster-analytic effort was conducted by Vangelisti (1994). In this work, a large sample of undergraduate students was asked to recall and describe in writing situations in which people had said things to them that had hurt their feelings. Examples of such hurtful messages include "He never liked you anyway. He just used you to get back at me" (romantic relations), "God almighty,

Table 2.3—Greenberg Sentence Rating Results Based on Mosher and Proenza Verbal Abuse Clusters

Aggressive level	Mean rating	Sentence
Criticism ($\overline{X} = 1.60$)	2.02	1. I wonder why you keep breaking them when no one else does.
	1.37	2. No, no, that's wrong.
	2.51	3. You say the wrong thing at the wrong time.
	.51	4. You seem to have trouble with that.
	1.59	5. You do that too slow.
Stereotypic derogation ($\overline{X} = 2.97$)	2.13	6. You're just plain nuts.
	3.54	7. You're dishonest.
	2.36	8. You're kind of malicious.
	3.28	9. I end up thinking you're a fool.
	3.50	10. You act like you're stupid.
	5.55	11. Anybody who pulls shit like you do is a pain in the ass.
Stereotypic derogation with cursing ($\overline{X} = 5.29$)	5.05	12. I end up thinking you're a son-of-a-bitch.
	4.64	13. You act like an asshole.
	5.18	14. You fuck up the whole damned thing.
	6.00	15. Then we find out that you're a god-damned liar.
	4.77	16. Jokes about faggots and lesbians make me think of you.
Severe derogation ($\overline{X} = 4.92$)	4.36	17. A lot of people rob the cradle, but you're really weird picking 'em under the age of ten.
	5.38	18. The mere mention of a nose-picking pervert brings you to mind.
	4.95	19. The reason you act so messed up is because your parents aren't even married.
	5.54	20. I see perverts come in here, but you're the worst.

Severe derogation with cursing ($\overline{X}$ = 5.80)	6.13	21. Kissing your boss's ass must get to be a drag for a brown-nose shit like you.
	4.77	22. You goddamned, self-destructive alcoholic, you act like you're trying to drink yourself to death.
	5.39	23. I'll bet you work in that mortuary just so you get a chance to screw those dumb-ass corpses.
	6.64	24. You act like a mother-fucking idiot with shit for brains.
	5.73	25. The reason I don't like to eat with you is because you pick your fucking nose and fart at the table.
	6.26	26. You goddamned weird asshole. I'll bet you eat your own stupid shit.
Stream of profanity ($\overline{X}$ = 6.23)	6.28	27. You little asshole, shithead dick-face, you make me want to puke.
	7.00	28. Do it that way, you son-of-a-bitch queer-ass bastard.
	4.97	29. You little bastard-ass son-of-a-bitch shithead, get the hell out and from now on knock.
	7.48	30. I don't give a mother-fucking shit if you stick your ass out the goddamned window.
	6.16	31. I'll pulverize the hell out of you.
Threat of physical attack ($\overline{X}$ = 7.08)	7.10	32. He might leave you alone, but I'll beat the living shit out of you.
	6.55	33. I'm going to kick your ass.
	7.33	34. Correct your mistakes, or I'll break this club over your goddamned head.
	7.92	35. Just to teach you a lesson, I'm going to smash your mother-fucking face in.

Note. From "The Effects of Language Intensity Modification on Perceived Verbal Aggressiveness" by B. S. Greenberg, 1976, *Communication Monographs, 45,* 130–139. Used by permission of the National Communication Association.

you're fat!" (physical appearance), "I guess it's hard for you teenage illiterates to write that stuff" (abilities/intelligence), "Well, I think you're selfish and spoiled" (personality traits). The hurtful message topics Vangelisti provides were cast into the following verbal abuse clusters: accusation, evaluation, directive, advice, expressed desire, information, question, threat, joke, and lie. Informative messages, Vangelisti suggests, are typically more hurtful than evaluative messages. The former are difficult to discount; the latter, in a sense, are a matter of disputable opinion or belief.

> When accused or evaluated, recipients have the control to either overtly or covertly "defend" themselves against hurt. [However,] when informed of something [factual], there are few such arguments available. If, for example, a person is accused of being selfish or inconsiderate, that person can point out instances in which that has not been the case. However, if the same person is informed by a lover that the lover is "seeing someone else," there is little the person can say to counter the statement. (p. 64)

In addition to informative or evaluative content, Vangelisti (1994) was also able to demonstrate four other qualities of the message and its delivery context that influence its level of experienced hurtfulness. One is attributed intent. For example, the recipient will perceive the message as more hurtful if he or she interprets the sender's intent as to blame rather than to explain. As T. A. Kinney (1994) had found, messages will also be experienced as more hurtful in the context of marital and romantic relationships when they refer to stable, global qualities of the recipient rather than more ephemeral or localized characteristics. More generally in such a context, message recipients who report close, intimate relationships with their partners experience less hurtful message impact than do those with less intimate, more distant relationships. Finally, Vangelisti also demonstrated that messages delivered by a family member (i.e., from someone with whom the recipient has a permanent relationship) will often have less impact than messages from persons with whom one is in relationships that can be terminated.

These four cluster-analytic systems for organizing verbally abusive messages are a particularly valuable beginning for both understanding and evaluating such low-level aggression. J. D. McCarthy (1991) shares this perspective:

> Developing taxonomies of social elements is unsung labor in sociology as it is in other disciplines. Steven Jay Gould remarks that it "occupies a low status among the sciences because most people view the activity as a kind of glorified bookkeeping dedicated to pasting objects into preassigned spaces in nature's stamp album. But classifications are . . . theories of order, not simple records of nature. . . . They shape our thoughts and deeds." (p. xvi)

The taxonomies just described, therefore, will be of special value to both practitioners and researchers as they undertake to comprehend the nature of verbal abuse and seek to alter its frequency and hurtful impact.

Common, everyday experience readily reveals that being on the receiving end of the types of messages examined in this chapter can be at best an unpleasant experience and often quite hurtful. Verbal abuse may well be the prime example, among all forms of low-level aggression, of behavior that is both frequent and frequently prone to escalate to higher rungs on the ladder to violence. And frequent in occurrence it is. Vissing, Straus, Gelles, and Harrop (1991) analyzed data on a national sample of 3,346 American parents with children under age 18 living at home. They found that 63% of the parents reported one and often more instances of cursing and insulting their child. Data reporting or reflecting similarly frequent incidences of verbal abuse are not hard to come by in marital (Stets, 1990; Straus, 1974), work (Allcorn, 1994), school (Goldstein & Conoley, 1997), and other contexts. In a national survey of over 5,000 American couples, for example, Straus and Sweet (1992) found that men and women engage in approximately equal amounts of verbal maltreatment of their partners. The probability of the occurrence of such behavior increases with alcohol or drug use and abuse, decreases with age and the number of children in the family, and is independent of race or socioeconomic status.

A number of investigators have directly examined verbal abuse as a precursor to higher levels of hurtfulness and have found such a progression to be not uncommon (Hoffman, 1984; Stets, 1990; Straus, 1974; L. Walker, 1979), a conclusion further supported by the laboratory, criminal justice, and incivilities escalation studies examined in chapter 1. A finer-grained analysis of this escalation sequence by Follingstad, Rutledge, Berg, Hause, and Polek (1990) first identified six major types of verbal abuse operating in male-female marital relationships: threats of abuse, threats to change marital status, ridicule, jealousy, restriction, and damage to property. Only three of these proved to be reliable precursors of subsequent physical abuse. The authors observe:

> It is important to note that the best prognosticators of the ability to predict physical abuse from emotional abuse were the *types* of emotional abuse that were present. The three types that predicted physical abuse made conceptual sense. It may be that *threats of abuse* will conjure up imagery of physical incidents and therefore loosen inhibitions against using physical means for the man. *Restriction* of the woman may imply a need for greater control over her at the time, which may suggest a build-up of tension for the abusing man. And, *damage to the woman's property* may be an initial destructive step that translates easily into damaging the woman. (p. 118)

Physical aggression is certainly not the only hurtful sequela of verbal abuse. Dobash and Dobash (1977–1978) and L. Walker

(1983) report that women who received frequent sarcasm, humiliation, threats, and/or name-calling from their spouses experience lowered levels of self-esteem and heightened levels of loss of control and powerlessness. Kashani, Burbach, and Rosenberg (1988) and Rohner and Rohner (1980) report similar self-concept changes in children receiving such abusive messages from their parents. Similar outcomes have been reported by Garbarino and Vondra (1987), Martin (1980), and Marshall (1994).

There are four types of verbal abuse that appear to be particularly common and thus deserve separate attention here. They are teasing, cursing, gossip, and ostracism or shunning. Teasing can vary from mild and playful to severe and hurtful; at the latter end it shades into bullying. Cursing is a fact of life that apparently is becoming more and more common. In many American schools, for example, youngsters—sometimes freely—curse each other, curse the work, and curse the teacher. Gossip, like teasing, can be harmless or, at its other extreme, malicious. As we shall see, much of what is written about the functions of gossip is positive, but gossip as verbal abuse is nonetheless a frequent reality. Verbal abuse generally takes the form of one person's saying something nasty to another person. But verbal abuse may also be sharply communicated if nothing is said—about anything. The final type of verbal abuse I will consider is ostracism.

TEASING

Although in the hindsight of adulthood it may seem that the teasing often directed toward adolescents and younger children by their peers is merely harmless kidding, ask the adolescents and children themselves. For many, teasing can be painful, even traumatizing, aggression directed toward them. True, in the grand scheme of things, it is not the most damaging type of aggression. But it can lead to serious enough effects on the target person that better understanding it and controlling it is important. In addition, teasing is by far not an uncommon event. School surveys at several grade levels reveal that at least two-thirds of students are at times, and sometimes frequently, teasing targets (Kelly & Cohn, 1988; Mooney, Creeser, & Blatchford, 1991).

Teasing embodies three qualities: aggression, humor, and ambiguity about its seriousness (Shapiro, Baumeister, & Kessler, 1991). It may mask criticism and insult and thus actually be aggressive, or it may be gentle and friendly and thus contain little aggression. Research shows that its most common form entails making fun of someone or something. Delivering sarcasm, tricking the target person into believing something, using exaggerated imitation, pointing, making faces, physically pestering, taking an item such as the target's hat and refusing to give it back—these are among the several forms that teasing can take (Shapiro et al., 1991).

What are children and adolescents teased about? Mostly physical appearance (especially being overweight) but also intellectual performance (being either too slow or too smart), physical and athletic performance, family members, interest in the opposite or the same sex, personal hygiene, race, fearfulness, promiscuity, psychological problems, handicapping conditions, and more (Cash, 1995; Kelly & Cohn, 1988; Tizard, Blatchford, Burke, Farquhar, & Plewis, 1988). The list is long; a youngster seeking to tease another indeed has many choices.

When asked, young people say they tease others because someone teased them first; as a joke; because they disliked the other person; because they were in a bad mood; or because the rest of their group was teasing someone. Much teasing also seems motivated by an effort to rein in any behaviors that are too different from the group norm. Thus, not only are unpopular, obese, or intellectually slow children teased a lot; so are those who are popular, good-looking, and intellectually advanced.

Teasing may be an effort to communicate aggression in a safe way, as happens when two youths engage in verbal dueling. It may also, in its more benign expressions, communicate affection and do so in a way that is less embarrassing to the teaser than its direct expression would be.

The person being teased must decode the message, must figure out how much is humor and how much is aggression, as well as determine exactly what the teaser was intending to say. The parties' relationship, the teaser's tone of voice and facial expression, and what was going on just before the tease all go into this decoding effort.

In families, especially early in children's lives, teasing is more a paternal than either a maternal or a sibling behavior (Labrell, 1994). Fathers tease by blocking their infants' ongoing actions, by pretend fighting or roughhouse play, and by sudden surprise (as in peek-a-boo games or "magic"). Such introduction of upended expectancies, challenge, and novelty, Labrell proposes, may contribute in positive ways to a youngster's emotional and cognitive development. Warm (1997) takes a quite similar position. When teasing moves beyond mild play, however, its consequences seem to be anything but benign.

When asked how being teased made them feel, 97% of the elementary school students in one survey said angry, embarrassed, hurt, or sad (Shapiro et al., 1991). The teaser may be creating what he or she thinks is harmless fun, but for the target person it is anything but fun. Of those surveyed, 10% respond by fighting, 40% by teasing back, and 25% by trying to ignore the teasing; only 12% said they usually laughed along with the teaser.

Adults who experienced in childhood substantial teasing about physical appearance are more likely to report body image dissatisfaction (Thompson, Fabian, Moulton, Dunn, & Altabe, 1991) and depression (Fabian & Thompson, 1989). Words can and do hurt. Teasing, especially teasing with a bite to it, is not playful behavior to be ignored. It is low-level aggression, to be actively discouraged.

CURSING

Cursing is a form of low-level aggression that begins quite early in life and grows in frequency over childhood and adolescence. Jay (1992) reports that by age 2, children typically know about 4 words that can be categorized as curse words. By age 4, the number is about 20, and it grows from there—with boys learning both more and more offensive words than girls. By age 10, children can produce between 30 and 40 different expressions containing dirty words. (For adults, the comparable number is 60 to 70.) Much of the content of curse words early in life concerns the rituals of toilet training and elimination. As the child grows to and through adolescence, terms focused on body processes and parts associated with sexual behavior become the most frequently used curse words (e.g., *shit, motherfucker, cocksucker*), as do those targeted to ancestral allusions (e.g., *bastard, son of a bitch*).

Vetter (1969) suggests that all curse words are related to either sex and excretion, blasphemy, or animal abuse. What words are in fact used, and how frequently? A survey conducted by Foote and Woodward (1973) revealed, for the male and female adults they sampled, the 20 most frequently used obscenities, listed in order of frequency in Table 2.4.

Categories of curse words, this survey reveals, are more diverse than Vetter (1969) proposed; they include body processes, parts, and products; ancestral allusions; blasphemy; social deviation; and ethnic and racial slurs. Essentially similar frequency-of-use results emerged in a second survey, reported by Jay (1977), with the added information that the rated frequency of use and the rated tabooness of terms were closely and positively associated.

Table 2.4—Most Frequently Produced Obscenities

Word	Denotative classification
Fuck	Body process
Shit	Body product
Bastard	Ancestral allusion
Cunt	Body part
Motherfucker	Body process/ancestral allusion
Cocksucker	Body process
Son-of-a-bitch	Animal/ancestral allusion
Bitch	Animal
God damn	Religious blasphemy
Prick	Body part
Damn	Religious blasphemy
Whore	Social deviation
Hell	Religious blasphemy
Asshole	Body part
Cock	Body part/animal
Piss	Body product
Tit(s)	Body part
Suck	Body process
Bullshit	Animal/body product
Nigger	Ethnic-racial slur

Note. From "A Preliminary Investigation of Obscene Language" by R. Foote and J. Woodward, 1973, *Journal of Psychology, 83,* 263–275. Reprinted with permission of the Helen Dwight Reid Educational Foundation. Published by Heldref Publications, 1319 Eighteenth St., NW, Washington, DC 20036–1802. Copyright © 1973.

Of interest for this book's primary focus, low-level aggression, Driscoll (1981) obtained level-of-aggression and frequency-of-use ratings from successive samples of adult raters, a process yielding the level-of-frequency data reported in Table 2.5.

Like all other forms of low-level aggression examined in this book, cursing is very much a person-environment event. What is said is determined not only by who is saying it but also by where the person is and when. P. Cameron (1969) found that curse words

Table 2.5—Level of Aggression and Frequency-of-Use Ratings for Cursing

	Aggression ratings	Frequency-of aggressive-use ratings
Asshole	4.90	4.80
Ball-buster	3.67	1.34
Bastard	4.81	4.17
Beast	2.26	2.85
Bitch	5.35	5.13
Blubberhead	2.09	1.56
Brown-noser	3.17	2.95
Bullshitter	4.02	4.32
Chicken	2.79	3.32
Chump	2.47	2.60
Clown	1.77	3.38
Cock	4.52	2.53
Cocksucker	5.31	3.65
Crazy	1.77	3.50
Dimwit	2.35	2.74
Dipshit	3.81	2.98
Dope	2.20	3.44
Dork	2.87	2.96
Fart	3.26	3.64
Fathead	2.65	3.04
Fuck-off	5.27	3.77
Goon	2.48	2.45
Ham	1.61	2.55
Hothead	2.95	3.22
Jackass	4.34	4.21
Liar	4.39	4.47
Maniac	2.97	3.00
Motherfucker	5.65	4.82
Nag	2.34	2.97
Numbskull	2.34	2.97
Prick	4.73	3.70
Punk	2.95	4.15
Sap	2.39	2.24
Schlemiel	2.29	.44
Schmo	2.00	.59
Screwball	2.57	2.82

	Aggression ratings	Frequency-of aggressive-use ratings
Shit	4.44	4.00
Skunk	2.00	1.92
Slut	5.33	3.79
Snake	2.11	1.52
Son-of-a-bitch	5.45	5.08
Stink	3.38	3.10
Sucker	4.18	3.75
Turkey	1.99	4.22
Wacko	2.06	1.82
Weirdo	2.78	3.59
Windbag	2.49	2.16
Wise-ass	4.02	2.91

Note. From "Aggressiveness and Frequency-of-Aggressive-Use Ratings for Pejorative Epithets by Americans" by J. M. Driscoll, 1981, *Journal of Social Psychology, 104,* 111–126. Reprinted with permission of the Helen Dwight Reid Educational Foundation. Published by Heldref Publications, 1319 Eighteenth St., NW, Washington, DC 20036–1802. Copyright © 1981.

constituted 3% of adult conversation on the job but 13% of what they said during leisure conversations. A college student sample (Jay, 1992) estimated the likelihood (0 to 100) of hearing a dirty word to vary considerably by campus location: dormitory (90), parking lot (54), bookstore (33), copy center (21), admissions office (7), dean's office (7), day care center (1). Some have suggested that cursing is more frequent in America's large cities than in other venues, perhaps because of higher stress levels, greater anonymity, and higher levels of tolerance (Goldstein, 1996b).

Why do people curse? Gilliam, Stough, and Fad (1991) propose several reasons: expression of anger, attention seeking, impression management (i.e., to appear "tough"), imitation, rebellion, and preoccupation with bodily organs and sexual acts. Attention seeking may be particularly significant. The youngster who says "fuck" or "shit" in class is immediately and unequivocally rewarded with teacher and classmate attention. Such attention, even if it takes the form of teacher alarm, anger, and criticism, is likely to serve as a positive reward that encourages cursing. For this reason, one of the frequently recommended tactics for reducing the likelihood of such inappropriate behavior is to withhold such attention (i.e., extinction or ignoring). Unfortunately, even when the teacher can refrain from attending to cursing (itself not an easy task), the perpetrator's peers are unlikely to do so. Behaviors rewarded are behaviors that continue. Beyond this concern, although extinction may work to diminish the frequency of some inappropriate behaviors, teacher-ignored cursing (just like ignored bullying, vandalism, or any other low-level aggressive act) is quite likely to both continue and escalate as a result of the attentional or other rewards it elicits from other persons.

Epstein, Repp, and Cullinan (1978) offer an alternative attention-providing perspective, but one targeted toward encouraging progressively diminishing levels of cursing. Rather than withholding attention, in this study each time a student used obscene language, a mark was placed on his or her individual "obscene language chart," displayed on the classroom bulletin board. If the student was able to stay below a given level, token reinforcements exchangeable for tangible rewards were provided. Employing a gradually lowering criterion of acceptability, three obscenities per day were permitted initially, diminishing to two, one, and none as the study's phases progressed. Study results demonstrated such differential reinforcement of progressively lower rates of cursing to be successful.

Certain nonviolent punishments may also work. In chapter 6, I propose the use of time-out, response cost, overcorrection, and contingency contracting as viable possibilities. Beyond these methods, I have three additional suggestions. One is negative practice, also known as satiation or instructed repetition. Here, the student is asked to go to a location where others cannot hear him or her (perhaps a time-out room) and repeatedly say the curse word used earlier in public. The repetitions should continue until saying the word becomes not only nonrewarding but even unpleasant. As Gilliam et al. (1991) observe, "Satiation . . . involves presenting a reinforcing stimulus at such a high rate that its reinforcing properties are lost" (p. 368). In addition to the use of such a "swear-down," Novelli (1993) proposes that youth be encouraged to substitute nonoffensive words, acceptable slang, or nonsense syllables for curse words. To be sure, if youngsters can follow this suggestion, "glug you" has a markedly different interpersonal effect than "fuck you" does. However, perhaps the most potent means for altering cursing (or any other form of low-level aggression) is the long-recommended but far too infrequently employed recommendation: "Catch them being good." I describe this splendid tactic fully in chapter 6 and exemplify its use to reduce the likelihood of cursing. Stated simply, it is a recommendation, based upon literally hundreds of studies of the consequences of positive reinforcement, to reward the youngster with praise, approval, and/or something tangible if he or she refrains from cursing in a situation in which he or she has cursed in the past—or even if the youngster curses but does so less often, less intensely, or more briefly. Cursing is a common and challenging form of low-level aggression. Considerable energy, creativity, and consistency on the part of the teacher, parent, or other change agent will be necessary to eliminate or even reduce it.

GOSSIP

In some cultures . . . we stick pins into the effigies of an unliked object; in modern society, gossiping is practiced in place of this mechanism of aggressive hostility and retaliation. (Fine & Rosnow, 1978, p. 166)

A good deal has been written about gossip, and, perhaps surprisingly, most of it is positive. *Webster's Third International Dictionary* defines it as "rumor, report, tattle, or behind-the-scene information, especially of an intimate or personal nature." Gossip is both process and content, verb and noun. In common parlance, it is "idle talk," but a number of writers emphasize its constructive functions. Fine and Rosnow (1978), for example, speak of gossip as purposeful communication that serves the function of information, influence, and entertainment. It is information in "its transmission of culture and illumination of ambiguous areas of behavior, [that] maps the social environment" (p. 162). It is a means for persons at all ages to become informed about norms for appropriate social behavior. As Szwed (1966) observed, gossip is "a sort of tally sheet of public opinion" (p. 435). It is a means of informal communication that can serve as an information grapevine. Gossip serves its information transfer function especially in those situations, personal or impersonal, in which the need for news is great. Gossip also serves an influence purpose. It is an opportunity not only for social comparison (Suls, 1977) but also for social control (Levin & Kimmel, 1977). Gossiping provides the opportunity to both receive and send opinions and evaluations. It is not about the weather that gossiper and gossipee exchange information; it is about norm-relevant standards and departures therefrom—about "improper" behavior, "inappropriate" dress, "inopportune" timing, and the like by one or more third parties. Gossip may also entertain, be a "satisfying diversion" (Fine & Rosnow, 1978, p. 164) or "intellectual chewing gum" (Lumley, 1925, p. 215).

In addition to its informational, influence, and entertainment purposes, gossip has been noted to provide the pleasure of simply talking to other people (Morreall, 1994), promote a sense of solidarity or closeness with others (Levin & Arluke, 1987), and maintain the dividing line between in-group members (who share the gossip) and out-group members (who do not) (Hannerz, 1967). If the substance of the gossip proposes that its targets are somehow inferior or immoral, then gossiping may enhance one's own sense of self-worth and respectability (Levin

& Arluke, 1987). In children, Fine (1977) suggests, gossip serves four functions: socialization, evaluation, impression management, and competency development. Indeed, as noted earlier, the collective "take" on gossip by social and behavioral scientists is indeed a positive one.

There is, however, a darker side to gossip. Gossip can be malicious, demeaning, degrading, and in other ways harmful not only to absent third parties, but even indirectly to its participants. Levin and Arluke (1987) conducted two studies, one in a college student lounge and the other in a nearby bar, and found that between 25 and 30% of student-to-student gossip was about negative personal habits, manners, appearance, or behavior. As Jaeger, Skleder, and Rosnow (1994) suggest, "Although it is described as a pleasurable activity, its consequences may be anything but pleasurable for its targets" (p. 154). These researchers examined gossip patterns and contents over time among members of a university sorority and found that a full half of remarks made emphasized negative themes and target characteristics. D. A. Kinney (1994) reports similar outcomes among high school students. Over a 2-year period, observations and interviews were conducted involving a large sample of female students attending an urban high school. Kinney notes that "the pervasive and intense gossip incited fights in the hallways, altered friendship patterns, and sustained separation between crowds" (p. 42).

In describing the public reputation of gossip, Emler (1994) observes:

> It has a reputation for triviality, for preoccupation with the thoroughly superficial and ephemeral in human affairs. . . . It is unreliable and inaccurate, an entirely fallible source of information about other people. Its motivations are disreputable; tellers are motivated by mischief, rancor, or spite, listeners by a prurient and improper interest in matters that are none of their business.

> Gossipers are often guilty of despicable violations of trust.
> The effects of gossip are frequently damaging—and
> sometimes catastrophically destructive—to the lives and
> livelihoods of those who are gossiped about. (p. 177)

Who gossips? Perhaps almost everyone. Folklore has it that
women do so more than men, but there is little evidence to support this view. Being generally more relationship oriented,
women tend more than men to engage in gossip about friends
and family members, whereas men focus on celebrities, sports
figures, and the like (Levin & Arluke, 1987). People who are more
anxious tend to gossip more (Jaeger et al., 1994), as do individuals in people-oriented versus non-people-oriented professions
(Nevo, Nevo, & Derech-Zehavi, 1994). Because participation in
gossiping may place the individual at the center of the created
communication network, it may temporarily enhance the gossiper's status. Thus, Levin and Arluke propose, it is the most isolated, least popular member of a group who may be most prone
to gossip.

In evaluating the positivity or negativity of gossip, it is well to
remember, as Taylor (1994) points out, that there are two quite different sorts of relationships associated with any act of gossip. For
the several reasons described at the beginning of this section, the
relationship between gossiper and gossipee may be positive to
start with and become even more so as a result of the gossip
communication act. However, the relationship between the parties
sharing the gossip on the one hand, and the person(s) being gos-
siped about on the other, may well be made substantially more
negative because of this same gossip action. In this sense gossip is
indeed a verbal abuse example of low-level aggression. As Levin
and Arluke (1987) note, "It permits the gossiper to communicate
negative, even nasty, information about other people with impuni-
ty, regardless of its consequences for the well-being of the targets" (p. 21).

OSTRACISM

Being isolated, ignored, avoided, excluded, rejected, shunned, exiled, banished, cut off, frozen out, made invisible—all are experiences that give the sense of ostracism. Williams (1997) suggests four types of ostracism, the first two of which I view as verbal maltreatment by what is not said. One is *physical ostracism,* which includes expulsion, banishment, exile, time-out, and, more generally, physically arranging a person's absence, departure, or isolation. In the second type, *social isolation,* the person remains visible to others but is ignored, given the silent treatment or the cold shoulder, "frozen out." *Defensive ostracism* is a self-protective, preemptive self-isolation in anticipation of negative, threatening feedback (including ostracism) from others. Finally, Williams notes, *oblivious ostracism* is the perhaps unintentional ignoring of certain people or types of people one views as not somehow worthy of one's time and energy—the elderly, people from low-income environments, people from particular ethnic groups. Ostracism varies not only by type but also by intensity. Such low-level aggression may vary in degree from coolness of tone and denial of eye contact to total ignoring—no speaking, looking, or attending.

Williams, Sherman-Williams, and Faulkner (1996) conducted a survey of over 2,000 men and women in the United States regarding their personal experiences of the "silent treatment." Three-quarters of those surveyed reported they had used this approach with loved ones; the same percent revealed it had been used on them. In a second such survey of long-term users and victims of the silent treatment, Williams (1997) found that "almost all of the victims we interviewed reported that the effects of long-term ostracism have been devastating . . . chronic or repeated exposure to the silent treatment elicited many negative emotions, such as anger, frustration, sadness, and despair" (p. 158).

Buss, Gomes, Higgins, and Lauterbach (1987) found the use of ostracism common between married couples in conflict. Cairns and Cairns (1991) found that over a third of the conflicts among middle school–age girls involved ostracism. Similar heavy use of such peer rejection behavior has also been reported among elementary-age children (Asher & Coie, 1990). Evans and Eder (1993) draw the distinction between neglected children, who tend to be viewed neutrally by their peers, and rejected children, who are actively disliked. Both are, in a sense, ostracized, but for the former it is "oblivious ostracism"; for the latter it is a much more active social rejection. Coie and Dodge (1983) found that youngsters rejected during one school year were quite likely to be rejected in subsequent years. A number of studies note that youngsters with mental handicaps or learning disabilities are disproportionately prone to receive such ostracism from their schoolmates.

Evans and Eder (1993) conducted a lengthy observational study of peer behavior among middle school students. Observations took place in the school cafeteria. Students who were negatively evaluated by peers for appearance, gender behavior, or mental maturity were most prone to be ostracized—to be ridiculed, to be rejected, to sit alone at lunch. In a sense, such youngsters took a double hit. Not only were they ridiculed and ignored by peers who initiated such behavior, but other youngsters seeking to avoid a sort of stigma by association similarly ostracized them for fear of also becoming victims. The investigators followed up this observational study by interviewing many of the observed youths some time later, when they had left middle school and were in high school. In a statement that offers a strong argument for smaller schools in which every student can find a school-associated role and none or few are marginalized, Evans and Eder note:

> They reported that the middle school status hierarchy
> was so rigid and so limited that only a few students felt
> successful, whereas the rest perceived themselves as

"dweebs" or "nerds." By giving only a few students positive visibility through select extracurricular activities such as basketball and cheerleading, a school tends to increase all students' concern with social status and peer acceptance. (p. 166)

Though I deal in this section with ostracism as low-level aggression, there is a constructive side to its use in some contexts. In the terminology of behavior modification, ostracism might be viewed as a sort of "extreme extinction" and employed as such to alter difficult-to-change inappropriate behaviors—including aggression. Barner-Barry (1986), for example, reports a case study in which a group of children, acting on their own, collectively and successfully used ostracism to reduce the chronic bullying behavior of one of their peers. In the same behavior modification spirit, DeAngelis (1998) notes the tribal banishment of those who commit crimes against the community and the prison use of solitary confinement to punish and, it is hoped, correct serious acting-out behaviors in the correctional context.

Ostracism has also been the focus of a small number of laboratory investigations. Geller, Goodstein, Silver, and Sternberg (1974) found that young women ignored during a conversation by two female confederates of the experimenters reported feeling anxious, withdrawn, frustrated, and bored compared to included participants. Similar feelings—rejection, unworthiness, anger— were reported by participants in a second study who were simply asked to imagine they were being ignored, whereas other participants were asked to imagine inclusion (Craighead, Kimball, & Rehak, 1979). In a third investigation (Williams & Sommer, 1997), one of two confederate participants, while supposedly waiting for the procedure to begin, noticed and began bouncing a racquetball, first alone, and then to others waiting (one of whom was another confederate, the other the real participant). After 1 minute of three-way play, and continuing for a 4-minute period, the two confederates then bounced and tossed the ball only between themselves, while totally ignoring the real participant. In this and a follow-on study that employed exclusive, two-person conversation and not ball bouncing, ostracized participants displayed substantial levels of disengagement and discomfort. Study findings also revealed reliable male-female differences. Ostracized women worked harder than did ostracized males on a subsequent collective task, perhaps as a means of gaining acceptance by the others involved. Women were also more likely to blame themselves for being excluded. Male participants neither compensated by working harder nor blamed themselves for being ostracized.

Ostracism, Williams (1997) concludes, deprives people of a feeling of belonging, threatens their self-esteem, robs them of a sense of control, and reminds them of the fragility of their sense of worth. Clearly, it is a form of low-level aggression worthy of continuing, serious attention.

REDUCING VERBAL MALTREATMENT

I have examined in this chapter a series of common verbally communicated forms of low-level aggression—verbal abuse, teasing, cursing, gossip, and ostracism. How may such hurtful behaviors be managed, reduced, or even eliminated? The parties involved in a verbal maltreatment exchange need to overcome three hurdles if they are to be successful in lowering their anger arousal levels and moving on to a more constructive dialogue. First, each person must calm down and seek to reduce his or her own anger level. Second, ideally, each person will take steps to help the other person calm down and reduce his or her anger level. Third, the two parties will engage in constructive communication about whatever issues had initially sparked the aggressive exchange. The sections that follow detail the procedures the disputing parties can follow to accomplish these three tasks (Goldstein & Keller, 1987; Goldstein & Rosenbaum, 1982).

Calming Yourself

To start to reduce your own anger level and combat the rush of adrenaline that causes your heart to beat faster, your voice to sound louder, and your fists to clench, try the following methods.

Deep breathing. Take a few deep breaths and concentrate on your breathing.

Backward counting. Count backwards. This is a good distractor from thoughts that keep anger pumping.

Peaceful imagery. Imagine yourself relaxed at the beach, by a lake, or in some similar place on a warm and balmy day.

Other relaxers. Try any other thoughts or actions that have helped you relax in the past.

In the final analysis, whenever any of us becomes angry, it is not directly because of what anyone else does but rather because of what we say to ourselves, including how we interpret the other person's words or actions. So after you begin calming yourself by the steps just listed, it is time to give yourself certain calming self-instructions. Try a simple "calm down," "chill out," or "relax." Perhaps you can tell yourself, "I'm not going to let him get to me" or "Getting upset won't help" or "I have a right to be annoyed, but let's keep the lid on." Further self-direction can include benign reinterpretations of what the other person did to provoke you: "Maybe he didn't mean to trip me. He always sits in that stretched-out way." "It's a shame she needs to pick arguments all the time, but it's her problem, not mine. No need for me to take this personally."

Calming the Other Person

When your self-calming steps are beginning to work, it is time to do what you can to help the other person calm down. Try using as many of the following steps as you can.

Model calmness.   One person's calmness in an argument can really help calm the other person down. Use facial expression, posture, gestures, tone of voice, and words to show you are getting your anger under control.

Encourage talking.   Help the other person explain why he or she is angry and what he or she hopes both of you can do to settle matters constructively.

Listen openly.   As things are explained to you, pay attention, don't interrupt, face the other person, and nod your head or give other signs that he or she is getting through to you.

Show understanding.   Say that you understand, that you see what the person means. Repeat in your own words the heart of what he or she said to you. Try to let the person know you understand what he or she is feeling.

Reassure the other person.   Point out that nonaggressive solutions to your conflict exist and that you are willing to work toward them. Reduce your threat; inspire a bit of problem-solving optimism.

Help save face.   Make it easier for the person to retreat or back off gracefully. Avoid cornering or humiliating the other person. Don't argue in front of other people. Try to compromise. Make your goal defeating the problem, not the other person.

Engaging in Constructive Communication

When a reasonable level of calm has been restored between yourself and the other person, it is time to try for effective discussion of the issue(s) under contention. Good communication, of course, begins with your intentions. If your goal is to defeat the other person and win the argument, it will be difficult to reduce aggression. If your goal is to join the other person to defeat the problem—what has been called a win-win strategy—you've made a good start at likely aggression reduction.

How do you get ready for effective, problem-solving communication? Here are some good starting steps.

Plan on dealing with one problem at a time.   Seeking to solve an argument with win-win solutions is not an easy task. Don't make matters more difficult by taking on too much at one time. If more than one problem is pressing, take them up in sequence.

Choose the right time and place.   Be careful where and when you try to communicate when you are or the other person is angry. Avoid audiences; seek privacy. Also, seek times and places in which you are not likely to be interrupted (by people, television, telephone, mealtime) and will be free to finish whatever you start.

Review your plan.   Try to open your mind before you open your mouth. Consider your own views and feelings as well as the other person's. Especially, ask yourself what you can do to bring about a win-win solution to your argument. Rehearse what you and the other person may say. Imagine this conversation in several different forms and outcomes.

Now you and the other person are face to face. Effective problem solvers follow such good communication rules as these.

Define yourself.   Explain your views, the reasons behind them, and your proposed solutions as logically as you can. Carefully spell out anything you think might be misunderstood.

Make sense to the other person.   Keep your listener constantly in mind as you talk. Encourage him or her to ask questions, to check out your meanings. Repeat yourself as much as necessary.

Focus on behavior.   When you describe to the other person your view of what happened and what you would like to happen, concentrate on actual actions you each have taken or might take. Try to avoid focusing on inner qualities that cannot be seen, such as personality, beliefs, intentions, and motivations.

Reciprocate.   As you describe how the other person contributed to the problem and what you think he or she can do to help solve it, be sure that you are equally clear about your part in both its cause and solution. Be specific. Avoid vague generalizations.

Be direct. Say your piece in a straightforward, nonhostile, positive manner. Avoid camouflage, editing, half-truths, or hiding what you honestly believe.

Keep the pressure low. To keep matters calm as your problem solving continues, try to listen openly to the other person, offer reassurance as needed, don't paint the other person into a corner, and show that you understand his or her position and plans. If anger and aggression return, take a temporary break and reschedule your discussion for a later time.

Be empathic. Throughout your discussion, communicate to the other person your understanding of his or her feelings. Even if your understanding is not quite accurate, your effort will be appreciated.

Avoid pitfalls. Much can go wrong when two people argue, even when they are both seeking positive solutions. There are many pitfalls to avoid: threats, commands, interruption, sarcasm, put-downs, counterattacks, insults, teasing, yelling, generalizations ("You never . . ."; "You always . . ."), not responding (silence, sulking, ignoring), speaking for the other person, kitchen-sinking (dredging up old complaints and throwing them into the discussion), and building straw men (distorting what the other person said, and then responding to it as if the other, not you, actually said it).

Such rules for good problem-solving communication are easy to present but hard to follow in the heat of the battle. Nevertheless, if you wish the battle to have a nonviolent, conflict-resolving outcome for both yourself and the other person, they are rules worth following.

CHAPTER THREE

Physical Maltreatment

The dual concerns of this chapter are bullying and sexual harassment. Unlike the several forms of verbal maltreatment that were the focus of chapter 2, the maltreatments to be examined here—predominantly in some settings and frequently in many settings—find expression in physical forms of aggression. Stated otherwise, verbal abuse, teasing, cursing, gossip, and ostracism may grow into physical aggression, but bullying and sexual harassment often actually *are* physical aggression. They are, furthermore, injurious behaviors that can occur almost anywhere but that are most likely in venues characterized by power differentials—for example, home, office, factory, military base, prison, and school. However, much of the theorizing about the causes of these behaviors, research into their processes, and intervention to reduce their occurrence has taken place in school contexts. The school, then, will be the primary though not exclusive focus of the following exploration of bullying and sexual harassment.

BULLYING

Definitions and Escalation

Bullying is harm-intending behavior of a verbal and/or physical character that is typically both unprovoked and repeated. As Stephenson and Smith (1997) note, it is aggressive behavior that is intended to and frequently does cause distress to its targeted victim. More than one bully and more than one victim may be involved in any given bullying incident. Olweus (1993) has employed a definitional distinction between direct and indirect bullying. The former entails face-to-face confrontations, open physical attacks by bully on victim, and the use in such contexts of threats and intimidating gestures. Direct bullying provides our primary rationale for the depiction of bullying as physical maltreatment. Indirect bullying is exemplified by social exclusion and isolation, scapegoating, the spreading of rumors, and similar behaviors more akin to the verbal maltreatments examined earlier.

Bullying has received relatively little attention in the United States (Hoover & Hazler, 1991). Its early recognition and research examination occurred primarily in Scandinavian countries (Olweus, 1993) and in Great Britain (Elliott, 1997a; Smith & Sharp, 1994a). The little that has appeared in American publications is largely anecdotal—opinion pieces and not useful research. One might even say we have been bully-shy in the United States. In spite of the substantial frequency with which bullying occurs, it is often the school's best-kept secret. Teachers and administrators may be preoccupied with acts reflecting higher levels of aggression, or they may simply ignore bullying because most victims, as we shall see, elect not to call it to their attention. When it does occur, it is more likely on the playground or in the school corridors between classes rather than in the classroom, so it usually doesn't disrupt the class. Further, even when its reality is acknowledged, it may still be ignored, given the belief of many school personnel (and parents) that bullying is a "natural" part of growing up and perhaps even a positive contributor to the toughening-up purported to be so useful in a competitive society. Thus, school staff may be unaware that bullying is taking place or, if aware, may ignore it. Others, too, may be blind or mute to its occurrence. The bully won't tell; why should he or she volunteer to get in trouble? The victim won't tell for fear of bringing on further and perhaps more severe episodes of the very behavior he or she wishes to avoid. Other students more often than not elect not to speak up, out of concern about becoming targets themselves and reluctance to break the code of silence that far too frequently prevails among students regarding such matters. The victim's parents are also likely to be unaware that bullying is taking place. They may wonder why their child comes home during the school day to use the bathroom, or how his clothing gets torn, or why she seems so hungry at supper time. They don't know that the school bathroom was too scary or that a bully had ripped the child's clothing or extorted the child's lunch money. Thus, bullying in American schools is little studied, little spoken about, and therefore seldom thwarted.

In consequence, like all other forms of low-level aggression similarly ignored, bullying continues and grows more frequent, and its sequelae emerge and escalate in intensity. Greenbaum, Turner, and Stephens (1989) report that adults who were childhood bullies are five times more likely to have serious criminal records by age 30 than are peers who were not bullies. In a longitudinal study conducted by Olweus (1991), 60% of the boys identified as bullies in grades 6 through 9 had, by age 24, at least one criminal conviction, and 40% of them had three or more arrests. That was true for only 10% of boys who earlier were neither bullies nor victims. Eron, Huesmann, Dubow, Romanoff, and Yarmel (1987) found that youths who bullied at age 8 had a 1-in-4 chance of having a criminal record by age 30, as compared to the 1-in-20 chance most children have. It is not only early adult arrest records that illustrate the escalation potential of physical maltreatment via bullying. So do school dropout, spouse abuse, drug dealing, and vandalism (Eron et al., 1987; Rigby & Cox, 1996). Findings concerning the escalation of bullying directly confirm the concern, expressed in chapter 1, about developmental pathways begun with low-level aggression. Bullying escalation findings also provide strong evidence of the collective need both to better understand its causes and to remediate its consequences.

Frequency and Forms

Because bullying, for the reasons noted, is often a hidden, ignored, or unreported event, its frequency is difficult to estimate. Further, as Hoover and Juul (1993) note, the several survey attempts to do so employ differing definitions of bullying as well as differing sample selection and data collection procedures. Thus, estimates of frequency differ widely and are at best approximations. Perhaps the safest answer to the question "How much bullying is there?" is "A lot!" The results of actual surveys vary widely, but they are invariably substantial. Bullying, these surveys reveal, is regularly perpetrated by 5% (Smith & Sharp, 1994a), 7% (Pearce, 1997), 12% (Hoover & Hazler, 1991), 13% (Boulton & Smith, 1994), 15% (Olweus, 1993), and 17% (Boulton & Underwood, 1992) of all children surveyed. Victims were 9% (Olweus, 1989), 11% (Pearce, 1997), 17% (Boulton & Smith, 1994), 18% (Rigby & O'Brien, 1992), 27% (Smith & Sharp, 1994a), 40% (Elliott & Kilpatrick, 1994), 68% (Elliott, 1997b), and 80% (Hoover & Juul, 1993) of youth surveyed. Beyond the quantifier "a lot," it is not easy to bring order into these arrays of outcomes. As noted, denial, indifference, reluctance to report, diversity of reporting formats, and exaggeration all play indeterminate roles in shaping the numbers. The two ranges are sufficiently broad that central tendency data (means, medians) are largely uninformative. Perhaps greater comfort with and openness of reporting in the future will combine with greater standardization of survey methodology to yield closer approximations to actual frequency of occurrence.

With somewhat greater confidence, however, one can assert that boys bully more frequently than do girls (Olweus, 1993; Ross, 1996), that frequency of bullying peaks in the middle school/junior high school years (Boulton & Underwood, 1992), and that bullying is not uncommon even in preschool (Manning, Heron, & Marshall,

1978) and the earliest years of elementary school (Smith & Levan, 1995). It is directed with particular frequency at special needs children (O'Moore, 1997). A final consideration regarding frequency concerns repetition. Once initiated, bullying behaviors are often prone to continue, depending on victim and contextual response. In Elliott's (1997b, 1997c) survey of 4,000 children in the United Kingdom, for example, almost 40% of victims were victimized multiple times. In Stephenson and Smith's (1997) survey of 1,000 Cleveland school children, 80% of those bullied report being targeted for a year or longer. Boulton and Smith (1994) report similar continuity of victimization.

A small body of literature has accumulated regarding types of bullying behavior as well as types of bullies and victims. The major behavioral distinction to be identified (alluded to earlier) is direct versus indirect bullying. Direct bullying, also termed *overt bullying* (Ahmad & Smith, 1994), consists of hitting, kicking, taking things, pushing, tripping, and shoving as well as yelling, cursing, and threatening. Direct bullying, more generally, is observable physical or verbal aggression. Indirect bullying consists of covert processes, typically conducted via a third party and concretized by spreading of rumors, backbiting, persuading of others not to associate with the target person, and similar behaviors. Such behaviors are examples of the social manipulation and relational aggression that characterize what Richardson (1999) labels "indirect aggression," defined as "behavior intended to harm another living being without confronting the target, through other people or objects" (p. 30).

Lagerspetz, Bjorkqvist, and Peltonen (1988) found that preadolescent girls made greater use of indirect means of bullying, whereas 11- to 12-year-old boys more frequently used direct bullying behaviors. Boys and girls differ little in means employed until about age 8. Starting around this age, girls become more indirect in bullying behaviors, a trend peaking, as just noted, around age

11 or 12. This trend is not apparent in boys until age 15 or older (Rivers & Smith, 1994). A number of investigators have verified these trends (Bjorkqvist, Lagerspetz, & Kaukiainen, 1992; Lane, 1989; Roland, 1993; Smith & Levan, 1995) and suggested that their bases lie both in the greater orientations to affiliation and interpersonal relationships in girls and to power assertion in boys, as well as in safety considerations.

> When in conflict, the individual makes his/her choice of aggressive strategy after an assessment based on the effect/danger ratio. . . . The object is to find a strategy as effective as possible, while at the same time exposing the individual to as little danger as possible. Therefore the usefulness of covert, indirect strategies. [They] put distance to the opponent, and they are accordingly less dangerous than physical aggression. Therefore, when verbal skills develop, verbal means of aggression tend to replace physical ones whenever possible. Since females are physically weaker than males, they may early in life learn to avoid physical aggression. (Roland, 1993, p. 185)

A few further findings regarding the frequency and form of bullying behavior are worth noting. Approximately half of the bullying that occurs comprises one-to-one confrontations, the other half being perpetrated by groups of youngsters. The latter are typically the bully and his or her peer lieutenants, in a form of bullying originally termed "mobbing" when it was identified in Scandinavian schools (Smith & Levan, 1995). Although the study of bullying in schools spotlights the aggressive behavior of individuals and groups of students, it has also been estimated that 10% of teachers regularly engage in bullying behavior. As instructors, disciplinarians, and models, through repeated use of threats and intimidation they can exert a powerful influence for the worse in the lives of targeted students.

In addition to different types of bullying, Olweus (1978) has suggested that there are different types of bullies. The *aggressive bully* is largely as stereotypically imagined—belligerent, coercive, and impulsive, with little tolerance for frustration. Ross (1996) describes such youngsters: "Their salient characteristics are an inflammatory combination of physical strength . . . a concern with power fueled by a strong need to dominate others, and a tendency to overreact aggressively in ambiguous confrontations" (p. 42). Bentley and Li (1994) report these to be youths who believe aggression is an appropriate, legitimate response to others. Miedzian (1992) describes the aggressive bully as one who views the world as made up of two kinds of people: those who dominate and those who submit. The bully is the former, inflicting pain with little remorse upon the latter.

The *passive* or *anxious bully* rarely takes the initiative in provoking a bullying incident but is rather an eagerly waiting lieutenant to the aggressive bully. This bully-helper may not start the action, but once it commences, he or she jumps on board. As Ross (1996) observes:

> The actions of the aggressive bully have a disinhibitory effect by appearing to legitimize the bullying, and this effect is strengthened in the anxious bullies by seeing the aggressive bully rewarded. . . . They appear to buy the approach of the aggressive bullies with intense loyalty. (p. 6)

Batsche and Knoff (1994) suggest that bullying is an intergenerational phenomenon in that the bully at school is often a bullying victim at home. Bullies typically come from home environments relying heavily on physical discipline, offering little warmth, evincing poor problem-solving skills, and reflecting a belief that it is appropriate for children to use physical means for settling conflict situations (Floyd, 1985; Greenbaum, 1988).

All acts of aggression, we would stress, are perpetrator-victim transactions. Although it is crucial to scrupulously avoid blaming the victim for the bullying visited upon him or her, victim characteristics and behaviors do much to influence who gets victimized, and how, and for how long. Olweus (1984) early described the typical victim (a.k.a. "whipping boy," "hostility sponge") as generally anxious, low in assertiveness, and often physically both smaller and weaker than most of his or her peers. Among young children, under age 5, victims have been described as sensitive and gentle youngsters, often unused to and confused by conflict (Elliott, 1997c). Bernstein and Watson (1997) suggest a victim pattern, a constellation of qualities that predispose certain children to be chronically bullied. As evidence in support of this assertion, they point first to the several qualities that these youngsters have in common and that differentiate them from children not victimized—for example, passivity, poor motor coordination, odd mannerisms, lower self-esteem, and poorer social information processing skills. Second, they note, children who are victimized early in life tend to remain victims for a long time, even though they may change schools and neighborhoods of residence. Finally, other children, such as classmates, are able to identify potential victims with high reliability.

Although some victims of bullying have themselves been described as provocative for their ineffectual but nonetheless aggressive behaviors, most are more likely to be social isolates (Ross, 1996). These are youngsters of poor social competence, with little social support, often caught in a downward spiral of growing rejection as nonbullying peers elect to ignore them for fear of a sort of stigma by association that might diffuse to their becoming targets for bullying themselves. Olweus (1991) has described this common group mechanism as one in which peers undergo gradual cognitive changes in perceptions of the victim. Bullying, it will be recalled, is repeated low-level aggression. As it continues, classmates or other peers increasingly see the victim as deviant, worthless, and—as Lerner's (1980) "just world" perspective would suggest—almost deserving of being bullied.

The victim becomes progressively less popular. As Salmivalli, Lagerspetz, Bjorkqvist, Osterman, and Kaukiainen (1996) note, "It becomes a social norm of the group not to like him or her" (p. 12).

Given what I have said about bullying frequently being a secret, hidden act, how might we identify which youngsters are in fact being victimized? According to Elliott (1997a), school officials, teachers, and other responsible adults ought to look for the following array of "telltale signs":

- Being frightened of walking to or from school

- Being unwilling to go to school

- Asking to be driven to school

- Changing the route to school every day

- Showing a marked drop in quality of school work

- Having torn or destroyed clothes, books, or school work

- Returning home from school very hungry

- Beginning bed wetting

- Crying frequently

- Developing stomachaches, headaches

- Having nightmares or other sleep disturbances

- Having unexplained bruises, cuts, or other injuries

- Missing possessions

- Asking for or beginning to steal money

- Frequently "losing" pocket money

- Refusing to describe what is wrong

- Giving improbable excuses for behavior

I have in this section examined the diverse forms bullying takes and explored a number of salient characteristics of both bullies and victims. In the following section, I offer some beginning notions of the reasons for such behavior.

Causes of Bullying: Person and Environment

At several points throughout this book, I speak of low-level aggression as behavior that grows from characteristics of its perpetrators as they interact with qualities of the social and physical environments in which they live and function. That is, aggression grows from a person-environment duet. Bullying grows not only from the several cognitive, dispositional, and behavioral qualities I described earlier as typical of the schoolhouse bully, but also from characteristics of the other persons and places both surrounding the bullying event and antecedent to it.

At the bullying event there is, first of all, the victim. Perry, Williard, and Perry (1990) found that the signs of distress emitted by victimized children often function as the very type of reinforcement to the perpetrator that encourages further bullying. Salmivalli, Karhunen, and Lagerspetz's (1996) study of bullying victims identified three common responses:

1. Counteraggression: The victim speaks up to the bully, tries to get others on his/her side, makes faces at the bully, attacks the bully, calls the bully names, calls to others for help, laughs or shouts at the bully.

2. Helplessness: The victim does or says nothing, starts to cry, stays home from school the next day, leaves in the middle of the day, tells his or her parents and/or teacher.

3. Nonchalance: The victim stays calm, acts as if he or she doesn't care, ignores the bully.

Salmivalli, Karhunen, and Lagerspetz (1996) found that 70% of all victims, even if they are repeatedly bullied, react with helplessness or nonchalance. Coie, Dodge, Terry, and Wright (1991) found that youths in their investigation employed escalation of the aggression, self-defense, conflict resolution, ignoring, and submission in response to bullying. Almost 50% of the time, as Salmivalli et al. had found, the alternative chosen was submission. Counteraggression-avoiding strategies also emerged predominantly in an inquiry by Smith and Sharp (1994a). Their respondents employed avoiding the perpetrator (67%), staying close to other students (57%), or staying home from school (20%).

Beyond the main actors—bully and victim—at least four other student roles may emerge at a school bullying incident and serve to either encourage or thwart its continuance and escalation (Salmivalli, Karhunen, & Lagerspetz, 1996; Sutton & Smith, 1999). At the "high end" of the encouragement for continuance is the *assistant*. This is the student who overtly and physically joins in the bullying, aggresses toward the victim, and perhaps helps escalate the event from an individual confrontation to a group mobbing incident. The *reinforcer* is verbally overt in his or her behavior. This is the student who shouts approval and encouragement to the bully, often as part of a gathering, observing crowd. The *outsider,* perhaps the most common of the auxiliary roles, ignores the bullying, does nothing to help it either end or escalate, and leaves the scene of the incident. (In an investigation by Slee [1993], 35% of the students surveyed responded affirmatively to the statement "It's none of my business." Ahmad and Smith [1994] found similar results.) Finally, the *defender* is the student

79

who actively intervenes to terminate the bullying by telling a responsible adult or actually attacking the bully. The student assuming this role often devotes substantial energy to comforting the victim.

What of the contribution of the school staff? I have already noted the manner in which some teachers and administrators may directly increase the frequency of student bullying by modeling it. Clearly, intimidation, humiliation, and other forms of direct and indirect bullying by school personnel are grossly inappropriate and highly damaging to bullying-reduction efforts. Staff may also encourage bullying by what they fail to do; I refer here to the need for adequate surveillance and timely intervention. Prime venues for bullying are the playground and school corridors, both locations often without adequate numbers of watching and supervising staff. As Higgins (1994) notes, the playground is often a site of overcrowding, exclusion, marginalization, and boredom. As such, it is a prime setting for bullying to take root. So, too, are school corridors and other locations often understaffed and thus underobserved (Ahmad & Smith, 1994). When insufficiency of monitoring is combined, as it too often is in the bully-friendly school, with an indifferent administration and staff prone to ignore bullying incidents or to blame the victim, or when students are taught not to "tell tales," bullying easily escalates.

To be sure, school budgets for supervising personnel are perpetually tight. In addition, as Besag (1997) notes, in the bustle of a large playground it is often quite difficult to distinguish bullying behavior from rough-and-tumble play. Yet, is it really too expensive to upgrade the *quality* of supervision? In one school, for very few additional dollars:

Teachers are now in class at least five minutes before pupils enter the building. The corridors are supervised on a rotating basis by teachers informally chatting to pupils

or among themselves. The outside play areas are observed from second-story classroom windows so that the
bird's eye view supports the supervision of staff in the
playground. (p. 43)

In this context, it is relevant that Olweus (1987) found a negative
correlation of .50 between the relative density of teacher supervision at playtime and the number of bullying incidents.

Stephenson and Smith (1997) illuminate the great importance
of school characteristics with their recommendations on "how to
encourage bullying":

1. The school should have many areas that are difficult for
   staff to supervise.

2. Students should be placed in these areas at times of least
   supervision—break time, lunch time, the beginning and
   end of the school day.

3. If supervision is provided at these times, it should be by
   untrained and underpaid staff.

4. The school day should be arranged so that the entire age
   range of the school arrives and leaves the school at the
   same time.

5. There should be no designated places of respite for students, and the majority of areas in which the students do
   gather should be dominated by fast and furious games.

6. Arrangements should be made that contribute to large
   numbers of students' having to move around the school in
   different directions at the same time.

7. The school should be designed so that the corridors used
   at class transition time are narrow.

8. There should be only one door into and out of each class-room.

9. Materials and supplies should be in short supply so that students have to share them.

10. Teachers should be encouraged to arrive at class late.

11. There should be no agreed, clear, and consistent way to record incidents of bullying.

12. There should be a lack of any clear policy on the use of sanctions.

13. Bullying should be viewed by school administrators and staff as part of the normal growing-up process.

14. The school should promote the view that high achieve-ment rather than relative achievement or effort is valued. This should ensure that many students will feel inadequate and marginalized at school.

15. Administrators should avoid developing a whole-school, antibullying policy.

Intervention

Beginning with the pioneering school bullying program developed by Olweus (1993) and progressing through the similarly compre-hensive interventions offered by Elliott (1997a); Garrity, Jens, Porter, Sager, and Short-Camilli (1994); Pepler, Craig, Ziegler, and Charach (1994); Roland (1989); and Stephenson and Smith (1997), it has become clear that the optimal intervention strategy for deal-ing effectively with bullying by and of students is a whole-school approach. As I have suggested at several points elsewhere in the book with regard to other forms of low-level aggression, all acts of aggression derive from a multiplicity of causes and, thus, will yield best when addressed by an equally complex and comprehensive intervention program. As chapter 6 describes in detail, whatever the program's components, it must be offered with integrity (i.e., true to plan), intensity, and prescriptiveness and in consultation with its recipients. Here, drawing upon and merging the several such comprehensive programs described earlier, I provide a menu or pool of useful school-based antibullying procedures and urge school-based readers to select and sequence whichever elements appear to fit their school's particular institutional climate, readiness, and resources. Following Olweus (1993) but expanding substantially on his specific offerings, I group program intervention components at the school, class, and individual levels. To flesh out the contents of components selected from this pool of alternatives, I especially recommend the training manuals *Bully-Proofing Your School* (Garrity et al., 1994) and *Bullying at School* (Olweus, 1993).

School-level interventions

- Schoolwide survey to determine amount, frequency, and locus of bullying

- Discussion of bullying (nature, sources, signs, prevention) at PTA/PTO meetings

- Discussion of bullying (nature, sources, signs, prevention) at whole-school and by-grade assemblies

- Increased quantity and quality of student surveillance and supervision

- Establishment of school antibullying policy concretized by mission statement distributed to all staff, students, and parents

- Creation of a schoolwide "telling" climate legitimizing informing about bullying and concretized in a phone hot line, an anonymous mail drop, or other means

- Regular staff meetings to exchange bullying-relevant information and monitor intervention effectiveness

- Development and dissemination of antibullying rules via posters, memos, and other means

- Restructuring of high-bullying school locations

- Separate break times for younger and older students

Class-level interventions

- Discussions of bullying (nature, sources, signs, prevention) at class meetings

- Regular role-plays of bullying response measures

- Announcement of use of nonviolent sanctions in response to bullying behavior

- Training of students to be helpful bystanders/informers when bullying occurs

- Formation of victim support groups

- Increased use of cooperative learning for curriculum delivery

- Use of student-run "bully courts" to adjudicate incidents

- Avoidance of use of bullying behavior by teachers

- Monitoring of student understanding of and compliance with schoolwide antibullying policy and rules

- Contracting with students for compliance with antibullying rules

- Use of stories, art, and activities to communicate and reinforce antibullying policy and rules

- Announcement and use of positive consequences for rule-following behavior in regard to bullying

Individual-level interventions

- With bullies

    Social skills training

    Sanctions for bullying behavior

    Employment as cross-age tutors

    Individual counseling

    Anger control training

    Empathy training

- With victims

    Assertiveness training

    Martial arts training

    Social skills training

    Changes of class or school

    Encouragement of association with new peers

    Individual counseling

Whole-school antibullying programs employing varied combinations of these several school-, class-, and individual-level components have been systematically evaluated by a number of investigators in widely dispersed locations and have consistently yielded substantial bullying-reduction outcomes (Arora, 1994; Olweus, 1993; Pepler et al., 1994; Roland, 1989; Smith & Sharp, 1994b). Whole-school intervention programming is a comprehensive strategy well deserving of implementation.

SEXUAL HARASSMENT

Of the times I was sexually harassed at school, one of them made me feel really bad. I was in class and the teacher was looking right at me when this guy grabbed my butt. The teacher saw it happen. I slapped the guy and told him not to do that. My teacher didn't say anything and looked away and went on with the lesson like nothing out of the ordinary had happened. It really confused me because I knew guys weren't supposed to do that, but the teacher didn't do anything. I felt like the teacher (who was a man) betrayed me and thought I was making a big deal out of nothing. But most of all, I felt really bad about myself because it made me feel slutty and cheap. It made me feel mad too because we shouldn't have to put up with that stuff, but no one will do anything to stop it. Now sexual harassment doesn't bother me as much because it happens so much it almost seems normal. I know that sounds awful, but the longer it goes on without anyone doing anything, the more I think of it as just one of those things that I have to put up with.

—*14-year-old girl*

The lines between bullying and sexual harassment are often blurred in the research and applied literature, with some seeing the latter as an example of the former with sexual content (Batsche & Knoff, 1994), and others suggesting that bullying is a common antecedent of sexual harassment (Stein, 1995). In either event, the two are close cousins and frequently adjacent steps in a sequence of verbal and physical maltreatment. A number of investigators have offered typologies of sexual harassment, in each case arraying subtypes according to one or another view of severity. In considering these typologies, it is well to recall the assertion in chapter 1 that level of severity rests in the perceptions of the maltreatment target. Thus, as Fitzgerald, Swan, and Magley (1997) observe regarding sexual harassment, "Severity of the stressor is not considered to inhere in the event itself; rather it is an individual's evaluation of the situation, as influenced by such factors such as ambiguity, perceived threat, loss and so forth that is determinative" (p. 15).

Classification Typologies

The earliest attempt at classification in the domain of sexual harassment was made by Till (1980), who worked with a female college student population. Till ordered behaviors from least to most severe as follows:

1. Generalized sexist remarks: These are insulting, degrading comments about women in general, and are not intended to elicit sexual cooperation.

2. Sanction-free sexual advances: These are solicitations for sexual activity, but with no penalty proposed for the woman's refusal to comply.

3. Solicitation of sexual activity: Here the proposal is accompanied by promise of reward for acquiescence.

4. Coercion of sexual activity: The proposal in this instance is accompanied by threat of punishment for refusal.

5. Sexual crimes: such as rape and sexual assault.

Fitzgerald et al. (1997) offer a three-category classification scheme. The first category, *gender harassment* (similar to Till's generalized sexist remarks), refers to verbal, nonverbal, and physical acts intended to convey hostility or insult to women, rather than solicit sexual cooperation. Acts of *unwanted sexual attention* are solicitations for sexual activity that are unwanted, offensive, and unreciprocated. Finally, *sexual coercion* is extortion of sexual cooperation in return for promised reward or threatened punishment. In addition to the intent of the perpetrator(s) and contents of the harassing communications, Fitzgerald et al. suggest that the severity of harassment experienced by its victim will also be a function of (a) characteristics of the victim herself; (b) characteristics of the context in which the harassment occurs, such as whether complaints are taken seriously, the victim incurs risks in reporting, or meaningful sanctions for perpetrators exist; and (c) qualities of the harassing behavior—for example, physical versus verbal, single versus multiple perpetrators, frightening versus annoying, focused on victim only or others also, status of the perpetrator, and possibilities for escape.

A final, finer grain category system for concretely defining sexual harassment has been offered by Gruber (1992). Within each of three main classifications—verbal requests, verbal comments, and nonverbal displays—the specific subtypes of sexually harassing behavior are arrayed from most to least severe (Table 3.1).

Like Fitzgerald et al.'s (1997) classification system, Gruber's (1992) severity rankings as reported in Table 3.1 derive from multiple criteria. An act of sexual harassment will be judged more severe the higher the status of its source, the more frequent its occurrence, the longer its duration, the more explicit and direct its

---

Table 3.1—Gruber Typology of Sexual Harassment

A. Verbal requests (more to less severe)
  1. Sexual bribery—with threat and/or promise of reward (quid pro quo)
  2. Sexual advances—no threat, seeking sexual intimacy
  3. Relational advances—no threat, repetitively seeking social relationship
  4. Subtle pressures/advances—no threat, implicit or ambiguous goal or target
B. Verbal comments (more to less severe)
  1. Personal remarks—unsolicited and directed *to* a woman
  2. Subjective objectification—rumors and/or comments made *about* a woman
  3. Sexual categorical remarks—about women "in general"
C. Nonverbal displays (more to less severe)
  1. Sexual assault—aggressive contact involving coercion
  2. Sexual touching—brief sexual or contextually sexualized
  3. Sexual posturing—violations of personal space or attempts at personal contact
  4. Sexual materials—pornographic materials, sexually demeaning objects, profanation of women's sexuality

---

Note. From "A Typology of Personal and Environmental Sexual Harassment: Research and Policy Implications for the 1990's" by J. E. Gruber, 1992, *Sex Roles, 26,* 447–464. Copyright 1992 by Plenum Publishing Corporation. Reprinted by permission.

---

contents, the greater its aversiveness or offensiveness, and the more threatening its quality.

Frequency of Occurrence

The diverse forms of sexual harassment indicated in Table 3.1 are far from uncommon. The first nationwide survey seeking to identify the prevalence of sexual harassment was conducted in 1981 by the U.S. Merit Systems Protection Board (USMSPB, 1981). It collected relevant data from a sample of more than 20,000 federal employees, and it showed that 42% of female respondents reported having experienced at least one of the six forms of sexual harassment presented in the survey. Substantial findings have subsequently been reported by others—53% (Gutek, 1985); 50% (Fitzgerald & Shullman, 1993); and in a review of 18 such surveys, a range of 28 to 75% with a median rate of 44% (Gruber, 1997). Particularly dismaying are frequency data among school children. A national survey of middle school children reported that 85% of girls and 76% of boys had experienced unwelcome behavior of a sexual nature at school (American Association of University Women, 1993). Table 3.2 provides frequency percentages from this survey by type of harassment for both girls and boys.

An independent survey, also targeted to middle school youth and conducted in 79 schools by Lee, Croninger, Linn, and Chen (1996), found directly comparable victimization outcomes—83% of the girls, 60% of the boys. One might guess, given the hormonal pressures of puberty, that sexual harassment of children by children begins at about this middle school age. Not so. The American

Table 3.2—American Association of University Women Survey of Students' Sexual Harassment in Schools

	Girls (%)	Boys (%)
Sexual comments, jokes, gestures, or looks	76	56
Touched, grabbed, or pinched in a sexual way	65	42
Intentionally brushed up against in a sexual way	57	36
Flashed or mooned	49	41
Had sexual rumors spread about them	42	34

Note. From Hostile Hallways: The AAUW Survey on Sexual Harassment in America's Schools (p. 9) by American Association of University Women Educational Foundation, 1993, Washington, DC: Author. Copyright 1993 by AAUW Educational Foundation. Reprinted by permission.

Association of University Women (1993) school survey further reports that 32% of students surveyed had been harassed by grade 6 or lower, and 6% were before grade 3! What are the behaviors that concretize sexual harassment in elementary school? Strauss (1994) reports those listed in Table 3.3, based upon a survey of a large sample of Midwestern U. S. teachers.

These findings combine with those of other surveys of sexual harassment at elementary school age (Paludi, 1997) to suggest, as Strauss (1994) has proposed, that the age for onset of sexually harassing behavior is moving from adolescence to early childhood. Our growing "adultification" of children in the United States vis-à-vis clothing, cosmetics, media exposure, and much more is appar-

Table 3.3—Elementary School Sexual Harassment Behaviors

Spiking (forcibly pulling down pants)

Snuggies (forcibly pulling up pants)

Flipping up skirts

Forcing kisses

Grabbing/touching another's genitals

Calling others sexually offensive names

Asking others to perform sexual acts

Threatening rape

Perpetrating sexual assault

Passing sexually explicit notes

Making gender-demeaning comments

Commenting on body parts

Using sexual profanity

Exposing genitals

Circulating pornography

Note. From "Sexual Harassment at an Early Age" by Susan Strauss, 1994, *Principal,* *74*(1), p. 27. Reprinted by permission of the National Association of Elementary School Principals. All rights reserved.

ently increasingly extending to realms of sexuality, including sexual harassment. Data on the frequency of sexual harassment at all school levels deserve wide and repeated dissemination to help us overcome denial of its reality and implement effective interventions. As earlier noted was true of bullying per se, such denial by both parents and school authorities is far from rare. Sabella and Myrick (1995) concur:

> Many parents resist the idea of their children discussing such delicate issues and, thus, have denied permission for systematic intervention and data collection among their children. To appease parents and others, administration may ignore or deny the problem and conclude that it rarely occurs in their schools. (p. 18)

Sexual harassment is a physical maltreatment example of low-level aggression. As such, it must be acknowledged to exist, identified when it occurs, and consequated to reduce or eliminate it. By the same token, it is equally important that we avoid a "moral panic" and that both children and adults learn not only what harassment is but also what it is not. For children (in this case adolescents), Sandler and Paludi (1993) offer guidelines to help distinguish flirtation from sexual harassment. Flirting feels good, makes one feel attractive, is a compliment, is two-way, and is positive. Sexual harassment feels bad, is degrading, makes one feel cheap, is one-way, and is negative. For teachers, the in-school behavior strategy for themselves, "Teach, don't touch," has become the gross overreaction. As Delisle (cited in Yaffe, 1995) admonishes:

> Every pat on the back has become suspect, each congratulatory squeeze to the shoulder a source of potential problems. Hugs have been demoted to handshakes. Private meetings with students have regressed to public forums. . . . In adopting this new philosophy our profession has quietly but surely taken a step back. (p. 10)

Although a significant portion of students experiencing sexual harassment—25% of harassed girls and 10% of boys—are victimized by school staff and not by students (Paludi, 1997) and such behavior must be vigorously discouraged and sanctioned, it is equally important to warn teachers and administrators against becoming overly cautious and forgetting the power of appropriate touching.

Response to Sexual Harassment

Fitzgerald, Gold, and Brock (1990; cited in Paludi, 1997) constructed a valuable classification system for categorizing student responses to sexual harassment, as reflected in Table 3.4.

Other responses to and impacts of sexual harassment have been demonstrated. In the previously noted American Association of University Women (1993) survey, a number of negative academic and emotional sequelae to harassment were reported. In manifestations of the former, victims often wished to stop attending school (33% girls; 12% boys), found it more difficult to pay attention in class (28% girls; 13% boys), and preferred not to talk at all in class (32% girls; 13% boys). Negative emotional responses, of girls and boys respectively, included embarrassment (64%; 36%), loss of self-confidence (43%; 14%), increased self-consciousness (52%; 21%), and increased fearfulness (39%; 8%).

In work settings, as in schools, the consequences for victims of repeated sexual harassment can be both broad and deep. Paludi (1997) points to decreased morale, damaged interpersonal relations, a sense of helplessness, depression, sleep and eating disturbances, and a host of additional psychological and physiological reactions. Dansky and Kilpatrick (1997) note decreased job satisfaction and performance; lessened motivation and morale; increased absenteeism; heightened anxiety, irritability, and sense of vulnerability; fatigue; loss of appetite; and more. Clearly, sexual harassment is a form of low-level aggression whose negative consequences can be and are considerable.

Table 3.4—Student Responses to Sexual Harassment

Internally focused strategies

Detachment	Minimizes situation; treats it like a joke
Denial	Denies it occurred; attempts to ignore/forget it
Relabeling	Reappraises event as less threatening; offers excuses for harasser's behavior
Illusory control	Takes responsibility for the harassment
Endurance	Puts up with harassment, believing help is unavailable or fearing retaliation

Externally focused strategies

Avoidance	Avoids situation by staying away from harasser
Assertion/confrontation	Refuses sexual offer, verbally confronts harasser
Seeks organizational relief	Reports the incident and files a complaint
Seeks social support	Seeks support of others to validate perceptions
Appeasement	Attempts to evade or placate the harasser

Intervention

Whether in school, office, factory, or elsewhere, intervention designed to control, reduce, and eliminate sexual harassment—like interventions for all other forms of low-level aggression—must consist of comprehensive, whole-facility, total-push approaches. In close parallel to my recommendation of multilevel intervention for bullying (school, class, individual), Strauss (1994) recommends administration, teacher, staff, parent, and student involvement in an ongoing intervention process that begins with a broad, frequency-determining survey, development and dissemination of policy statements, and establishment of reporting procedures; moves to personnel awareness and intervention training, establishment of grievance procedures, and monitoring for violations; and seeks evaluation of efficacy and feedback at each level on a continuing basis. Roscoe, Strause, and Goodwin (1992) suggest that a comprehensive intervention for sexual harassment directed to (early adolescent) students optimally will include the following components:

1. Definitions of sexual harassment

2. Specific behaviors that constitute sexual harassment

3. Information about who can be perpetrators and victims

4. Potential effects of sexual harassment on the victim

5. Consequences of sexual harassment for the perpetrator

6. Reasons why sexual harassment occurs

7. Steps students should take if sexually harassed

Valuable manuals detailing comprehensive intervention programming for dealing effectively with sexual harassment have been prepared by O'Donohue (1997) and Ross (1996).

Bullying and sexual harassment are both pervasive forms of physical maltreatment. Considerably more often than not, they are hidden abuses. Our schools and work sites, propelled by law and good conscience, have increasingly begun to acknowledge their existence more fully, identify their causes, consequate their perpetrators, support their victims, and offer intervention programming intense enough to contribute meaningfully to their prevention and elimination. I applaud these healthy developments, acknowledge that we as a society have a long road ahead, and urge that the effort continue.

CHAPTER FOUR

Criminal Maltreatment

Several forms of low-level aggression are crimes. Commit them and you can go to jail, be fined, or both. As previous chapters have sought to do regarding verbal and physical maltreatment, this one examines the definitions, causes, and diverse forms of criminal maltreatment and, to the extent they are available, describes apparently useful intervention responses.

VANDALISM

Definition and Typologies

Vandalism has been defined as

> the willful or malicious destruction, injury, disfigurement, or defacement of property without the consent of the owner or person having custody or control by cutting, tearing, breaking, marking, painting, drawing, covering with filth, or any such means as may be specified by local law. (Federal Bureau of Investigation, 1978, p. 217)

Motivational typologies seeking to specify subtypes of vandalistic behavior have varied greatly in their relative emphases on person-centered versus environment-centered perspectives. Viewing vandalism causation as essentially an intrapersonal phenomenon, Cohen (1973) offers acquisitive, tactical, ideological, vindictive, play, and malicious subtypes. In contrast, holding that vandalism resides not in persons but in the nature of buildings, school or park equipment, or other public facilities, Weinmayer (1969) proposes the following vandalism subtypes: overuse, conflict, curiosity, leverage, deleterious and irresistible temptation, and "no-other-way-to-do-it" vandalism. My own view is that vandalism, like all other forms of aggressive behavior, grows from *both* person and environment characteristics, a perspective on which I elaborate further later in this chapter (Goldstein, 1994).

Across the several typologies suggested, school (and other) vandalism is an expensive fact of U. S. life. Comprehensive monetary cost estimates collectively illustrate that the expense of vandalism, like its incidence, is both absolutely high and increasing. In the approximately 84,000 schools in the United States, for example, monetary vandalism cost estimates over the past 25 years show a near-linear upward trend, peaking in recent years at $600 million (Stoner, Shinn, & Walker, 1991).

Arson, a particularly dangerous form of vandalism, perhaps deserves special comment. Whereas window breaking is the most frequent single act of aggression toward property in schools, arson is clearly the most costly, typically accounting for approximately 40% of total vandalism costs annually (Mathie & Schmidt, 1977).

The costs of vandalism are not only monetary but social. Vestermark and Blauvelt (1978) describe its expensive impact in school settings:

> By limiting criteria of vandalism's impact to only monetary costs, we overlook those incidents which have low monetary cost but, nevertheless, tremendous impact upon the school. The impact of a seventy-nine cent can of spray paint, used to paint racial epithets on a hallway wall, far exceeds the monetary cost of removing the paint. A racial confrontation could result, which might force the closing of the school for an indefinite period. How does one calculate that type of expense: confrontation and subsequent closing of a school? (p. 138)

Causes and Correlates

In a school context, the vandal may be a youngster who feels particularly alienated from the school, believes that he or she has been unjustly placed in detention, or has received a grade that he or she deems unfair. According to Tygert (1988) and Zweig and Ducey (1978), vandalism reaches its peak frequency in seventh grade and then progressively decreases with each succeeding grade. Socioeconomically, typical school vandals are as likely to be from middle-class as from low-income backgrounds (Howard, 1978); emotionally, they are no more disturbed than are youngsters less prone to vandalize (Richards, 1976). However, vandals are more likely to have been retained (Nowakowski, 1966), to have often been truant (Greenberg, 1969), or to have been suspended from school altogether (Yankelovich, 1975).

Youngsters prone to vandalism also often appear to have poor understanding of the impact of their behavior on others and are primarily concerned with the consequences of such behavior for themselves, such as getting caught. In their view, public property in a real sense belongs to no one. In contrast, for youngsters less prone to vandalism, public property belongs to everyone—a view reflecting their sense of themselves as part of a larger community (Goldstein, 1996a). As with all forms of aggression, the single best predictor of future vandalistic behavior is similar past behavior (Tygert, 1988).

To turn from individual to environmental correlates, vandalism has been shown to be associated with autocratic or laissez-faire versus "firm but fair" school administration; inconsistent or weak administrative support and follow-through (Casserly, Bass, & Garrett, 1980); school governance that is overly impersonal, unresponsive, nonparticipatory, overregulated, oppressive, arbitrary, or inconsistent (Greenberg, 1969; Ianni, 1979); high teacher turnover rates (Leftwich, 1977); such teacher inadequacies as disrespectfulness, callousness, lack of interest, and middle-class bias

(Bayh, 1978; Rubel, 1977); overuse of punitive control methods; and inadequate clarity of school and classroom rules and discipline procedures (Mayer & Sulzer-Azaroff, 1991). In contrast, aggression toward property in schools is lower in venues whose social ecology is characterized by high teacher identification with the school, even-handed rule enforcement, parental support of school disciplinary policies, teacher avoidance of the use of grades as disciplinary tools, and teacher avoidance of hostile or authoritarian behavior toward students (Bayh, 1978; Goldstein, 1992).

The school's physical ecology also bears importantly upon the frequency of vandalism in its context. Noteworthy are the school's age, as reflected in obsolescence of facilities and equipment (Greenberg, 1969; Howard, 1978); its size, with larger schools having more incidents per capita (Garbarino, 1978; Goldman, 1961; Kingston & Gentry, 1977; Stefanko, 1989); its physical appearance (DeBunza, 1974; Pablant & Baxter, 1975); its density—little space per student (Stefanko, 1989); and the general facts that it is often unoccupied, is easily accessible, and is a public place owned by no one in particular (Vestermark & Blauvelt, 1978). In an attempt to determine physical-ecological correlates of low school vandalism levels, Pablant and Baxter (1975) studied 16 pairs of schools. One school in each pair had a high vandalism rate and the other had a low rate; the two schools were matched for similarity in other respects (size, ethnic composition, grade level, and location). The schools with lower rates, as the authors had predicted, (a) were characterized by better aesthetic quality and maintenance of school property, (b) were located in more densely populated areas with higher activity levels, (c) furnished less obstructed views of school property to surrounding residents, and (d) were located in better-illuminated neighborhood areas.

A school is thus a prime ecological context for vandalism not only because of the presence of a large number of youths at a highly vandalism-prone age (the person component) but also because of a number of real and symbolic qualities of the school itself (the environmental component). Size, age, aesthetic appearance, public ownership, maintenance level, and location vis-à-vis possible sources of surveillance have been mentioned. Community characteristics are also often important influences upon in-school events: School vandalism tends to be correlated with community crime level and the degree of nonstudent (intruder) presence in the school (Casserly et al., 1980; Irwin, 1976). Furthermore, several of the vandalism-relevant physical-ecological characteristics of the school site and its community location appear to constitute relevant contexts for vandalism elsewhere—libraries, museums, highway signs, trains, buses, mass transit stations, public telephones. All of these are easily accessible public sites; many have low levels of formal or informal surveillance; and many, because of low maintenance effort, display the "releaser cues" of already vandalized property that permit and encourage further destruction. In addition, they are all "symbols of the social order" (Zimbardo, 1973) and hence handy targets of dissatisfaction or frustration.

The ecology of vandalism has a temporal dimension as well. When does it occur? For many of the same contextual reasons that contribute to site determination—especially accessibility and presence or absence of surveillance—a high proportion of vandalism (in schools and elsewhere) occurs before and after school hours, at night, on weekends, during vacation periods, later in the school week, and later in the school year (Anderson, 1977; Casserly et al., 1980; Massucci, 1984; McPherson & Carpenter, 1981; Rautaheimo, 1989).

Intervention Strategies: Changing the Ecology of the School

The ecological perspective on vandalism control and reduction has appeared and reappeared under a variety of rubrics: "utilitarian prevention" (Cohen, 1973), "deopportunizing design" (Wiesenthal, 1990), "architectural determinism" (Zweig & Ducey, 1978), "crime prevention through environmental design" (Wood, 1991), "situational crime prevention" (Clarke, 1992), and "environmental criminology" (Brantingham & Brantingham, 1991). Unlike the person-oriented strategies, all of which in a variety of ways seek to reduce the potential or actual vandal's motivation to vandalize, the environment-oriented strategies seek to alter the physical setting, context, or situation in which vandalism might occur so that the potential or actual vandal's opportunity to vandalize is reduced. This ecological strategy, of altering the physical or social environment to prevent or reduce the occurrence of vandalism, has been an especially popular choice, particularly in a society as technologically oriented as the United States. Thus, venues as diverse as school districts, mass transit systems, museums, shopping malls, national and state parks, and many others have time and again opted for target hardening, access control, offender deflection, entry-exit screening, surveillance increase, inducement removal, and similar environment-altering intervention strategies as the first, and often only, means of defense against vandalism. Later in this chapter, I enumerate and catalog the several dozen strategies of this sort that have been implemented. I suspect the reader will respond (correctly) to this lengthy, technology-oriented enumeration with the sense that we Americans certainly love our hardware!

Yet, paradoxically, very little other than anecdotal, impressionistic, or testimonial "evidence" exists for the actual vandalism control effectiveness of these widely used strategies. Furthermore, the very scope of their implementation—in their most extreme form, the "Bastille response" (Ward, 1973) or the "crimeproof fortress" (Zweig & Ducey, 1978)—has in some settings had highly negative impact on the very mission for which the setting was created in the first place. For example, "More and more high schools are becoming mechanical systems ruled by constraints on timing, location, and behavior. The similarity between schools and jails is becoming ever more pronounced" (Csikszentmihalyi & Larsen, 1978, p. 25).

Not only may the setting's mission be compromised, but in a sort of paradoxical self-fulfilling prophecy, the environmental alterations made to reduce vandalism may be experienced by a vandal-to-be as an inviting, potentially enjoyment-providing challenge to vandalistic skills and thus may actually serve to increase such behavior (Wise, 1982; Zweig & Ducey, 1978). The fence around the school, the graffiti-resistant wall surface, the theftproof parking meter, the slashproof bus seat, the toughened glass, the aisle store camera—each is a possible opportunity-reducing deterrent; as such, each is also a challenging invitation to vandalism.

Thus, the downside of reliance on alterations to the physical environment as the means of vandalism control and reduction is not inconsiderable. Yet an important "upside" also exists. First, without concurring with an assertion as extreme as Weinmayer's (1969) that "ninety percent of what is labeled vandalism can be prevented through design" (p. 286), one may still accept and act on the belief that venue changes can be significant components of effective person-environment interventions. First, design innovations may help deopportunize vandalism in more than one way. Wiesenthal (1990), for example, observes that "property damage can be avoided by design elements that do more than resist attack; design can be used to subtly steer the user away from destruction or defacement" (p. 289). Wise (1982) suggests that design may be employed to channel attention away from potentially damaging activities, to reduce the effects of natural processes (e.g., erosion, weathering) that vandalism may augment, and to eliminate or reduce the type of environmental feedback that may serve to reinforce vandalistic behavior.

Levy-Leboyer (1984) expands the case for design-as-intervention by noting that some locations are more prone to vandalism than others—a view also put forth by Christensen, Mabery, McAllister, and McCormick (1988) in their call for a predictive framework for identifying various degrees of site vulnerability. Public sites, newer sites, sites previously vandalized, those previously damaged by something other than vandalism, those located in "low-status" institutions, and the venues providing inadequate service are all common targets—and thus desirable sites for environmental alteration. R. Wilson (1977), writing as an architect, summarizes the case for design-as-intervention succinctly:

> The shape of buildings can dictate patterns of use and the circulation of people around them and hence help to structure the networks of social relationships that develop. In addition, buildings, by the amount of surveillance they afford, may prevent or offer opportunities for certain activities to take place unobserved. Finally, attrition and damage to buildings can be prevented to an extent by careful use of materials and finishes. It is eminently sensible to suppose that there is some connection between design and behavior, including vandalism. (p. 795)

Those taking a deterministic view believe that individuals choose to engage in vandalistic behavior in response to characteristics not only of their physical environments, but also of their social environments. This is purported to be the case at both micro and macro levels. At the micro, immediate level, the central social-ecological intervention concept is perceived and actual surveillance. Vandalism, it is held, is less likely to occur if the potential perpetrator believes he or she will be observed and perhaps apprehended. Thus, for example, Blauvelt (1980) urges making the school "occupied." He claims:

> The key to controlling vandalism is to make the school a place that in some sense is continuously occupied by some form of human or mechanical presence, which will deter or respond to the vandal. The heart of any effective approach to controlling vandalism will be establishing that sense of "presence" which defines the building as no longer being an inert target. (p. 47)

Added bus conductors, real and dummy TV cameras in stores, neighborhood watch programs, improved neighborhood lighting, and increased numbers of store employees are all examples of opportunity-reducing, surveillance-increasing social-ecological interventions.

Blauvelt (1980) extends the notion of presence in his emphasis on shared responsibility. The broader the responsibility within an institution for deopportunizing vandalism, the more likely such an approach is to succeed. Thus, in a school setting, such matters are ideally the concern not only of security personnel or administration but also of all teachers, secretaries, custodians, kitchen personnel, and students. Porter's (1980) "place defense model" suggests a taxonomy of means for citizens in general, and not only institutional personnel, to join the social-ecological intervention efforts against vandalism. Included are incident-specific personal confrontations, in which citizens are urged, when it is appropriate, to threaten transgressors and physically stop vandalistic behavior; incident-specific appeals to authority, in which police or other authorities are requested to confront transgressors; and non-incident-specific social interventions, such as formation of a crime watch group or hiring of security personnel. Ducey's (1976) call for heightening citizen involvement via antivandalism public relations efforts, and Yambert and Donow's (1984) highlighting of the need for enhanced "community instincts" and "ecological commandments" are further citizen-oriented social-ecological calls for intervention.

Finally, and in quite a different manner, Shaw (1973) also accords the vandal's social ecology a central intervention role with this macro-level observation:

> Vandalism is a rebellion with a cause. To prevent it, we must combat social indifference, apathy, isolation and the loss of community, neighborhood and family values. We must reaffirm the principle that human rights are more

important than property rights, and property rights are acknowledged by all only when all have a share in them. (p. 18)

Intervention Strategies: Changing the Vandal

Contrasting with intervention efforts directed toward the actual or potential vandal's physical or social environment are strategies in which the intervention target is the vandal himself or herself. Cohen (1974) suggests three such person-oriented strategies:

Education. In these strategies, the effort is made to increase the potential vandal's awareness of the costs and other consequences of vandalistic behavior. The assumption is that once this awareness is increased, the person will consider the possible consequences and choose to refrain from perpetrating vandalism.

Deterrence and retribution. These strategies rely on threat, punishment, or compulsory restitution. Punishment strategies are especially widely employed. Ward (1973) comments:

> The most frequent public reaction to vandalism is "Hit them hard": all that is needed is better detection by the police and stiffer sentences by the court. The general tendency is to support heavier fines, custodial sentences. . . . Other, extra-legal sanctions include banning offenders from swimming baths, sports fields, youth clubs or play centers. Some local authorities have suggested the evicting of tenants whose children are responsible for vandalism. (p. 256)

Deflection. These strategies "attempt to understand and redirect the motivational causes of vandalism into non-damaging means of expression" (Cohen, 1974, p. 54). They include allowing controlled destruction, providing substitute targets, or furnishing alternative outlets for energetic activity.

Koch (1975) describes a parallel array of person-oriented strategies, employing coercive controls, indoctrination with information, legal regulations, or substitution of functional equivalents:

> The first model has as its goal the total prohibition or elimination of some objectionable behavior. It implies strict enforcement and punishment of offenders. The second is an educational and/or propagandistic strategy. It has as its major goal the objective of changing behavior and attitudes. The third model is a regulative approach which utilizes rules or laws and prescribes allocations of time, space, age groupings, and monetary costs, in order to influence behavior. . . . The final alternative involves the substitution of some functional equivalent for an identified objectionable behavior. (p. 61)

To repeat a previously mentioned distinction, environment-focused interventions target opportunity reduction; person-oriented efforts seek to alter motivation. Although punishment, as noted earlier, appears to be an especially frequently used person-oriented strategy (M. C. Heller & White, 1975; Stoner et al., 1991), there is evidence that heavy reliance on it may often actually result in an increase, not a decrease, in the frequency of vandalism (Greenberg, 1969; Scrimger & Elder, 1981). These latter investigators, as well as others, report a substantial decrease in vandalism as punitiveness decreases and such interventions as increased teacher approval for desirable student behaviors are used more frequently (Mayer & Butterworth, 1979; Mayer, Butterworth, Nafpaktitis, & Sulzer-Azaroff, 1983; Mayer, Nafpaktitis, Butterworth, & Hollingsworth, 1987).

In contrast to such use of extrinsic rewards (e.g., teacher approval) targeted toward altering vandal behavior, Csikszentmihalyi and Larsen (1978) focus more directly on a strategy calling for enhancement of intrinsic processes. Reliance on extrinsically provided rewards or reinforcement, they propose, is cumbersome and cost-ineffective; most significantly, in their view, it functions to diminish the individual's intrinsic motivation to refrain from vandalistic behavior. A second vandal-oriented strategy, of which they are similarly critical on these very same grounds of diminished intrinsic motivation, is that of "strengthening the means-ends connection between adherence to school constraints and achievement of desired future goals" (p. 29). This is a difficult strategy to implement, as it requires a considerably closer correspondence between school performance and future rewards. For many youths and in many schools, such a connection is not easy to perceive. And when it is perceived, it is yet a second instance of training youths to guide their behavior on the basis of extrinsic rather than intrinsic motivations. As an alternative strategy, Csikszentmihalyi and Larsen recommend reorientation of school procedures and curriculum in a manner designed to stimulate and respond to youths' intrinsic motivation for challenge, for extension of their skills, for mastery, for growth, and for (in their terms) the experience of "flow." In their view:

> The state of enjoyment occurs when a person is challenged at a level matched by his or her level of skill. . . . Ideally, learning should involve systemic involvement in sequences of challenges internalized by students. . . . In the absence of such opportunities, antisocial behavior provides an alternative framework of challenges for bored students. Disruption of classes, vandalism, and violence in schools are, in part, attempts of adolescents to obtain enjoyment in otherwise lifeless schools. Restructuring education in terms of intrinsic motivation would not only reduce school crime, but also accomplish the goal of teaching youth how to enjoy life in an affirmative way. (p. 1)

My own strategic perspective regarding vandal-oriented intervention suggests that both externally imposed incentives and intrinsic motivators serve the cause of vandalism reduction well.

Vandalism is a domain of interest that has a remarkably meager research base. When rigorous and relevant studies on aspects of this topic do exist, they need to be heeded especially closely. Mayer and colleagues' extrinsic-reward studies (Mayer & Butterworth, 1979; Mayer et al., 1983, 1987), as well as relevant intrinsic-motivation studies (deCharms, 1968, 1976; Deci, 1975), support the value of both orientations in enhancing vandals' prosocial motivation.

One final point must be offered regarding vandal-oriented intervention strategies. I urge the consideration of a prescriptive intervention response plan. Ideally, both who the vandals are (Griffiths & Shapland, 1979) and what levels their vandalistic behaviors have reached (Hauber, 1989) will help determine the nature of the intervention implemented. Griffiths and Shapland correctly assert that the vandal's motives and the meaning of the act itself change with age and context and that strategies need to vary accordingly:

> The preventive measures that need to be taken to make any given environment vandal-proof may be different according to the nature of the vandal. . . . As an example of this, look at how a window in a deserted house may be broken. This may have been done by kids getting in to play; by older children as a game of skill; by adolescents or adults in order to remove the remaining furniture or fittings; by someone with a grudge against the person or previous landlord; by a pressure group to advertise the dereliction of empty property; or by [a vagrant] to gain attention or to [get in to spend] the night. (pp. 17–18)

Intervention Strategies: Person-Environment

Every act of vandalism, I hold, springs from both person and environment sources—a duality that must similarly characterize efforts directed towards its prevention and remediation. The separate person-oriented and environment-oriented vandalism intervention strategies I have explored—along with their strengths and shortcomings—will optimally be implemented in diverse, prescriptively appropriate combinations. Casserly et al. (1980), Cohen (1973), Geason and Wilson (1990), Kulka (1978), Vestermark and Blauvelt (1978), and S. Wilson (1979) are among the vandalism theorists and researchers also championing multilevel, multimodal, person-environment intervention strategies. Several practitioners have already put in place such joint strategies and at least impressionistically report having done so to good advantage (Hendrick & Murfin, 1974; Jamieson, 1987; Levy-Leboyer, 1984; Mason, 1979; Panko, 1978; Scrimger & Elder, 1981; Stover, 1990; Weeks, 1976; White & Fallis, 1980). The following section provides a comprehensive listing and cataloging of the many environment-oriented and person-oriented tactics that have been employed in an array of commonly vandalized settings in implementation of the strategies we have considered.

Intervention: Implementation Tactics

The vandalism intervention tactics cataloged in this section have been employed in school and, at times, other settings. In arranging this listing, I have incorporated and built upon Clarke's (1992) taxonomy for categorizing methods of situational crime prevention. I have employed his taxonomic system elsewhere to good advantage in an ecological analysis of aggression interventions targeted more broadly than at vandalism alone (Goldstein, 1994), and I believe that with the modifications and new categories I have added to it, it will serve the current purposes well. It should be noted that Clarke's categories (I through XI) list vandalism interventions directed at the physical and social environment, and that my own categories (XII through XVII) are interventions directly or indirectly targeted toward changing the potential or actual vandals themselves.

I. Target Hardening

This situational crime prevention approach involves the use of devices or materials designed to obstruct the vandal through physical barriers:*

1. Toughened glass (acrylic, polycarbon, etc.)

2. Latticework or screens to cover windows

3. Fire-retardant paint

4. High-impact plastic or steel fixtures

5. Hardened rubber or plastic swing seats

6. Concrete or steel picnic tables, benches, bleachers

7. Trash receptacles bolted to concrete bases

8. Rough-play-tolerant adventure playgrounds

9. Original planting of large-diameter trees

10. Slashproof transit vehicle seats

11. Steel-framed bus seats

12. Antigraffiti repellent spray on bus seats

13. Tamperproof sign hardware and fasteners

14. Door anchor hinges with nonremovable pins

II. Access Control

This approach involves architectural features, mechanical and electronic devices, and related means for maintaining prerogatives over the ability to gain entry:

---

* Categories I through XI are from *Situational Crime Prevention: Successful Case Studies* (pp. 12–21) by R. V. Clarke (Ed.), 1992, New York: Harrow & Heston. Reprinted by permission of the publisher.

15. Key control systems

16. Locked gates, doors, windows

17. Electromagnetic doors unopenable from outside

18. Deadbolt and vertical-bolt locks

19. Metal door/window shutters

20. Protective grills over roof access openings

21. Fenced yards

22. Vertical metal or small-mesh (unclimbable) fencing

23. Reduced number of building entrances

24. Unclimbable trees/bushes planted next to building

25. Prickly bushes planted next to site to be protected

26. Sloped windowsills

27. Elimination of crank-and-gear window mechanisms

28. Steeply angled roofs with parapets and ridges

29. Use of guard dogs

30. Use of student photo identification

31. Partitioning off of selected areas during "downtime" hours

32. High curbs along areas to be protected

III. Deflection of Offenders

This is the channeling of potentially criminal or aggressive behavior in more prosocial directions by means of architectural, equipment, and related alterations:

33. Graffiti boards, mural programs

34. Schools/studios to give graffiti writers exposure and recognition

35. Interesting wallpaper, daily newspaper, chalkboard on bathroom wall

36. Litter bins

37. Wash fountains and towel dispensers in school hallways

38. Steering of pathway circulation:

     Paving the shortest walk between connecting points

     Avoiding sharp changes in direction

     Paving natural shortcuts after demonstrated use

     Installing or landscaping traffic barriers (e.g., benches, bushes)

39. "Next step" posters on broken equipment

IV. Control of Facilitators

This is the alteration of the means to criminal or aggressive behavior by making such means less available, less accessible, or less potentially injurious:

40. Control over sales of spray paint and indelible markers

41. Removal of debris from construction/demolition sites

42. Removal of waste paper, rubbish, and other combustibles

43. Use of tamperproof screws

44. Placement of permanent signs, building names, and decorative hardware out of reach from ground

45. Placement of school thermostats, fire alarms, and light switches far from "hang-out" areas

V. Exit-Entry Screening

Instead of seeking to exclude potential perpetrators (as in access control), this set of tactics seeks to increase the likelihood of detecting persons who are not in conformity with entry requirements (entry screening) or detecting the attempted removal of objects that should not be removed from protected areas (exit screening):

46. Closed-circuit TV

47. Metal detectors

48. Vibration detectors

49. Motion detectors

50. Perimeter alarm system

51. Library book tags

VI. Formal Surveillance

This is surveillance by police, guards, monitors, citizen groups, or other paid or volunteer security personnel:

52. Police, citizen, senior citizen, tenant, parent patrols

53. Neighborhood watch, school watch, block watch, rail/bus watch groups

54. Provision of on-site living quarters for citizens or security personnel (e.g., "school sitters," "campground hosts")

55. Informant hotlines (e.g., "rat-on-a-rat program," "secret witness program")

56. Crime Solvers Anonymous reward program

57. Mechanical, ultrasonic, infrared, electronic intruder alarm system

58. Automatic fire detection systems

59. After-hours use of school public address system for monitoring

VII. Natural Surveillance

This is surveillance provided by employees, homeowners, pedestrians, and others going about their regular daily activities:

60. Community after-school use

61. Reduced teacher-student ratio

62. Increased number of employees (e.g., playground supervisors, bus conductors, teachers)

63. Round-the-clock custodial staffing

64. Live-in custodian/caretaker

65. Distribution of faculty/staff offices throughout the school

66. Assignment of additional faculty/staff members to hall, cafeteria duty

67. "Youth vacation vigil" student surveillance program

68. Use of bus/train employees to report vandalism on their routes

69. Improved exterior and interior lighting

70. Low trimming on shrubbery and plants

VIII. Target Removal

This is the physical removal or decreased accessibility of potential vandalism targets:

71. Use of graffiti dissuaders

    Teflon, plastic laminate, fiberglass, or melamine covering

    Rock cement, slanted siding, or deeply grooved surfaces

    "Paint-outs" or use of contrasting colors in patterned surfaces

    Fast-growing wall vines or shrubbery, or construction of wall barriers

72. Removal of pay phones from high-loitering areas

73. Removal of corner bus seats, hidden from driver's view

74. Removal of outside plant bulbs

75. Windowless school or other buildings

76. Omission of ground-level windows

77. Concealed school door closers

78. Concealed pipework

79. Fittings moved out of reach (e.g., from wall to ceiling)

80. Signs/fixtures made flush with wall or ceiling

81. Key-controlled light fixtures in public areas

82. Removal of (or not replanting of) easily damaged trees/bushes

IX. Identification of Property

This is the physical identification or marking of potential vandalism targets:

83. Property marking with school district identification

84. Property marking with business logo

85. Property marking with identification seals

86. Property marking with organization stencil

87. Property marking with individual's Social Security number

X. *Removal of Inducements*

This is the physical alteration of potential vandalism targets:

88. Rapid repair of damaged property

89. Rapid removal of graffiti

90. Use of small windowpanes

91. Elimination of school washroom and toilet stall doors

92. Elimination of bars over toilet stall doorways

93. School restroom thermostats kept at 62°F

94. Removal of gates and fences

95. Repainting of playground equipment in bright colors

96. Beautification programs (e.g., landscaping, painting, maintenance)

XI. *Rule Setting*

This is the making of explicit prior statements about acceptable and unacceptable behaviors as well as about penalties for noncompliance:

97. Model "hate crime" bill

98. Antivandalism laws

99. Building design specifications

100. Building security codes

101. Parental liability statutes

102. Prohibition of sale of spray paint and indelible markers

103. Codes of rights and responsibilities

104. School rules of student conduct

105. Rigorous, irregular, no-warning fire drills

XII. Education

These are direct efforts to inform potential and actual vandals, as well as the general public, about vandalism costs, consequences, and alternatives.

106. Vandalism education programs

107. Arson education programs

108. Vandalism awareness calls

109. Vandalism case-study classroom discussions

110. Classroom brainstorming on vandalism reduction

111. Year-round education

112. Student orientation handbook

113. Student orientation

114. Multicultural sensitivity training

115. Antivandalism lectures by older students to younger ones

116. Antivandalism films

117. Antivandalism games

118. Antivandalism slide or tape projects

119. Antivandalism brochures

120. "Ride with pride" antivandalism transit program

XIII. Publicity

These are indirect efforts to inform potential and actual vandals, as well as the general public, about vandalism costs, consequences, and alternatives.

121. Antivandalism advertising

122. Antivandalism news releases

123. Milk carton/grocery bag antivandalism messages

124. Antivandalism decals on mass transit vehicles

125. Antivandalism slogan contests

126. "Sign amnesty" day (a day of no fines or other penalties for those who return stolen signs)

127. "Help the playground" campaigns

128. Antivandalism buttons, T-shirts, bookmarks, posters

XIV. Punishment

These are negative experiences directed to perpetrators consequent to their vandalistic behavior:

129. Suspension from school

130. Monetary fines

131. Restitution

132. Student vandalism account

133. Group billing for residence hall damage

XV. Counseling

These are remedial experiences directed to perpetrators consequent to their vandalistic behavior:

134. Student counseling programs

135. Conflict negotiation skills training

136. Moral reasoning training

137. Interpersonal skills training

138. Aggression Replacement Training

139. Behavior modification treatment for arson

    Stimulus satiation

    Contingency management

    Assertion training

XVI. Involvement

These are efforts to increase the sense of involvement with and ownership of potential vandalism targets:

140. Encouraging students in residence halls to personalize (paint, furnish) their rooms

141. Permitting students in residence halls to retain the same rooms several semesters

142. Student participation in school decision making

143. School administration collaboration with student organizations

144. School-home collaboration

145. Hiring of unemployed youths as subway vandalism inspectors

146. "Adopt-a-station" antivandalism program

XVII. Enhancement of Organizational Climate

These are procedures for enhancing the quality of the potential or actual vandal's social/educational/daily living context:

147. Teacher/staff approval/reward for student prosocial behaviors

148. Teacher respect toward students

149. Teacher/parent modeling of respect for others and for property

150. Regular, visible presence of school principal

151. Involvement of school principal in community activities

152. School curriculum revision

153. Improved student-custodian relationships

154. Improved school-community relationships

155. Reorganization of large schools into schools-within-a-school or house plans

This extended list of context-oriented and vandal-oriented interventions forms a substantial pool of diverse means for seeking to prevent, control, and reduce vandalistic behavior. In the next section, I propose and examine rationales for selecting wisely from this pool, in order to assemble synergistic sets or programs of interventions that are likely to have significant impacts.

Intervention: Combinations and Evaluation

Viewed collectively, the array of preventive and remedial tactics employed in schools and other venues frequently targeted for vandalism is diverse and creative; it reflects the substantial energy that a wide variety of professionals continue to expend in their attempts to control and reduce this costly antisocial behavior. This array of potentially effective interventions is the good news. The bad news is the plain lack of anything approaching hard evidence (or even "soft evidence" in most instances) that would aid potential users in sorting through and selecting from among these numerous interventions.

One issue that can be addressed with certainty, however, is the need to identify potent *combinations* of interventions. Vandalism, like all instances of aggression, is a complexly determined behavior. Every act of vandalism derives from a complexity of causes and therefore is best combated with equally complex interventions. In the next two sections, I seek to examine and elaborate these assertions.

Complexity of Cause

Suppose that a teacher walking down a school corridor turns a corner and comes upon one of her students spray-painting his initials across the doors of several other students' lockers. Later that day, the teacher meets with the assistant principal to discuss the incident—both its causes and its consequences. In my experience, it is quite common, in discussions such as these, for both teacher and administrator to focus their attention exclusively on the perpetrator. "Johnny is a chronically bad kid [or a good kid]. He is angry [or aggressive, or misunderstood, or abused, or sleepy, or whatever]. We should caution him [or deny him certain privileges, discipline him, detain him, or suspend him]."

Is something missing here? Are the teacher's and the administrator's views of both causality and cure too limited? Every act of aggression, including vandalistic acts, is a person-environment event. This perspective on complexity of cause is elaborated in Table 4.1. If the table's assertion of complex causality for all acts of aggression is correct, then it logically follows that such complexity must also characterize optimal intervention attempts. Cure must follow cause. In a related context, I have sought to describe this perspective more specifically:

Table 4.1—Multiple Causes of Aggressive Behavior

General category	Specific factors
Person variables	
Physiological predisposition	Male gender and associated testosterone and temperament levels
Cognitive-affective patterns	Attribution of hostile intent; projection of blame; mislabeling; low level of moral reasoning
Interpersonal skills	Absence of self-control, anger management, prosocial skill alternatives
Environmental variables	
Cultural context	Societal traditions and mores that encourage aggression
Immediate interpersonal	Parental/peer criminality; peer environment pressure; video, film, live models of aggression
Immediate physical environment	Temperature; crowding; low probability of surveillance; incivilities
Presence of disinhibitors	Alcohol, drugs; successful aggressive models
Presence of means	Weapons, tools (spray paint, markers, bricks, etc.)
Presence of targets	Windows, walls, transit vehicles, fencing, etc.

The call for complexity of solution has been heard before, from the community psychologist (Heller, Price, Reinharz, Riger, Wandersman, & D'Aunno, 1984), the ecological psychologist (Moos & Insel, 1974), the environmental designer (Krasner, 1980) and the systems analyst (Plas, 1986) . . . [to] have even [a] modest chance of enduring success, interventions designed to reduce aggression towards persons or property in school contexts must be oriented not only towards the aggressor himself, but also at the levels of the teacher, school administration and organization, and the larger community context. Furthermore . . . an optimally complex intervention designed to reduce school violence ought to seek to do so via a variety of modes or channels. The first requisite, therefore, which we propose as necessary for the effective planning of a successful aggression reduction intervention is multilevel, multichannel complexity. (Goldstein, 1988, p. 294)

Next, I draw upon the pool of vandalism interventions presented earlier in order to illustratively reorganize samples of these interventions into just such multilevel, multichannel configurations. In the absence of efficacy evaluations, no particular interventions or configurations can be singled out for recommended use at this time. However, I believe that this emphasis on the selection and implementation of meaningful intervention combinations is likely to prove a major step toward truly effective vandalism prevention, control, and reduction.

Complexity of Interventions

Table 4.2 presents a level [×] mode intervention schema targeted to the reduction of vandalism in school contexts. My intent here is to urge both implementers and evaluators of vandalism prevention/reduction efforts to ensure that their packages of interventions include interventions at all levels and through all channels.

A second factorial schema seeking to reflect in its particulars the desirability of complex vandalism intervention programming is that offered by Harootunian (1986). Instead of mode or channel of intervention, Harootunian's proposal crosses level of intervention with intended goal. In a later publication (Goldstein, Harootunian, & Conoley, 1994), he observes:

Table 4.2—A Multilevel, Multichannel Schema for the Reduction of School Vandalism

Level of intervention	Mode of intervention				
	Psychological	Educational	Administrative	Legal	Physical
Community	"Youth vacation vigil" programs	Arson education programs	"Adopt-a-school" programs	Monetary fines	Citizen, police, parent patrols
School	Conflict negotiation programs	Year-round education	Schools-within-a-school	Code of rights and respon-sibilities	Lighting, painting, paving programs
Teacher	School-home collaboration	Multicultural sensitivity training	Reduced teacher-student ratio	Property marking with school ID	Distribution of faculty offices throughout school
Student	Interpersonal skills training	Vandalism awareness walks	School detention, suspension	Restitution, vandalism accounts	Graffiti boards, mural walls

Various actions taken against aggression are initiated to prevent or discourage hostile acts directed against persons or school property. Such measures as 24-hour custodial service and better lighting are designed to prevent aggression. The use of Plexiglas windows may not prevent aggressive acts, but it will certainly reduce the incidence of broken windows. Compensatory interventions do not in themselves change aggressive or disruptive students, but they do offset the consequences of their actions. Remedial interventions, on the other hand, are aimed at changing students, not simply providing them with ways of circumventing their aggressive acts. (p. 204)

Table 4.3 illustrates this level [×] goal perspective.

Beyond the multilevel, multigoal vandalism intervention combinations derivable from Table 4.3, the schemas of Tables 4.2 and 4.3 may be combined in the actual practice of planning and implementing vandalism prevention/reduction programs. Such a three-dimensional schema based simultaneously on intervention levels, channels, and goals may be a bit complex to conceptualize, but it is no more complex than the multiply determined behavior it seeks to alter—vandalism. Furthermore, as Harootunian (Goldstein et al., 1994) notes:

Any one strategy in isolation often has resulted in confusion, if not contradictory findings. A multiple perspective strategy makes it possible to determine where a suggested intervention or approach fits and how it may influence or be influenced by adjacent solutions. Also, a comprehensive view of school aggression may reveal gaps, and overloads in the system. There is evidence, for example (Zwier & Vaughn, 1984), that almost one-half of the literature on school vandalism focuses on the physical dimensions of the school. (p. 206)

Table 4.3—A Multilevel, Multigoal Schema for the Reduction of School Vandalism

Level of intervention	Goal of intervention		
	Prevention	**Compensatory**	**Remediation**
Community	"Adopt-a-school" programs	Less restrictive child labor laws Short-term treatment centers	Family support services
School	24-hour custodial service	Use of Plexiglas windows	Prescriptively tailored courses
Teacher	Programs to enhance knowledge of ethnic and minority milieu	Better skills, e.g., teacher-pupil ratio	Acquisition of new training techniques in psychological structured learning
Student	Identification cards	School transfers Part-time programs	Interpersonal training Behavior modification

Note. From "School Violence and Vandalism" (p. 131) by B. Harootunian, 1986, in S. J. Apter and A. P. Goldstein (Eds.), *Youth Violence: Programs and Prospects,* New York: Pergamon. Copyright 1986 by the authors. Reprinted by permission.

In quite the same factorial spirit as Tables 4.2 and 4.3, Zwier and Vaughn (1984) propose a schema for combining vandalism interventions—one that crosses level of intervention (defined differently than it was defined previously) with ideological orientation. Educational practices in U. S. public schools have long been fair game for broad and often intense public concern and debate. This spotlight of attention most certainly includes disciplinary practices. Harootunian (Goldstein et al., 1994) quite correctly notes that for a specific intervention to be accepted, to be implemented, and to have a chance of succeeding, the values it elicits must overlap appreciably with the values or ideologies of those who are asked to accept and participate in its implementation. Table 4.4 details this level [×] ideology perspective.

As noted earlier, the different ideological perspectives represented in Table 4.4 have generated considerable historical and current debate and contentiousness in the United States. My own belief is that the appropriate position at this point is an empirical one. Whether a set of vandalism interventions reflecting one or another ideological orientation (crossed with levels) proves most efficacious, or a mixing of ideological implementations is to be preferred, is a matter for yet-to-be-conducted efficacy evaluations. Whichever ideological stance or stances guides the selection and implementation of interventions, and whichever levels, channels, or goals are also reflected therein, I believe that three qualities of such programming are essential to success: Vandalism interventions must be comprehensive, prescriptive, and appreciative—qualities that also apply equally well to change efforts targeted at any other form of low-level aggression. I will discuss these desirable intervention characteristics in more detail in chapter 6.

SHOPLIFTING

Specific crimes often become hot topics for both the general public and the social scientists who study such transgressions. Thus,

Table 4.4—The Relationship between Ideological Orientations and Assumptions Concerning the Causes of School Vandalism and Types of Solutions Offered

Ideological orientation and assumptions about cause	Type of solution		
	Specific ➤ *Physical environment*	*School system*	*Community at large* ➤ Diffuse
Conservative Vandals are deviant. They must be caught and punished.	Protection of school and school grounds, employment of security officers and caretakers[a]	Encouragement and enforcement of school rules, use of contingency contracts	Involvement of community in antivandalism patrols and (parent) restitution programs, dependence on judicial system
Liberal The school system is malfunctioning. Vandals capitalize on this.	(Superficial) improvement of the design, appearance, and layout of the school grounds	Modifications in school climate, curriculum, and use of special conflict management programs[a]	Extension of recreational activities, use of school after hours for health and social services
Radical The school system is debilitating. Vandalism is a response of normal individuals to abnormal conditions.	Promotion of radical changes in the structure and appearance of the school, approval of policy to decrease the sizes of large schools and maintain small schools	Provision of student involvement in decision-making process, adoption of changes in assessment procedures, and exploration of alternative schooling methods	Involvement of the whole community in school affairs, installment of community education programs, improvement of social situation in society at large[a]

[a]The solution considered most favorably by the particular ideological orientation.

Note. Reprinted from "Three Ideological Orientations in School Vandalism Research" by G. Zwier and G. M. Vaughn, 1984, *Review of Educational Research, 54*, p. 269.

we have seen significant bursts of interest in and research on missing children, domestic violence, sex abuse, gangs, serial killers, and drug abuse. Shoplifting, however, has rarely caught on among either average citizens or social science researchers as a worthy social problem. This may be because shoplifting does not result in eye-catching "body counts" or astronomical dollar losses being generated by *individual* shoplifters. Without sensational evidence of cataclysmic harm to foster and fuel public concern, most people consider shoplifting an interesting but not a very serious type of crime (Klemke, 1992).

If aggression is properly defined as intentional physical or psychological injury to persons or property, perhaps it is not stretching things too far to view shoplifting as an aggressive act. Clearly, such theft behavior results in damage—to the business in which it occurs, to the other customers of that business, and often to the perpetrator himself or herself. It has been estimated that the annual cost of shoplifted goods in the United States is $16 billion (McGuire, 1997).

Among early adolescents, the most frequently stolen goods are low-cost food items (Jackson, 1990). For those over age 17, clothes are the most frequently shoplifted items (Munday, 1986). There is a common tendency for shoplifting to be perpetrated by groups (Baumer & Rosenbaum, 1984). Both males and females commit this form of low-level aggression, with some evidence that the ratio of female to male shoplifters increases with increasing age (McGuire, 1997). Large stores are more common targets than are smaller shops (Lo, 1994), perhaps because of easier access to hiding spots, more escape routes, and a belief among perpetrators that large firms can more easily handle the losses. Walsh (1978) and Lo (1994) found that most shoplifting occurs in April and during the pre-Christmas buildup of goods and shoppers in November, as well as on Fridays and Saturdays and during the noon hour any day. Such timing corresponds closely to the perceived and actual levels of surveillance: That is, shoplifting is most likely when fewer salespeople are present and the density of shoppers is high. Those who shoplift most, according to a study by Kraut (1976), are persons who see the least risk in doing so, whether risk was defined as likelihood of getting caught, as severity of penalty if one were caught, or as severity of informal social disapproval. Some shoplifters specialize (e.g., stealing cigarettes, meats, particular articles of clothing); others take more of a cafeteria approach (Klemke, 1992). Some, with seeming impulsiveness, snatch merchandise and run to the nearest exits; others, alone or with accomplices, contrive elaborate shoplifting con jobs.

In chapter 1, I examined the various criteria researchers have used for establishing the seriousness of various aggressive and criminal acts. When rating the seriousness of shoplifting, Warr's (1989) raters appear to have used the degree of harm to the victim, as shown in Table 4.5.

Moore (1984), using a battery of measures, identified five subtypes of shoplifters, listed in declining order of frequency: Amateur

Table 4.5—Average Perceived Seriousness of Selected Offenses

Offense description	Mean seriousness score
Robbing a store and killing two employees	9.87
A father sexually abusing his teenage daughter	9.36
Ten high school boys beating up a classmate	7.63
Breaking into a house and stealing a TV set	6.69
Shoplifting merchandise worth $600 from a store	6.63
Writing a bad check for $350 to a store	5.78
Breaking into a parking meter and stealing $2	4.71
Painting obscenities on a highway billboard	3.92
Shoplifting a pair of socks from a store	3.13
Trespassing in a railroad yard	2.37

Note. From "What Is the Perceived Seriousness of Crime?" by M. Warr, 1989, *Criminology, 27,* p. 795–819. Copyright 1989 by the American Society of Criminology, Reprinted by permission.

(56%), Impulse (15%), Occasional (15%), Semiprofessional (11%), and Episodic (2%). McShane and Noonan's (1993) cluster analysis yielded a taxonomy of four shoplifter types: (a) Rebels—younger, mostly female perpetrators with histories of other criminal activity; (b) Reactionaries—older males, occupationally stressed, typically married and well educated, with no previous involvement in criminal activities; (c) Enigmas—of either gender, with no apparent precipitating stress, middle aged; and (d) Infirm—elderly, with histories of chronic illness and like the "Enigma" cluster in marital and socioeconomic status.

Persons committing this crime have also been identified as either out-of-necessity or nonsensical shoplifters (Yates, 1986). The first, for example, may be a poor, unemployed parent stealing needed clothing or food. The second may be a middle- or upper-class individual, with ample funds, stealing for perhaps more complicated reasons.

Nonsensical, irrational, or not-out-of-necessity shoplifting may occur, one criminologist suggests, out of revenge against the store for real or imagined complaints, because of poor impulse control, to help finance a substance addiction, to somehow moderate difficult life stresses, or—in the case of adolescents and younger children—as a result of peer pressure and a desire to win group acceptance. An estimated 90% of shoplifting is done by amateurs (known as snitches) and 10% by professionals (boosters; M. O. Cameron, 1964).

Ray (1987), in a large shopper survey at 10 Western shopping malls, also inquired into motivations for shoplifting in the 1 of every 12 persons surveyed who admitted to such behavior. The major reasons they gave were economic need, hostility toward "the system," desire for the merchandise, relief of personal and social stresses, and a belief that they would probably not be caught. Klemke's (1992) study of adolescent shoplifters yielded two motivational clusters. Approximately 45% of his sample were primarily *economically* motivated (e.g., "I needed something and couldn't afford to pay for it").

About a like number reported *sporting* motivations (e.g., "I wanted to see if I could get away with it"). The remainder of youths acted primarily out of *peer pressure* motivations ("My friends were doing it") or *illicit market* motivations ("Taking items I couldn't buy, like cigarettes and beer"). Turner and Cashdan (1988), in a similar motivational inquiry directed at college student shoplifters, report economic need and self-indulgence as primary motivations, followed by excitement and the thrill of the act, and also hostility or revenge toward the store involved. For some shoplifters, the intensity, repetitiveness, and salience of the experience; the need for higher and higher levels; the aversive feelings when one ceases; the rush when one perpetrates; and the frequency of relapses all suggest a motivational level equivalent to an addiction (McGuire, 1997).

Thus, it is evident that all shoplifters are certainly not alike. Their motivations may indeed differ widely. Yet frequently accompanying these motivations are a set of beliefs, heavily subscribed to by shoplifters in one study (Soloman & Ray, 1984, p. 1076), that seem to free up the perpetrator or make the shoplifting easier:

- If I am careful and smart, I will not get caught.

- Even if I do get caught, I will not be turned in and prosecuted.

- Even if I am prosecuted, the punishment will not be severe.

- The merchants deserve what they get.

- Everybody at some time has shoplifted.

- Shoplifting is not a major crime.

- I must have the item I want to shoplift.

- It's OK to shoplift because the merchants expect it.

At the risk of imparting a sense of blaming the victim, which I certainly do not wish to do, I quote the observation of Cox, Cox, and Moschis (1990):

> Many people are contingently honest; they behave honestly most of the time, but will occasionally slip into dishonesty if the circumstances are right. Such circumstances include temptation, ability to rationalize, and perceived low risk of apprehension and punishment. . . . If one compares these three conditions (temptation, ease of rationalization, and perceived low risk of apprehension) to the characteristics of most modern retailers, the pervasiveness of consumer shoplifting becomes less puzzling. To begin with, retail stores are designed with the express purpose of tempting customers with merchandise. . . . In fact, Russell (1973) has argued that stores' efforts to increase impulse buying (e.g., enticing displays that encourage customers to handle merchandise) may also increase shoplifting. . . . In addition, retailers are increasingly large, impersonal institutions. . . . Finally, retail theft may be perceived as relatively risk free. As noted earlier, only about one in every 30 shoplifters is apprehended by store officials. (p. 152)

As the work of Charles Dickens and others portrays, shoplifting no doubt goes back as far as the first shops and stalls that brought varied goods together for purchase. Its seriousness as a costly and widespread crime, however, began with the opening of the first 5- and-10-cent store by F. W. Woolworth in 1879. Shoplifting reached full bloom as a 16-billion-dollar-a-year offense in the United States as, in recent years, the neighborhood mall became the community mall, then the regional mall, and now the megamall. Items stolen may be as inexpensive as food or drink consumed but not paid for during shopping (known as grocery grazing) to very expensive clothing, electronic equipment, or other costly goods. A perpetrator may wear the stolen item out of the store, conceal it under clothing, or hide it in various props brought into the store (a booster box, a bad bag, a klepto bag). Another may take an item and, without leaving the store, attempt to obtain a refund by claiming to be returning something received as a gift.

Bring more and more people together, add movies (attracting teenagers), bars (attracting drinkers), and public transit stops (attracting nondrinking, low-income populations), and both motivation and opportunity have been brought together in a way that makes "I see it, I want it, I take it" more likely.

Will other (nonshoplifter) shoppers who observe the shoplifting report it? About a quarter of such shoppers did so in a simulated shoplifting study by Gelfand, Hartmann, Walder, and Page (1973). The simulating shoplifter's appearance (hippie, youth-culture clothing or conventional, conservative clothing) did not make a difference in whether or not they were reported. Female "shoplifters," however, were reported more frequently than were males, especially by male shoppers. Contradictory results were found by Steffensmeier and Terry (1973) in a similar simulated shoplifting investigation. "Shoplifter" appearance did matter; gender of shopper or "shoplifter" did not. Shoplifter appearance differences also led to significant reporting differences in a study by Fedler and Pryor (1984). Two "shoplifters," one 5 foot 6 and 140 pounds, the other 6 foot and 255 pounds, took turns "stealing" a bottle of wine from a convenience store. The confederates alternated appearing well dressed (in shirt and tie) and poorly dressed (in pullover and jeans). As the researchers had predicted, there was significantly more reporting when the "thief" was well dressed, observers commenting that anyone who could afford a suit like that shouldn't need to steal. Also as predicted, the smaller shoplifter was reported twice as frequently as the larger man. This latter result may be a fear-of-retaliation effect, a supposition also supported by the fact that 30 of the 33 witnesses who reported the crime first waited until the shoplifter had left the store. In yet

other staged shoplifting research, female shoppers were more likely than males to report the shoplifter (Bickman & Green, 1977;
Destke, Penner, & Ulrich, 1974).

As noted earlier, it has been estimated that only about 1 in 30
shoplifters is ever caught, though some store security personnel
claim to detect shoplifters skillfully by focusing more on shoppers'
actions (e.g., a customer looking much more at other people than
the merchandise) than on appearance. Others claim to focus on
persons with large purses or shopping bags, those wearing bulky
or out-of-season clothing, those shopping very rapidly, or those
who linger or hang around back areas of the store (Klemke, 1992).
That so many get away with shoplifting is rather surprising because businesses invest a great deal of energy, creativity, and
money to combat it.

Intervention

Several efforts to combat shoplifting consist of physical changes in
the way merchandise is packaged (large and unwieldy wrapping
and boxing) or displayed (locked cabinets, inaccessible counters).
Others have incorporated in-store posters ("Shoplifters—All Eyes
Are on You"); random in-store announcements ("Security, report to
department X"); and even, as Klemke (1992) reports, random,
highly visible "shoplifting arrest incidents" staged by hired actors.
Other efforts have focused on various ways to increase the
chances that perpetrators will be seen or apprehended—or at least
make them think that they will be seen or caught. These efforts include hiring more security and sales staff and training them in surveillance techniques, using in-store video cameras and aisle
mirrors, widening between-counter aisles to improve viewing of
store customers, and regulating the number of customers occupy-
ing the store at any given time.

In addition to prevention and witnessing shoplifting as it occurs, a third approach is attempting after the fact to catch perpe-

trators with stolen goods before they leave the store premises. Electronic price tags and various types of exit alarms are examples of this strategy.

With these many and varied human surveillance and high-tech approaches, why are so few shoplifters caught? There likely are many answers, involving customer traffic volume, store and merchandise layout, public relations, and more. But one answer concerns the high skill level plus low guilt level of many shoplifters. Carroll and Weaver (1986) conducted a fascinating study that made this point very well. Through various means, they hired two groups of persons for their experiment. One was a group of "novices," who reported that they had never shoplifted. The other was a group of "experts," each of whom had done so at least 100 times, including at least 10 times in the past year. Each expert or novice was wired to a tape recorder and a lapel microphone and was walked individually through a series of stores by the researchers. As the participants walked, they were asked to imagine that they were contemplating shoplifting incidents and asked to describe all their thoughts about the incidents into their microphones. An extensive analysis of these many comments about perceptions, feelings, strategies, tactics, and the like revealed that the experts, far more than the novices, were highly focused on the security and sales personnel and customers present, store layout, security devices, item size, and other aspects of "stealability." Novices, in sharp contrast, zeroed in not on the act but on the possible consequences of shoplifting: arrest, trial, fines, jail.

Additional approaches to the control and reduction of shoplifting have been rehabilitative and directed to actual perpetrators. These include psychoeducational training groups to deal with supposedly precipitating stressors (Mac Devitt & Kedzierzawski, 1988), covert desensitization (Gauthier & Pellerin, 1982), systematic desensitization (Marzagao, 1972), social casework (Schwartz & Wood, 1991), relaxation self-instruction training (Henderson,

1981), film-mediated aversion treatment (Kellam, 1969), aversive breath holding (Keutzer, 1972), and rational emotive therapy (Soloman & Ray, 1984). Still another approach has been the public information campaign seeking either to communicate anti-shoplifting messages to potential offenders or to increase public awareness and the likelihood of reporting (Sacco, 1985).

Thus, different paths to shoplifting intervention are available: in-store technology, merchandising, and personnel deployment; a variety of quasi-therapeutic approaches; public education efforts; and, of course, the punitive sanctions of arrest and incarceration. In my view, each of these alternatives is necessary; none by itself is sufficient. Earlier in this book, in proposing effective interventions for bullying, harassment, vandalism, and other forms of maltreatment, I sought to underscore the necessity of *comprehensive* intervention strategies. As with those expressions of low-level aggression, each act of shoplifting occurs for a multiplicity of reasons, from several possible causes. The complexity of cause must be matched by complexity of intervention.

Hiew (1981) describes one such comprehensive intervention—Operation S.O.S. ("Stop Our Shoplifting"), a collaboration of merchants, community organizations, schools, media firms, and the city's local university. As the latter's community survey revealed:

> One implication of the survey findings is that all sectors
> of the community are contributing to the problem of
> shoplifting and changing behavior in this area requires
> that everyone—merchants, students, parents, adults, law
> enforcement agencies—has to become more responsible.
> Effective solutions can only be found by their involve-
> ment. (p. 61)

This diversity of involvement was reflected in the program components of Operation S.O.S.:

- An antishoplifting presentation by police officials at all city junior and senior high schools

- A student-developed shoplifting information pamphlet distributed to all students

- A Chamber of Commerce–sponsored essay contest, "Why I Don't Shoplift"

- Student-designed antishoplifting posters (e.g., "What you take today may be your tomorrow") displayed in all city malls and in downtown stores

- S.O.S. buttons distributed in all city schools, S.O.S. placemats distributed in restaurants, S.O.S. bookmarks distributed in bookstores and libraries

- Training sessions by police for store employees, covering apprehension of shoplifters, methods of shoplifting, merchandise display, and so on

- A mass media public awareness campaign, culminating in a citywide "Antishoplifting Week"

- Repeated antishoplifting and S.O.S. radio spots

- Local newspaper advertisements covering S.O.S. campaign activities and interviews

Such broadly based, comprehensive intervention programs are rare and are much to be commended. Even rarer and more commendable is this program's systematic evaluation component, which showed substantial, significant reductions over an extended period in the frequency of shoplifting. Hiew (1981) comments in conclusion:

Most shoplifting prevention strategies are aimed at either increasing public awareness of the severity of their consequences or increasing the threat and likelihood of detection. Present research indicates that awareness campaigns using strategies which organized the community for joint participation and action effectively reduced shoplifting rates. The . . . campaign directly involved several thousands of people including junior high, high school and university students, merchants, store employees and managers, shoppers, the media and members of the criminal justice system. . . . The success of Operation S.O.S. indicates that crime prevention in the area of shoplifting is highly feasible. (p. 66)

SABOTAGE

Although sabotage can occur in any form of organization—governmental, educational, business/industrial—it is primarily with regard to the latter setting that the literature on this topic has developed. Thus, Rosow (1975) defines sabotage as any employee behavior whose purpose is to inflict a production loss on the targeted organization. Dubois (1979) describes it broadly as any act seeking to lower the quantity or quality of production, including strikes, go-slows, working without enthusiasm, theft, and absenteeism. According to Brown (1997), sabotage is deliberate damage to machinery, product, or work environment and includes intentional poor workmanship and the withholding of effort. Crino (1994) views sabotage as acts that

constitute deliberate interference with normal company activities and relationships, and . . . characterized by prior thought and appreciation of likely consequences. The intention is to damage, disrupt or subvert the organization's operations for the personal purposes of the saboteur by creating unfavorable publicity, embarrassment, delays in production, damage to property, the destruction of working relationships, or the harming of employees or customers. (p. 312)

Sabotage may be carried out by a wide variety of means. Giacalone and Knouse (1990) polled a large sample of business students who identified 51 different means (see Table 4.6). A factor analysis of this large methods pool yielded four categories: (a) profits and production sabotage, (b) information sabotage, (c) violent illegal sabotage, and (d) labor methods sabotage. A second such listing (Table 4.7), provided by DiBattista (1991) and only partly overlapping the large pool displayed in Table 4.6, combines with it to reveal the unusually large number of harm-inflicting means available to the motivated saboteur.

Why sabotage? What motivates such aggressive behavior? Linstead (1985) proposes that sabotage stems from an intentional desire to reduce frustration, ease the work process, or assert control. Crino (1994) provides a more comprehensive answer:

1. To make a statement or send a message: These attention-calling acts of sabotage are often made out of moral, political, or religious beliefs.

2. To prevent or encourage corporate change: In this instance, the central feature may be fear—of work methods changes, of possible new ownership of the company, and so forth.

3. To establish one's personal worth in the eyes of others: Here the sabotage is carried out as an attention-seeking attempt, to impress others, to enhance one's perceived status.

4. To gain competitive advantage over co-workers: Perceived or actual competition is the motivation in this case, as when an employee damages a co-worker's work product or means in order to gain advantage in salary, position, or status.

Table 4.6—Methods of Sabotage

1. Arson
2. Using explosives to destroy company property
3. Disassembling key parts of machinery
4. Instructing others to engage in activities which will be harmful to the company
5. Altering or deleting the data stored in computer databases
6. Embezzling money
7. Falsifying information on company records
8. Disclosing secret information to competitors
9. Allowing defective products to pass inspection
10. Lowering the quality of the product by purposely using lower-quality parts
11. Blackmailing the company
12. Taking quality merchandise and disposing of it via the garbage or the toilet
13. Spreading rumors about the organization's plans so that other employees will do destructive things
14. Continuously taking merchandise from the organization
15. Purposely breaking a piece of machinery to slow down production
16. Altering company records
17. Placing a false order
18. Talking other workers into going on strike
19. Purposely forgetting maintenance procedures so that machinery will break
20. Graffitiing the walls
21. Packaging the products improperly so that they break during shipping
22. Destroying tools so that you don't have to work
23. Wrecking the office of an executive you don't like
24. Damaging someone else's work

25. Destroying the power lines
26. Using too much of a product so that there is a lot of waste
27. Extorting funds
28. Being unproductive by not meeting quotas
29. Stealing needed equipment
30. Starting a union
31. Purposely delaying work processes
32. Insulting customers
33. Losing important files and papers
34. Destroying a project in a way that would prevent its completion in time
35. Scaring other employees so that they won't work
36. Hurting a key person in the organization
37. Ruining relations with other companies
38. Putting poison in the products
39. Lying to management about important data
40. Distracting other employees, thereby causing errors
41. Failing to record money received
42. Tampering with the books
43. Destroying the reputation and credibility of the company
44. Only partially assembling merchandise and sending out
45. Destroying company vending machines
46. Ordering fewer supplies than needed so that company runs out of everything
47. Using physical violence against other workers
48. Overloading machine capacity
49. Littering
50. Training new employees poorly
51. Intercepting mail so that it fails to get to people on time

Note. From "Justifying Wrongful Employee Behavior: The Role of Personality in Organizational Sabotage" by R. A. Giacalone & S. B. Knouse, 1990, *Journal of Business Ethics, 9,* 57–58. Reprinted with kind permission from Kluwer Academic Publishers.

Table 4.7—Forms of Sabotage

1. Doing "personal work" on company time with company supplies and telephone
2. Writing on company furniture and walls
3. Flattening tires and scratching company cars
4. Stealing to compensate for low pay and poor work conditions
5. Self-creating "downtime"
6. Switching paperwork around the office
7. Snipping cables on word processors
8. Passing on defective work and parts to the next station
9. Calling the OSHA representative as a scare tactic
10. Altering the time on the punch clock
11. Punching someone else's time card
12. Calling upon the union to intervene
13. Setting up the foreman to get him/her in trouble
14. Pulling the fire alarm and making bomb threats
15. Turning on a machine and walking away, knowing it will crash

Note. From "Creating New Approaches to Recognize and Deter Sabotage" by R. A. DiBattista, 1991, *Public Personnel Management, 20,* 347–352. Reprinted by permission of the International Personnel Management Association, 703-549-7100, www.ipma_hr.org.

5. To gain revenge against management or co-workers: Believing one has been treated unfairly—not given a raise, passed over for promotion, denied needed resources—one may use sabotage for payback purposes.

6. To have an impact in a large, faceless bureaucracy: Sabotage of this type is an effort to affect a difficult-to-impact work environment, to feel one is making a difference, to gain a measure of control over one's work life.

7. To satisfy a need to destroy or seek excitement: Boredom is often a major industrial problem; sabotage for some may be the thrill-generating solution.

8. To avoid work or responsibility for failure: To shift blame, get off the hook, or simply do less work are the motivations in this instance.

9. For personal gain: Sabotage may be employed as a route to obtaining additional compensation—for example, by creating opportunities for overtime.

10. To express anger engendered by nonwork problems: Motivation here resides in the expressive act of sabotage itself, in response to frustrations experienced off the job.

Although the traditional image of an act of sabotage conjures up the destructive, disgruntled, or dissatisfied employee as perpetrator, management too may engage in sabotage—broadly defined. Sartin (1970) points to errors in product design or production, poor manufacturing methods, wasted time, machine downtime, shortage of raw material, poor plant maintenance, and similar failures or intentional acts.

In part, but only in part, the occurrence and escalation of sabotage have been controlled by a variety of means (Crino, 1994; Giacalone, 1990). Whom does one hire? The screening and assessment of applicants can be helpful, perhaps shedding light not only on past destructive behaviors but also on its possible precursors and correlates—frequent job changes, claims of multiple incidents of past maltreatment by employers, and so forth. After a new employee is hired, proper orientation to the firm and the position as well as proper skills training for the job itself may minimize, respectively, misunderstanding and a frustrating sense of inadequacy. Team-building activities may enhance employees' positive identification with the company. Once employees are on the job, creating an atmosphere of trust and fair treatment, keeping employees informed, employing equitable personnel policies, implementing a fair reward system, ensuring due process when disciplinary actions are necessary, and conducting frequent and fair performance reviews will enhance both company-worker relations and employees' sense of self-identity, both potent inhibitors of anticompany behaviors such as sabotage.

ANIMAL CRUELTY

In this section I will examine the relationship of aggression toward animals and toward humans, consider the history of cruelty toward animals, and focus on target (animal) qualities apparently related to the likelihood of victimization. To briefly place these topics in broad perspective, it is useful to note that approximately nine and a half *billion* animals are killed each year in the United States. Nine billion are killed for food, approximately two hundred million by hunters, fifty million in animal experiments, fifteen to twenty million by trappers, and five million in animal "shelters" (Beirne, 1998; Dunayer, 1995; Plous, 1993). Further, as Agnew (1998) notes, the vast majority of the animals that are killed live their lives in crowded, restricted, stressed, and often tortuous conditions. Though in the following discussion I consider animal cruelty as abnormal human behavior, it is clear that from this broader point of view that such behavior is quite fully the norm in our society.

Aggression directed toward animals, although often not low level in terms of the degree of injury inflicted, is worthy nonetheless of inclusion as one more expression of low-level human aggression that frequently constitutes a step on the ladder to interpersonal violence. Both Ascione (1993) and Felthous and Kellert (1987) have reviewed the approximately two dozen existing studies examining the relationship between childhood cruelty to animals and later violence toward people. At first glance, results of this array of investigations appear mixed, with several studies finding no relationship and several others reporting a strong, positive association. Felthous and Kellert have helped clarify these discrepant patterns. The majority of the studies with negative outcomes tended strongly to inadequately define either the predictor (animal cruelty) or the criterion (adult violence), weaknesses much less characteristic of the studies with positive outcomes. Even more consequential, the majority of the former were "chart studies," whereas the latter were investigations employing direct interviews. Stated otherwise, in much of the research failing to link cruelty toward animals in one's youth and aggression toward other persons in one's adulthood, the investigators sought both the animal cruelty and human aggression information by reviewing patient charts of research participants in a VA hospital (Macdonald, 1961), a private psychiatric hospital (Felthous & Bernard, 1979), a prison hospital (Prentky & Carter, 1984), a hospital emergency room (Clement, Hyg, & Ervin, 1972), and similar settings. Unlike all of the studies inquiring into this relationship via interview (e.g., Felthous, 1980; Hellman & Blackman, 1966; Kellert & Felthous, 1985), the chart studies did not clarify whether the patient was even asked about animal cruelty behaviors. We may presumptively conclude, then, that a relationship between early cruelty toward animals and later aggression toward humans is at least possible for many persons and quite likely is probable. At minimum, the methodologically stronger interview studies warrant our tentative decision to view animal cruelty for many persons as a low-level step toward higher levels of violence.

History and Current Definitions

Before the 19th century, there was no concern in law for the rights of animals and, with only occasional exceptions (Bentham, 1781; Primatt, 1776, cited in Favre & Tsang, 1998), very little humanistic or philosophical awareness expressed regarding their suffering. Early American legislation began to alter this picture, but only for commercially valuable animals such as horses and cattle. The pre-1900 view of animals as mere property was maintained in these early statutes but altered to take account of property that was able to experience pain. An 1821 Maine statute, for example, read:

> Be it further enacted, That if any person shall cruelly beat any horse or cattle, and be thereby convicted . . . he shall be punished by fine not less than two dollars nor more than five dollars, or by imprisonment in the common gaol for a term not exceeding thirty days, according to the aggravation of the offense. (Favre & Tsang, 1998, p. 39)

Many other states enacted similar, misdemeanor-level legislation during this period. As these statutes were adopted, their scope was expanded—from prohibition against only killing, to killing and torture; from prohibition of such cruelty to other people's animals (i.e., property), to other people's and one's own. Even this earliest anticruelty legislation reflected a budding awareness of the dangers of progression and escalation to aggression against humans:

> Initially, the societal concern about cruelty to animals contained mixed motives. While some did not believe moral duties were owed to animals, they did accept that cruelty to animals was potentially harmful to the human actor, as it might lead to cruel acts against humans. (Favre & Tsang, 1998, p. 42)

Anticruelty legislation expanded broadly and rapidly in scope with the arrival on the legal scene of Henry Bergh in 1866. In this year, Bergh asked for and received from the New York State Legislature a charter to establish the American Society for the Prevention of Cruelty to Animals (ASPCA). As its first and highly activist president, he succeeded in having New York State change its animal cruelty statutes to prohibit not just killing, but also maiming, wounding, injuring, torturing, beating, and even neglecting an animal—in fact *any* animal "belonging to himself or another," not only horses or cattle. In a year, this statute itself was expanded to cover "any living creature," not just owned animals, and the ASPCA itself was accorded the police power to arrest any person in violation of the statute. In the late 1800s, passage of such legislation, and the ASPCA itself, spread broadly across the United States. As cases emerged, courts subsequently came to define animal cruelty concretely to include beating a horse, burning a goose, pouring acid on an animal's hooves, overworking a mule, starving a horse or depriving it of proper shelter, freeing a captive fox in the presence of a pack of hounds and allowing them to tear the fox apart, and passively permitting a dog to attack or kill other dogs (Favre & Tsang, 1998). Today, as Vermeulen and Odendaal (1993) note, a greatly expanded definition of animal cruelty is widely accepted (Table 4.8).

These several categories of cruelty to animals show it to be a highly diverse form of aggression. As Ascione, Thompson, and Black (1997) observe, each of these acts of animal cruelty can vary in severity, frequency, and duration, thus presenting a difficulty in establishing whether an act of cruelty to an animal should be viewed as low-, mid-, or high-level aggression, the same difficulty that we faced in chapter 1 in attempting to establish what behaviors are best defined as low-level aggression toward humans.

Targets of Animal Cruelty

The vast majority of person-oriented research on human aggression examines who does it rather than who receives it. Given that aggression is (at least) a two-person, transactional event, we need much more research, such as that summarized in Baenninger's (1991) important book *Targets of Violence and Aggression*. Perhaps Kellert and Berry's (1980) speculations regarding which animals

Table 4.8—Typology of Companion Animal Abuse

Physical abuse, intentional or nonintentional

Active maltreatment
- Assault
- Burning
- Poisoning
- Shooting
- Mutilation
- Drowning
- Suffocation
- Abandonment
- Restriction of movement
- Incorrect methods of training
- Inbreeding
- Trapping
- Transportation
- Fireworks
- Bestiality

Passive neglect or ignorance
- Lack of food and water
- Lack of shelter
- Lack of veterinary care
- Lack of sanitation
- General neglect

Commercial exploitation
- Labor
- Fights
- Indiscriminate breeding
- Sport
- Experimentation

Mental abuse, intentional or nonintentional

Active maltreatment
- Instillation of fear, anguish, and anxiety
- Isolation

Passive neglect
- Deprivation of love and affection
- Lack of recreational stimuli

Note. From "Proposed Typology of Companion Animal Abuse" by H. Vermeulen and J. J. Odendaal, 1993, *Anthrozoös, 6,* 248–257. Copyright 1993 by the Delta Society. Reprinted by permission.

are and are not typically targeted for cruelty may, as a model, be useful in this regard. Felthous and Kellert (1987) suggest that the following qualities may determine the extent to which an animal or type of animal is valued and hence is more or less likely to be abused:

> aesthetic appeal of the animal; intelligence of the animal; phylogenetic relatedness to humans; size of the animal; economic value of the animal; perceived dangerousness to humans; likelihood of causing property damage; cultural and historical importance; relationship to human society (for example, pet, farm animal, fame, pest); predatory tendencies; skin texture and morphological structure; and means of locomotion (for example: swimming, flying, walking, crawling). (p. 1714)

Regarding its aesthetic value, Kellert (1983) asks, Is it a butterfly or a slug? Its phylogenetic closeness to humans: A bear or a jellyfish? Its presumed threat to human health: A cricket or a cockroach? Its cultural and historical importance: A bald eagle or a vulture? Its economic value: An oyster or a starfish?

One researcher has speculated that an important factor in the way we feel about and treat animals is how similar we think they are to humans. Perhaps, he suggests, if we believe they think and feel pain, fear, anger, and affection and therefore are more like us, we are less able to hurt them. If they differ from us in such ways, on the other hand, cruelty is more possible. Such us-versus-them perception underlies much human-to-human aggression—why not human-to-animal also (Goldstein, 1996b)?

Felthous and Kellert (1987) moved beyond these interesting speculations in their animal cruelty study of "diffusely, recurrently aggressive subjects" (p. 1714), namely, prisoners at two U. S. penitentiaries. Cats were revealed to be the most frequently abused target, apparently a not uncommon finding (Dale-Green, 1963; Felthous, 1981; Oldfield, 1956).

151

Physical features of cats render them suitable for some specific methods of abuse. Cats have long flexible tails that can be joined together. Fur burns. Their bones are easily broken. Cats are small enough to be carried about and dropped from heights. But physical features alone do not adequately explain the high incidence and severity of cat abuse or the considerable prejudice that abusers harbor against cats. Cultural prejudices against cats appear to be prevalent. (p. 1719)

Such feelings were not reported toward dogs, but dogs were the second most frequently abused species. Several subjects reported abusing dogs to elicit compliance, others to encourage ferocity. Other targets were horses, cows, pigs, rats, birds, small game, fish, frogs, and other species. Most targets were small; only very rarely was the target an animal dangerous to the perpetrator.

The abusers' motivations, derived from their own descriptions of their abusive behavior, included control, retaliation, satisfaction of a prejudice against a species, expression of aggression, an urge to shock or amuse observers, or a displacement of hostility felt toward another person.

Types of abuse were as varied as the underlying motivations. Beating, stoning, and shooting were most common. Animals being dismembered, set on fire, exploded, having bones broken, and being thrown from heights were also reported expressions of animal cruelty.

A substantial number of studies of human aggression have shown its magnitude to vary inversely with empathy (Chandler, Greenspan, & Barenboim, 1974; Feshbach, 1978; Miller & Eisenberg, 1988; Reed, 1981; Selman, 1980): the more of the former, the less of the latter. Perhaps animal cruelty takes on significance in human affairs via its reflection of a diminished capacity for empathy. As Ascione (1992) found, a year-long humane education program "not only enhanced children's attitudes towards animals, but this change generalized to a measure of human-directed empathy" (p. 240).

Perhaps a fitting way to conclude this examination of animal cruelty as low-level aggression is to urge the heeding of Lockwood and Hodge's (1986) advice:

> Perhaps the most important approach to the problem of animal cruelty is *prevention*. . . . Without proper intervention, children may graduate to more serious abusers including violence against people. Do not ignore even minor acts of cruelty. Correct the child and, when possible, express your concerns to his or her parents. Appropriate interventions may, in this way, stop a cycle of escalating abuse. (p. 6)

STALKING

Stalking is a crime involving acts of pursuit of an individual over time that are threatening and potentially dangerous. Stalking is repeated behavioral intrusion upon another person that is unwanted, that results in communication to that person of implicit or explicit threat, and that causes the threatened person to experience fear. A large national survey (Tjaden & Thoennes, 1998) revealed that 8% of women and 2% of men have been stalked at some time in their lives—that is, 8.2 million women and 2 million men. For just the year 1997, comparable victimization figures are 1 million women and 370,000 men. Some additional data: Approximately 80% of stalking victims are women; 87% of stalkers are men. About three-quarters of the victims know their stalkers, who tend to be current or past intimate partners. Of the victims reporting, 21% said the stalking occurred before the relationship ended, 43% after it ended, and 36% both before and after. Among stalking victims, 51% are ordinary citizens, 13% are former employers of stalkers, 17% are highly recognizable celebrities, and the remainder are lesser known entertainment figures (Meloy, 1998).

Stalking takes many forms, including making unsolicited phone calls, following the victim home or to work, sending unwanted letters, vandalizing the victim's property, killing or threatening to kill a family pet, going through mail or stealing it, stealing underwear, entering the victim's home to move objects around, going through the victim's garbage, threatening suicide, wiretapping the victim's telephone, going through the victim's handbag or briefcase, ordering items in the victim's name, canceling items (leases, utilities) in the victim's name, harassing the victim's family or friends, leaving harassing or malicious e-mail messages (cyberstalking), and other forms of trespass, following, or intrusion (Hall, 1998, Meloy, 1998).

Stalking is not merely, by definition, a repeated occurrence; in numerous instances, it is repeated many, many times. About two-thirds of stalking cases last 1 year or less, about a quarter continue for 2 to 5 years, and about a tenth last more than 5 years. On average, a stalking case lasts 1.8 years. According to the Tjaden and Thoennes (1998) survey, victims' explanations of the reasons such stalking behaviors took place included beliefs that the stalkers wanted to keep them in the relationships, control them, or scare them; that the stalkers wanted attention or wanted to catch them doing something; or that the stalkers were mentally ill. Victim responses include, in order of frequency, taking extra precautions, getting help from family and friends, getting a gun, changing one's address, moving out of town, avoiding the stalker, talking to an attorney, varying one's driving habits, moving to a shelter, stopping going to work or going out altogether, and hiring a private investigator.

Clearly, stalking is a painful event. It is also an event that may turn violent. It may begin, Walker and Meloy (1998) suggest, mildly, even positively, such as with one member of a couple querying about the other's activities, or calling occasionally to ask about the other's day, or offering an opinion about a friend or family member. However, it may grow to frequent instances of the foregoing and become monitoring, surveillance, overpossessiveness, intrusion, and stalking. Hall (1998) describes this escalation process as one moving from relational harassment through pathological pursuit to criminal stalking. For some victims, it is a sequence that can end in violence. Lloyd-Goldstein (1998) reports that about half of all stalkers threaten violence, and that about a quarter of these actually carry out the threats.

Stalkers: Background and Dynamics

Who are the perpetrators of stalking behavior, and why do they carry out such behavior? I have already indicated that most are males and that only a minority are strangers to their victims. Harmon, Rosner, and Owens (1995) and Kienlen (1998) report that stalkers tend to be older, educated men with unsuccessful personal and employment histories. Zona, Palarea, and Lane (1998) suggest that there are three types of perpetrators. The first they label *simple obsessionals*. Most of these individuals are people who know their victims and were in intimate relationships with them. As these investigators note, many such cases are postscripts to domestic violence situations. The other major subgroup of simple obsessional stalking is seen in the work environment—a terminated employee stalking the employer he believes is responsible for his firing or a rejected suitor pursuing the co-worker who has not responded to his advances. Zona et al. note a final subgroup of simple obsessional stalking in the context of such nonintimate relationships as teacher-student, doctor-patient, psychotherapist-client, and business partners. A second major type of stalker is the *love obsessional.* Here there is no relationship between perpetrator and victim, intimate or otherwise. Victims of this type of perpetrator are usually celebrities, public figures, or others known to the stalkers only through the mass media. *Erotomanic* stalkers, the third category proposed, share two features in particular. Most are females, and they suffer from the delusional belief that the victims love them. Of the three types of stalkers, Meloy (1998) reports, it is the simple obsessionals who are most likely to perpetrate high-level violence. When violence is perpetrated, it most likely will be directed to the victim, but a second, not uncommon target is the person the stalker perceives as interfering with his access to the victim (a parent, a new boyfriend, etc.).

In part because of the common observation, noted earlier, that stalkers often have histories of unstable or nonexistent personal relationships, Meloy (1992, 1996) speculates that many such persons suffer from a "pathology of attachment." Indeed, Kienlen (1998) finds a not uncommon pattern of what has been called "preoccupied attachment," a picture in which the perpetrator's early-life caregivers were inconsistent, were insensitive, and generated in the stalker-to-be a poor self-image combined with an acute need for approval and validation from others. Kienlen (1996) suggests that "individuals with a preoccupied attachment style actively seek to gain their attachment figure's approval in order to validate their tenuous sense of self worth" (p. 59).

Obscene Phone Calls

Obscene phone calls are a particularly common, often repetitive, and frequently fear-arousing type of personal intrusion and are therefore a phenomenon appropriately examined in a consideration of stalking. Katz (1990) estimates that phone companies receive 6 million complaints each year about annoying, harassing, or explicitly obscene phone calls. It is a phenomenon much more typically experienced by women than by men. The typical call recipient is a young to middle-aged female, single or divorced, living alone, and residing in a metropolitan area (Katz, 1994; Smith & Morra, 1994). Callers are most frequently adult males who are strangers to the parties they call. Mead (1975) proposes that there are three types of obscene phone callers. The first, frequently juveniles, typically open their calls with immediate use of profanity or obscene propositions. The second, whom Mead labels "ingratiating seducers" string the callees along with believable statements regarding previous acquaintanceships or mutual friends and, the listening trap thus set, spring the obscene contents. The third, far less common type is the trickster, who poses as a survey taker, businessperson, or other with a legitimate reason for talking to the callee about personal matters. As noted, obscene calls are far from uncommon events. Prevalence rates vary widely from survey to survey, but in almost all instances they are quite substantial (Clarke, 1990; Fine, 1989; Savitz, 1986; Sheffield, 1989). Obscene calls are common not only in terms of the numbers of recipients, but also regarding the average number of calls each one receives. Among Smith and Morra's survey respondents, 86% of those receiving obscene calls got more than one, and 36% got six or more.

For the call recipients surveyed by Savitz (1986), the most common caller opening statement was explicitly sexual (41%), followed in frequency by a neutral or inquisitive opening (20%). Smith and Morra (1994) found sexual or threatening openings reported by 78% of the callees they surveyed, whereas 22% of the calls received were silent. Both types of calls generally came after dark (61%). About a quarter of those called hung up immediately, whereas about 40% responded to neutral openings with similarly neutral responses like "Who are you?"

Warner (1988) has provided a fine-grain analysis of the structure of typical obscene phone calls in her examination of "aural assault." She describes well the various subterfuges, ploys, and related tactics callers may use to gain control of the call's pace and contents in order to deliver their obscene messages. The consequences following from receipt of such messages can be substantial. Warner's (1988) respondents at minimum felt threatened, and many experienced the added burden of self-blame and a sense of further possible vulnerability.

Even without making overtly threatening remarks, callers were perceived as possible assailants. Several respondents stated that they believed callers had "sinis- ter" or "criminal" motivations. . . . Women worried about how callers had discovered their telephone num- bers and whether, as a result, callers knew where they lived. (p. 310)

Smith and Morra (1994) report similar emotional conse- quences. Three-quarters of their callee sample responded to calls with fearfulness, ranging from uneasiness to outright terror. One- fifth reported anger, ranging from annoyance to outrage. Others spoke of repulsion, violation, or shock.

Across these several surveys, respondents report a variety of coping strategies—changing phone numbers, using answering ma- chines or caller ID to screen calls, informing the phone company or the police. Matek (1988) offers what for many callers may be use- ful responding tactics:

The best thing to do is to hang up the phone gently with the realization that this is an obscene phone caller. Bang- ing the receiver down or trying to retaliate by screaming or scolding only plays into the wishes of the obscene phone caller who takes this as a reward. Some women have re- ported success by partially covering the mouthpiece of the phone and saying out loud, as though talking to a third party, "This is him officer—hurry." Other tactics that seem to have worked are to pretend to be hard of hearing and to complain that it is difficult to understand him; or to say one is going to another phone extension, but instead, just let the phone sit off the hook for a while. (p. 125)

Although obscene phone calls are an example of low-level aggression that usually remains in its original low-level form, its repetition (Katz, 1994) and instances of its progression to a physical assault (Sheffield, 1989; Warner, 1988) are both examples of circumstances under which it may have an escalating aggressive impact.

Intervention

Why does stalking stop? The Tjaden and Thoennes (1998) national survey revealed reasons, in descending order of frequency: The victim moved, the stalker got a new love interest, police warned the stalker, the victim warned the stalker, the stalker was arrested, the stalker moved, the stalker got help, the victim got a new love interest, the stalker died, or the stalker was convicted of another crime.

Clearly, stalking is a common, fear-arousing, quite unpleasant form of low-level aggression that, in a significant minority of instances, can and does engender violent, injurious consequences for the victim and for others. We strongly concur with Walker and Meloy (1998), who urge, "Stalking is a risk factor for further physical abuse or a lethal incident just by virtue of the tenacious proximity-seeking toward the victim. . . . It needs to be identified at its earliest stages, even before the behavior becomes serious enough to bring in law enforcement" (p. 142).

ROAD RAGE

By its use, its abuse, its advertising images, and many of its names (Charger, Gladiator, Ram, Firehawk, Impulse, Blazer, Samurai, Trooper, Cutlass, Bronco, Tracer, Storm, Probe, Stealth), the automobile is not only a vehicle for transportation but too often also a vehicle for aggression. Studies of driver behavior over the past 40 years show not only that aggressive road behavior has been with us a long time but also that it is growing worse (Marsh & Collett, 1986; Parry, 1968; Whitlock, 1971).

In the 1960s and 1970s, driver aggression took mostly such low-level forms as rude gestures, the desire to injure another driver, excessive use of the horn, and racing other drivers. The surveys of the 1980s showed an escalation to tailgating, deliberate blinding with high headlight beams, deliberate blocking of passing or changing lanes, throwing of objects, and displaying of weapons. In the 1990s, auto aggression has reached new levels of intensity to include roadway shootings and suicide and murder crashes.

Who are the aggressive drivers? They tend to be persons who are competitive, irritable, distractible, impulsive, extroverted, and male (Macmillan, 1975; Michalowski, 1975). They are drivers who agree with such survey items as "It is each man for himself on the roundabout [traffic circle]"; "I would rather accelerate than brake to get out of a difficult situation"; and "If you are stuck in the wrong lane, you may have to cut across in front of other cars" (Macmillan, 1975). They frequently have more accidents and more convictions for motoring offenses (Macmillan, 1975). But auto aggression, like all aggression, springs not only from the hearts and fists of its perpetrators; the setting, the circumstances, and the situation also contribute in important ways.

One research team (Doob & Gross, 1968) created a frustrating circumstance for drivers by arranging to have a car, which was stopped at a traffic light, fail to move when the light changed. On some occasions, the stopped vehicle was an expensive one, a new black Chrysler Imperial. At other times it was a rusty old Ford station wagon or a decrepit Rambler. Backed-up drivers honked their horns more, and more quickly, when stuck behind either of the older cars than when blocked by the Chrysler. Male drivers honked more, and more quickly, than female drivers, especially when the driver of the stopped car was female. Because aggression is always at least a two-person affair, auto aggression depends not only on the qualities of the aggressive driver but also on the surrounding circumstances: who the other driver is, the type of car, and, as other studies have shown, even the outdoor temperature and humidity (Kenrick & MacFarlane, 1986).

One further study of the context for road rage is instructive. Hauber (1980) arranged for an experimental confederate pedestrian to enter the street at a predetermined point as an automobile approached. Approximately 1,000 drivers were exposed to this procedure, and their responses were recorded and judged. The behavior of 25% of the drivers was rated as aggressive—fist shaking, cursing, horn honking, and similar actions. Younger drivers (those judged to be under 40), both male and female, displayed more such aggression than did older drivers. The gender of the pedestrian also mattered. There was twice as much aggression when it was a male starting to cross. Finally, there was a time-of-day effect, with more frequent aggression in the afternoon than in the morning. In this last regard, Novaco, Stokols, and Milanesi (1990), too, report that drivers find the evening commute more stressful and aggression-engendering than the morning commute.

A growing minority of drivers are carrying guns in their cars. A recent study of drivers required to attend traffic school revealed that 44% of them had been charged at by other drivers, 36% had had objects thrown at them while they were driving, 13% had been bumped or rammed, 8% had had physical fights with other drivers, 4% had been threatened with guns, and 5 of the 412 drivers surveyed had actually been shot at while driving (Novaco, 1991). What driving conditions appear to contribute to road rage? Deffenbacher, Oetting, and Lynch (1994) presented 1,500 college students with an extended series of driving-related situations and, using their responses, constructed the Driving Anger Scale, a measure consisting of six clusters of precipitants, as shown in Table 4.9.

What goes on inside drivers that promotes aggression? Novaco (1991) suggests four processes that encourage aggression. The first is anger arousal. Chronic exposure to traffic congestion, long

Table 4.9—Driving Anger Scale Items

Cluster 1: Hostile gestures

Someone makes an obscene gesture toward you about your driving.

Someone honks at you about your driving.

Someone yells at you about your driving.

Cluster 2: Illegal driving

Someone is driving too fast for the road conditions.

Someone is weaving in and out of traffic.

Someone runs a red light or stop sign.

Someone is driving way over the speed limit.

Cluster 3: Police presence

You see a police car watching traffic from a hidden position.

You pass a radar speed trap.

A police officer pulls you over.

A police car is driving in traffic close to you.

Cluster 4: Slow driving

Someone in front of you does not start up when the light turns green.

A pedestrian walks slowly across the middle of the street, slowing you.

Someone is driving too slowly in the passing lane, holding up traffic.

Someone is driving slower than reasonable for the traffic flow.

A slow vehicle on a mountain road will not pull over and let people by.

Someone is slow in parking and holding up traffic.

Cluster 5: Discourtesy

Someone is driving right up on your back bumper.

Someone cuts in right in front of you on the freeway.

Someone cuts in and takes the parking spot you have been waiting for.

Someone backs right out in front of you without looking.

Someone coming toward you does not dim their headlights at night.

Cluster 5: Discourtesy *(continued)*

At night someone is driving right behind you with bright lights on.

Someone speeds up when you try to pass them.

Someone pulls right in front of you when there is no one behind you.

A bicyclist is riding in the middle of the lane and slowing traffic.

Cluster 6: Traffic obstructions

You are stuck in a traffic jam.

You hit a deep pothole that was not marked.

You are driving behind a truck which has material flapping around in the back.

You are driving behind a vehicle that is smoking badly or giving off diesel fumes.

A truck kicks up sand or gravel on the car you are driving.

You are driving behind a large truck and you cannot see around it.

You encounter road construction and detours.

Reproduced with permission of authors and publisher from: Deffenbacher, J. L., Oetting, E. R., and Lynch, R. S. Development of a driving anger scale. *Psychological Reports,* 1994, 74, 83–91. © Psychological Reports 1994. This scale may be copied and used, either in hard copy or computer format, for research purposes only, without further permission from the authors. The user is responsible for assuring that any research using this measure meets the ethical standards of the American Psychological Association. No commerical use is allowed without specific permission of the authors.

---

commutes, and many other stressful features of routine driving are associated with lowered tolerance for frustration, increased blood pressure, and increasingly negative mood. In a second process, aggression also stems from the difficulty of the trip. The longer the trip; the greater the number of roads and interchanges traveled; the heavier the traffic; the more the delays and obstacles to moving ahead, getting home, or getting to the office—the worse the driver's mood.

The third process concerns the anonymity of the driving situation. The typical driver is anonymous, can usually easily leave the scene of his aggression and remain unidentified, and can avoid accountability for his behavior if he desires, much as with the deindividuation that occurs in groups, crowds, or mobs. Such ability to fade into the shadows makes auto aggression more likely, especially when combined with the disinhibiting consequences of alcohol or drug consumption. The contribution of anonymity to the expression of aggression on the road is well demonstrated in a study conducted by Ellison, Govern, Petri, and Figler (1995). In this investigation, a confederate of the experimenter, driving a convertible, pulled in front of waiting cars at a stoplight. When the light turned green, the confederate driver remained stationary and recorded the other driver's horn honking (the study's measure of low-level aggression). This was done to 60 cars—30 times with the convertible's top up (the confederate in an anonymous condition) and 30 times with the top down (an identifiable condition). When the top was up and the confederate was thus anonymous to the blocked drivers, the latency of horn honking (seconds till first honk) was shorter, its duration was longer, and its frequency was greater—all differences being significant.

Finally, Novaco (1991) points to a fourth process: scripts. These are the routine ways that people interpret what they see going on around them. Such scripts help determine how people respond. As the United States continues to become a more aggressive nation, and as the roadway is increasingly seen as a major playing field for aggression, drivers' scripts increasingly promote violent behavior.

There is yet a fifth process that may contribute to the likelihood of driver aggression: the degree to which one's automobile becomes an extension of oneself. At some personal level, an injury to it feels not so much like an injury to an object one owns as an injury to oneself. Marsh and Collett (1986) approach this notion when they speak of one's car "as a special territory with personal space zones" (p. 259). Going even further, however, I refer here to a process of *apersonation,* in which inanimate objects—because of their use, proximity, and so on—come to feel as if they are a part of oneself. Lifelong users of crutches and wheelchairs sometimes comment about these objects in such a manner. Many drivers, I believe, experience their cars as part of themselves.

One of this book's major assertions is that we as a society have failed to pay sufficient attention to low-level aggression in its diverse forms (including road rage) and, as a result, have inadvertently encouraged its continuance and even its escalation. According to Fumento (1998), road rage is an exception to this indictment of inattention. If anything, he asserts, we have paid too much attention to it! He claims it is largely a media-hyped, pseudophenomenon whose reality rests on weak, inadequate, and over-inclusive evidence. Though there are strands of truth in his argument, I believe it is substantially overstated.

Road rage at the level of excessive horn honking, cursing, headlight blinding, and tailgating can often escalate to seriously high levels of violent behavior. Novaco (1991) reflects on a series of 100 roadway shootings. His typology of roadway aggression includes the categories of shootings, throwings, assaults with a vehicle, sniper/robber attacks, drive-by shootings, suicide/murder crashes, and roadside confrontations—with and without weapons. All of these criminal maltreatment events appear to be a recurrent and serious reality on the American roadway today.

Some good advice: If you are out driving and find yourself about to become involved in an auto aggression confrontation—as either perpetrator or victim—stay in the car, take a deep breath, count from 10 to 1, think of that nice balmy day you spent at the lake last summer, imagine that you are already home or wherever you are heading. Then, drive on.

CHAPTER FIVE

Minimal Maltreatment

In the same catch-it-low, escalation-retarding spirit that informed earlier chapters focused on verbal, physical, and criminal maltreatment, in this chapter I consider behaviors whose characteristic levels of injuriousness makes them best viewed as possible preludes to low-level aggression. In themselves, they may or may not be classifiable as low-level aggression, but, intuitively, they are close. I speak here of rough-and-tumble play, hazing, baiting, booing, and tantrum behavior.

ROUGH-AND-TUMBLE PLAY

Hank and Terry are 12-year-old classmates on a school trip to a local park. About 2 P.M., after a ball game they both enjoyed, they are sitting together on a park bench out of teacher view. Hank grabs Terry firmly but gently around the neck and, laughing, wrestles him off the bench as he verbally teases him for hitting into the game-ending double play. They roll on the grass, both now laughing. Terry winds up sitting on Hank as he tries to pin his arms to the ground. After 5 or so minutes of such horseplay, a bit winded and by mutual consent, they return to the bench, talking about the game, to sit and finish their drinks. Their play fighting has remained play fighting.

At more or less the same time, in the playground at the other end of the park, Sal and Benji, two 9-year-olds, have been taking turns, along with changing groups of two or three other children, in using the playground's slide. On this particular run, Sal goes first as Benji stands on the slide's top step waiting for Sal to clear the slide. Benji then sits at the top of the slide, ready to go. But Sal, rather than returning to the line, stands on the bottom of the slide and starts trying to run up it. Rising to the challenge, Benji shoves off, and the two meet in the middle of the slide. They continue down to the bottom, a laughing, shouting heap of arms and legs. But Sal and Benji don't disengage at the bottom. At first, like Hank and Terry, they wrestle playfully. Shortly, their play hardens, becomes less playful. They become more intent on hurting each other. Kicks and punches are exchanged. Play fighting has become real fighting. A few minutes later a passing adult breaks up the fight. Sal walks away frowning, rubbing the bruise on his leg. Benji heads in the opposite direction, tissues pressed to his bloody nose.

In the first scenario, what began as horseplay ended as horseplay. In the second, the play fighting became real, and the two youngsters were hurt. Which scenario, in reality, is more likely? Is there a connection between play fighting and the real thing?

Parents, teachers, and others concerned with children's behavior have asked the same question. When children in their charge wrestle, push, play kick, splash or dunk in the pool, or engage in other rough-and-tumble play, should they leave the kids alone? Is it part of normal, healthy development? Or is it a training ground for later aggression, to be stopped as soon as possible?

A number of researchers have studied rough-and-tumble play, also known as play fighting or horseplay, and its consequences. Boys do it more than girls, men more than women (Boulton, 1996). Between men and women, there is more horseplay in close relationships than in casual ones, and there is more when one of the partners is a moderate or heavy drinker (Gergen, 1990).

What of horseplay and aggression? Superficially, they look similar, but there are reliable differences (Boulton, 1991, 1993, 1994; Costabile et al., 1991). Play fighting or horseplay—in which the motivation is to have fun—involves smiling, often laughing, self-handicapping by stronger partners, reversal of positions, absence of threats, relaxed muscles, very few injuries, and the two parties remaining together afterward. It is gamelike, often beginning with an invitation, and a child may decline to participate without losing face. It occupies as much as 10% of children's free playground time (Humphreys & Smith, 1987). Aggression—in which the goal is to hurt—involves a fixed gaze, frowns, less restraint in delivering blows, less variety of actions, injuries, and the parties going their separate ways after the fight. It often begins with an attack, consists of unrestrained blows, and, unlike play fighting, frequently draws an audience of other children. Compared to rough-and-tumble play, real fighting involves more strength and, later, more regret. In an observational study of 3- to 8-year-old children, Fry (1990) found that rough-and-tumble play episodes occurred significantly more often than aggressive episodes (5.3 versus 0.6 per hour), lasted significantly longer (16 seconds versus 4 seconds), were more variable in content, and were more likely to involve multiple participants. DiPietro (1981) and Smith and Lewis (1985) report similar relative frequencies and characteristics. Children as young as 4, according to Boulton (1992), can tell which is which, though in one study (Schafer & Smith, 1996) employing video of 20 fighting episodes, some play and some aggression, teachers had difficulty distinguishing the two about a third of the time. Costabile et al. (1991) provide a comprehensive list of the criteria employed by (British) children in distinguishing between rough-and-tumble play and aggression (see Table 5.1).

Does rough-and-tumble play lead to aggression? Are those who play roughly likely to be those who seek to hurt others? Research results are mixed (Boulton, 1992; Frey & Graff, 1994; Pellegrini, 1995). It seems quite probable that for the large majority of children, the two are most often unrelated. Play is play; aggression is aggression. Two important exceptions have been identified, however: (a) children who are frequently rejected by their peers and

Table 5.1—Criteria Used to Distinguish between Playful and Serious Fighting

Criterion	Definition
Length of episode	Refers to the duration of the encounter (e.g., "If it was a fight it would have lasted longer" and "It didn't last long enough to be a fight").
Stay together or separate	Refers to what the participants do or try to do at the end of the encounter (e.g., "It was a fight 'cos that boy was trying to get away" and "It was only a mess about 'cos that boy stayed with him").
Facial expressions	Refers to the facial expression of the participants (e.g., "It was a mess about 'cos he were smiling" and "You could tell it was a real fight because he had a right angry face").
Physical actions	Refers to the presence, absence, or qualification of physical acts, or all three (e.g., "It was only a play fight 'cos he didn't hit him hard" and "That was a real fight because he ran after him and kicked him in the leg").
On the ground (position)	Refers to whether or not the participants were upright or on the ground (e.g., "He was really fighting 'cos he got the other boy on the ground").
Crowd	Refers to the presence or absence of spectators (e.g., "It was real 'cos they all came round" and "That were a toy fight as the other boys didn't watch them").
Actions of nonfocal peers	Refers to the actions of other children (e.g., "It were real because his friend tried to break it up" and "That were only a mess about 'cos another boy tried to join in").

Criterion	Definition
Inference about affect	Refers to the (presumed) affect of the participants, without reference to other criteria (e.g., "It was a real fight because they were both angry" and "That was a toy fight 'cos he didn't mind him doing that").
Inference about action, intent, or both	Refers to the (presumed) actions, intentions, or both of the participants (e.g., "It was a play fight 'cos that probably didn't hurt him" and "That were a true [fight] 'cos he tried his best to get him").
Stereotyped knowledge	Refers to what children think usually happens (e.g., "That were a mess about 'cos girls don't fight with boys" and "It was really aggressive 'cos boys usually do that when they are mad").
Knowledge about focal child or children	Refers to how the participants had been seen to behave in the past (e.g., "That were a toy fight 'cos I know them and they're best friends" and "Real fight because he is always picking on him, he's a bully").

Note. From "Cross-National Comparison of How Children Distinguish Serious and Playful Fighting" by A. Costabile, P. K. Smith, L. Matheson, J. Aston, T. Hunter, and M. J. Boulton, 1991, *Developmental Psychology, 27,* 881–887. Copyright 1991 by the American Psychological Association. Reprinted by permission.

(b) chronically aggressive youngsters (Dodge & Frame, 1982; Pellegrini, 1988). These children are prone to errors when they try to read or decode the behavior of others, especially in falsely assuming that others have hostile intentions. Both of these types of children often find their rough play blending into serious aggression.

After puberty, the line between rough-and-tumble play and aggression often gets fuzzier, at least for some adolescents and young adults (Neill, 1976; Pellegrini, 1994). Two groups are especially prone to an increased blending of play fighting with real fighting: young males trying to build macho reputations by displays of toughness and young couples—especially those who have been dating long or are going steady—when one or both parties have consumed too much alcohol (Gergen, 1990). With regard to the young males, a study by Pellegrini (1995) of rough-and-tumble play as it relates to aggression by adolescent boys was able to dismantle horseplay into two constituent components—chase and physical roughness. The latter but not the former proved to correlate significantly and positively with subsequent instances of aggressive behavior. Frey and Graff (1994) have found the relationship between rough-and-tumble play and acts of aggression to hold for adolescent girls as well as boys, but at substantially lower levels of covariation.

For the rest of us, horseplay may not only be transitory fun, but there is some evidence that for many children it may even be valuable practice for the learning of a number of physical and social skills (Blurton Jones, 1972; Humphreys & Smith, 1987). Fagan and Wilkinson (1998), for example, suggest that rough-and-tumble play may be of functional value in three ways: affiliations and friend selection, development of fighting skills, and initial establishment of one's position in a peer dominance hierarchy. Unfortunately, as we have noted, for too many youngsters such behavior fails to remain playful in character and intent and, instead, grows into low-level aggression with all that such growth implies for possible escalation and harm infliction.

HAZING

Hazing is an organizational initiation ritual consisting in large part of low-level verbal and physical aggression directed to the initiate. Such rites have long been employed within civic organizations, military services, professional schools, high schools, and, especially, college fraternities. The occurrence of hazing in this last context is the focus of this section.

Baier and Williams (1983) identified a representative sample of specific member behaviors, directed toward pledges or applicants for membership, that constitute hazing. They are presented in Table 5.2.

Hazing may be perceived as playful by its perpetrators, but in far too many instances it is experienced as anything but play by its recipients. Its nasty nature ("collective stupidity, insensitivity, and irresponsibility," according to Buchanan, Shanley, Correnti, & Hammond, 1982, p. 57) is captured in the abstract by the Texas and Florida antihazing statutes, legal definitions similar to that employed in antihazing statutes now in effect in most states.

The Texas statute defines hazing as follows:

(1) any willful act by one student alone or acting with others, directed against any other student of such educational institution, done for the purpose of submitting the student made the subject of the attack committed, to indignity or humiliation, without his consent;

(2) any willful act of any one student alone, or acting with others, directed against any other student of such educational institution, done for the purpose of intimidating the student attacked by threatening such student with social or other ostracism, or of submitting such student to ignominy, shame, or disgrace among his fellow students, and acts calculated to produce such results.

(3) any willful act of any one student alone, or acting with others, directed against any other student of such educational institution, done for the purpose of humbling, or that is reasonably calculated to humble the pride, stifle the ambition, or blight the courage of the student attacked, or to discourage any such student from longer remaining in such educational institution or reasonably to

Table 5.2—Fraternity Hazing Activities

1. Calisthenics
2. Nudity
3. Wearing/carrying unusual items
4. Dropping food into mouth
5. Paddle swats
6. Throwing substances on pledges
7. Loud or repetitious music
8. Pushing, shoving, tackling
9. Yelling, name-calling
10. Forced drinking of alcohol
11. Pledge class lineups
12. Non-fraternity-related memorizing
13. Kidnaps, road trips, walks
14. Confining in uncomfortable room
15. Repeated disturbances of sleep
16. Pranks against other groups
17. Misleading about initiation chances
18. Pledges used for entertainment
19. House duties not shared by actives
20. Any assignment actives won't also do
21. Unusual, embarrassing, uncomfortable clothing
22. Eating unpalatable foods

Note. From "Fraternity Hazing Revisited: Current Alumni and Active Member Attitudes toward Hazing" by J. L. Baier and P. Williams, 1983, *Journal of College Student Personnel, 24,* p. 301. Copyright 1983 by American College Personnel Association. Reprinted by permission.

cause him to leave the institution rather than submit to such acts; or

(4) any willful act by any one student alone, or acting with others, in striking, beating, bruising, or maiming; or seriously offering, threatening, or attempting to strike, beat, bruise, or maim, or to do or seriously offer, threat-

en, or attempt to do physical violence to any student of any such educational institution or any assault upon any such student made for the purpose of committing any of the acts, or producing any of the result, to such student as defined in this section. (Texas Code Annotated, Section 4.19)

In the Florida statute, hazing is defined as follows:

As used in this section, "hazing" means any action or situation which recklessly or intentionally endangers the mental or physical health or safety of a student for the purpose of initiation or admission into or affiliation with any organization operating under the sanction of a university, hereinafter referred to as "university organization." Such term shall include, but not be limited to, any brutality of a physical nature, such as whipping, beating, branding, forced calisthenics, exposure to the elements, forced consumption of any food, liquor, drug, or other substance, or any other forced physical activity which could adversely affect the physical health or safety of the individual, and shall include any activity which would subject the individual to extreme mental stress, such as sleep deprivation, forced exclusion from social contact, forced conduct which could result in extreme embarrassment, or any other forced activity which could adversely affect the mental health or dignity of the individual. For purposes of this section, any activity as described above upon which the initiation or admission into or affiliation with a university organization is directly or indirectly conditioned shall be presumed to be a "forced" activity, the willingness of an individual to participate in such activity notwithstanding. (Florida Code 240.262)

The aggressive nature of hazing may also be concretized in the fact that, state antihazing statutes and university antihazing policy statements notwithstanding, a substantial number of pledges each year are seriously injured, and some killed, as a direct result of hazing experiences (Bryan, 1987; Buchanan et al., 1982; Hammond, 1981).

Baier and Williams (1983) and Ramey (1981) have also noted that a large proportion of the attempts to limit or eliminate hazing on the university campus have been unsuccessful. Only twice in the over 100 years that university fraternities have existed has there been a decline in the incidence of hazing—in the late 1940s as a result of the large influx into university life of more mature returning veterans, and in the 1960s when student activist movements caused the Greek system to be relatively ignored and fraternity membership declined (Richmond, 1987). A survey of current and past fraternity members conducted by Baier and Williams (1983) revealed strong attachment to a series of justifications for the continuance of hazing, including (a) building pledge class unity, (b) instilling humility, (c) perpetuating chapter tradition, (d) proving the pledge can "be a man," (e) maintaining campus respect for the chapter, and (f) fulfilling the expectations of pledges, who "enjoy it." With such a broad wall of rationalization, it is no wonder that hazing continues. These rationalizations are further buttressed by belief that if hazing is a problem, it is a problem for other fraternities, not one's own, as a survey of current and past fraternity members by Baier and Williams revealed:

> Despite the fact that a large percentage of both active and alumni members acknowledge that certain activities are hazing, that their chapters occasionally or usually engage in these activities, and that hazing is a problem nationally and at their university, only 10% of the active members and 13% of the alumni members believe hazing is a problem in their own chapters. The "it's somebody else's problem" syndrome that is prominent in most fraternal organizations also appears to be a primary hin-

drance to the reduction or elimination of hazing in college fraternities. (p. 304)

Hazing as an initiation rite clearly seems to qualify as minimal maltreatment, sometimes innocuous and playful, at other times serious and harmful. Continued legal and administrative sanctioning to reduce and eliminate its use appears wise and worth encouraging.

BAITING

Harris Brown was very depressed. His marriage had slowly been going sour for many months, and he had begun to suspect that his wife had a lover. Today at work he had been given a firsthand lesson in the meaning of the word *downsizing*. He'd spent 22 years at the company, 22 faithful, hard-working years. And now a note: "Not needed anymore. Good-bye. Clean out your desk by Friday." He crossed the street to the office building he had seen from his office for years but never entered. Took the elevator to the 12th floor. Entered the men's room, opened the window, and crawled out on the ledge.

Harris stood there, gazing down but not really seeing. He looked across the street to his own office and thought about the memo. "Not needed anymore. Good-bye. Clean out your desk by Friday." Words broke through his fog of depression. They seemed to be coming from below, from the street.

"Jump! Jump! . . . Jump! Jump!"

This strange and repugnant expression of minimal maltreatment, the suicide-baiting crowd has been studied by Mann (1981). His data consist of 21 cases in which a crowd was present when a person threatened to jump off a building, bridge, or tower. Crowd reaction, he suggests, may be primarily concern, or curiosity, or callousness. This last group quality, he proposes, is what characterizes the suicide-baiting crowd, whose members jeer, taunt, and urge the victim to jump.

What conditions give rise to such behavior? Mann (1981) hypothesized that a callous crowd would be characterized by deindividuation—a condition of diminished self-awareness, a condition in which, in a sense, one's identity is lost in and merges with the crowd. Deindividuation is more likely to occur under some circumstances than others, and the research sought to find out if these circumstances were present when baiting occurred and absent when it did not. Here is what Mann found.

Crowd size. People should feel more anonymous in large crowds than in smaller groupings. In fact, there was significantly more baiting of the victim in crowds of more than 300 persons than in smaller ones.

Cover of darkness. Dim lighting should also contribute to deindividuation for the same reason as does crowd size: It increases anonymity. Again, analyses showed more taunting, jeering, and encouragement to jump in incidents occurring after 6 P.M. than before.

Physical distance between crowd and victim. Where the potential suicide is close to the crowd, making it difficult for crowd members to remain anonymous, little baiting should occur. Further, when so much distance intervenes that the victim would be unable to hear the taunts and jeers, it is also true that little baiting should occur. Most baiting should take place at an intermediate distance, when victim and crowd are far enough apart for crowd members to lose their identity, yet close enough for shouted communications to be heard. This is just what the research found: Baiting occurred only when the person threatening to jump was on the 6th to 12th floors of the building involved, not at a lower or a higher level.

Duration of the incident. It has been proposed that deindividuation is more likely when crowd members are tired and perhaps irritable. Consistent with this idea, baiting was substantially more frequent in those incidents lasting more than 2 hours as compared to briefer ones.

Baiting is an uncommon event. However, when it does take place, it may function as a type of minimal maltreatment that may encourage seriously self-injurious behavior in its target. It is thus desirable that such crowd reaction be better understood and minimized.

BOOING

Verbal expression of disapproval, disagreement, and dissatisfaction in the form of booing, razzing, whistling, hissing, or chanting has not been a focus of substantial theorizing or research inquiry. A small amount of relevant social science concern with such forms of minimal maltreatment does exist, however, and will be examined here.

Clayman (1993) studied audience behavior at a wide variety of public speaking events—U. S. presidential debates, congressional floor debates, television talk shows, and British party conference speeches. Certain types of speaker statements are more likely than others to elicit booing. Chief among these are unfavorable remarks concerning a political adversary. Criticisms, accusations, or derisive characterizations of the opposition preceded well over half of the booing episodes identified. A second booing stimulus is boasts of accomplishment by the speaker, with which members of the audience disagree. Also booed are straightforward factual statements, political opinions, and policy proposals.

The anatomy of booing episodes is of interest. Unlike applause, which typically occurs immediately after a well-liked presentation, lasts an average of 8 seconds, and results from independent decisions by individual members of the audience, booing typically begins after a delay of as much as 2 seconds following a disapproved presentation and usually only after audience members monitor one another's behavior to be sure they are not booing alone. Booing rarely continues for more than 3 seconds.

Clayman (1993) reports that audience behavior immediately preceding booing is of two general types. Some is disaffiliative: Audience members whisper or talk to their seat neighbors; they may talk out loud, jeer, or shout at the speaker. Disaffiliation may begin with a buzz or murmur and escalate to collective booing. As noted, pre-booing audience members monitor one another. The buzzing of others indicates current audience dissatisfaction and thus serves to disinhibit the subsequent booing.

Booing may also be immediately preceded by an affiliative audience response, such as applause or appreciative laughter. This sequence may occur when the positive response (applause, laughter) of some audience members is itself viewed negatively by other members, the latter's booing thus serving as a message of public disagreement with both the original stimulus and the initial positive response to it by others in the audience.

Some speakers, Clayman (1993) notes, engage the booing and, in explicit ways, reply to it by seeking to counter or refute the audience objection that it makes concrete. In this manner the speaker may score rhetorical points and even elicit applause from other, supportive members of the audience. Alternatively, a speaker may talk through the booing and, in a sense, behaviorally ignore it. Such a strategy makes the booing less conspicuous and perhaps less prolonged as well.

Booing may or may not be a precursor to low-level aggression. Intuitively and anecdotally, it has functioned at times as such a minimal maltreatment. What has been shown, however, is that to receive it is a stressful experience (Greer, 1983), one causing demonstrable decrements in skill behaviors. Its continued scrutiny as an emotional—and social—influence event seems clearly appropriate.

TANTRUMS

It's 3:30 in the afternoon, and the young mother is doing some late-day shopping at the supermarket to pick up a few things for supper. Her 3-year-old son is sitting in the cart as she hurriedly pushes it toward the store's fruit and vegetable section. By mistake, in her rush, she turns down the cookie aisle. Her son's eyes light up. "Cookies," he says, "I want a cookie!" Mom responds, "No, darling, we're going to have supper soon. You can have a cookie later." "No, no, no," he insists, "I want a cookie now!" "You can't have one, " the mother responds sharply, as she watches the boy's face get red and his arms and legs grow rigid. The escalation is rapid, and within a few minutes of louder demanding by the son and refusals by the mother, the child is in a full-blown tantrum—shouting, crying, flushing, arms and legs flailing, kicking anyone and anything in reach. Potegal and Davidson (1997) suggest that this array of vigorous behaviors reflects two underlying processes—anger and distress.

What is known about such tantrum behaviors? They usually begin between ages 1 and 2, occur in about half of all children, peak in frequency at about age 2, and usually are gone by age 4 or 5 (Bath, 1994). The typical tantrum lasts 1 to 4 minutes and involves a rapid sequence of four stages.

Prodrome. Although some tantrums seem to arrive out of the blue, most are preceded by a sometimes lengthy period of whining, irritability, defiant looks, and similar warnings of a storm cloud gathering. This has been called the "rumbling and grumbling" pre-tantrum arousal stage (Treschman, 1969).

Confrontation. The tantrum proper usually begins with a confrontation between the child and a parent or other individual. Refusal of a persistent request, such as for the cookie, seems to light the fuse. The most common tantrum behaviors are screaming, crying, shouting, hitting, kicking, and flailing. Not uncommonly, during this stage the child may hurt himself or herself and others. The most common source of self-injury is from head banging. Though both boys and girls throw tantrums, hitting and kicking as part of the tantrum is substantially more common in boys.

Sobbing. As the tantrum begins to wind down, sobbing replaces shouting, stillness replaces thrashing, floppiness replaces rigidity. The child starts to regain self-control and to reestablish contact and communication with the parent or other. He or she may, in this stage, even feel guilty and apologize. Einon and Potegal (1994) suggest that the transition from confrontation to sobbing reflects an inner transition from anger to distress.

Reconciliation. The tantrum ends, often (in 35% of instances) with a cuddle. Such need on the part of the child for what Potegal and Davidson (1997) describe as "post-tantrum affiliation" appears to increase with age, perhaps because with age the distress also lasts longer. What about the cookie (or whatever else lit the fuse in the first place)? In 30% of the instances, the child does not get his or her way (no cookie); 6% of the time, the child does (yes, a cookie); and about 20% of the time, a compromise (a cookie later) is the solution. In general, this last tantrum stage is a time of increased contact, communication, and reassurance. Only in about 12% of tantrums does the anger and sulkiness persist. Much more commonly, the argument fades away and life goes on as before (Potegal & Davidson, 1997). LaForge (1996) reports that typical tantrum behaviors vary by age, as indicated in Table 5.3.

The introductory example of the struggle over the cookie is probably a good one because the most common conflicts initiating tantrum behavior concern eating. Other frequent provocations have to do with confinement (to a stroller or shopping cart), dressing, and similar daily events in which parental and child preferences may clash. Tantrums peak in the late morning (before lunch) and the early evening, when the child is likely fatigued. More generally, LaForge (1996) suggests, triggers include frustration, fatigue, hunger, illness,

Table 5.3—Typical Tantrum Behaviors by Age

Under age 3

Crying	Arching the back
Biting	Throwing self on floor
Hitting	Pounding or flailing arms
Kicking	Breath holding
Screaming	Head-banging
Screeching	Throwing things

Ages 3 to 4—any of the above, plus

Stomping	Shaking clenched fists
Yelling	Slamming doors
Whining	Accidentally breaking things
Criticizing	

Ages 5 and up—any of the above, plus

Swearing	Deliberately breaking things
Self-criticism	Threatening
Striking out at a sibling or friend	

Reprinted with permission of Pocket Books, a division of Simon & Schuster, Inc., from TANTRUMS: SECRETS TO CALMING THE STORM by Ann E. LaForge. Copyright © 1996 by Peggy Schmidt. A New Century Communications Book from the Editors of *Child* magazine.

anger, changes in routine, jealousy, stresses at home, stresses at school, and insecurity about oneself or one's abilities.

Tantrums are unpleasant and at times harmful events. Although it is not easy to do, if parents or other caregivers can steel themselves and ignore the tantrum behavior, there is a good chance it will diminish in frequency. As a great deal of research on extinction has demonstrated, any behavior (including tantrums) that consistently fails to get that valuable reward of attention tends to disappear. True, not getting mother's or father's attention will at first result in more, not less, shouting, kicking, and crying (i.e., the "extinction burst"). But research shows quite clearly that giving in to the tantrum results in both longer and more frequent tantrums.

Give the reward of attention, instead, to the quiet, nontantrum behaviors that eventually follow the tantrum. Children who were cuddled (a great form of attention) at this quiet, post-tantrum stage had, subsequently, both shorter and less frequent tantrums than did those children who were not.

In addition to the combined use of extinction and "catch them being good," LaForge (1996) has offered a number of further strategies to minimize the frequency and intensity of tantrum occurrence.

Confer a sense of control. Give the child a sense of control by demystifying the tantrum. For example, use it in a game to make it seem less frightening and overwhelming, or tell the child, "The last tantrum lasted 9 minutes. I'm setting the timer for 7 minutes, and we'll see if you can stop it before the buzzer goes off."

Use foreshadowing. Before visiting the mall, the relative's house, or other likely tantrum site, tell the child what will happen, how he or she is expected to behave, and what to do if he or she feels overwhelmed.

Provide choices. Within a restricted range (two items of clothing, two types of breakfast cereal), let the child feel empowered and choiceful, rather than having a decision imposed on him or her.

Teach relaxation. Even quite young children can learn the positions, movements, and breathing patterns that effectively promote a sense of calm and relaxation.

Avoid nonconstructive responses. Avoid arguing, giving in, lecturing, pleading, shaming, or yelling.

And remember—next time be careful and don't turn down the cookie aisle!

The five behaviors I have elected to designate as minimal maltreatments, that is, behaviors with potential to grow to low-level aggression, are but a mere sampling—and a small one at that—of the myriad human behaviors possessing such potential. The interested researcher or practitioner would do well to consider additional candidates: insults (Cohen, Nisbett, Bowdle, & Schwarz, 1996), threats (Benoit, 1983), quarrels (Dawe, 1934), argumentativeness (Tannen, 1998), incivility (Carter, 1998), humiliation (Miller, 1993), meanness (Mills, 1997), intentional embarrassment (Sharkey, 1997), complaining (Kowalski & Erickson, 1997), guilt inducement (Sommer & Baumeister, 1997), annoyance (Cunningham, Barbee, & Cruen, 1997), deception (O'Hair & Cody, 1994), rivalry (Reit, 1985), revenge (Bies, Tripp, & Kramer, 1997), deceit (Ford, 1996), deficient information processing (Dodge & Coie, 1987), stress (Felson, 1992), sensation seeking (Arnett, 1996), competition (Franken & Brown, 1995), attribution (Crick, 1995), irritability (Smith & Taylor, 1985), jealousy (White & Mullen, 1989), showing off (Hold-Cavell, 1985), authoritarianism (Walker, Rowes, & Quinsey, 1993), macho values (Salisbury & Jackson, 1996), pro-aggression attitudes (Saunders, Lynch, Grayson, & Linz, 1987), dominance (Williams & Schaller, 1993), and impulsivity (McCown, Johnson, & Shure, 1993).

The variety of potential precursors to low-level aggression is quite substantial, presenting both challenge to those wishing to better understand causation and opportunity to those wishing to thwart escalation.

Intervention: Strategies, Tactics, and Evaluation

Whether it takes the form of verbal, physical, criminal, or minimal maltreatment, it is clear that low-level aggression is frequent, diverse, and often a step up to higher rungs on the ladder to violence. In the preceding chapters I have examined the many concrete forms such behavior may take and in several instances have also suggested viable intervention approaches. In this chapter I will offer a fuller statement regarding intervention and, in doing so, will explore apparently productive intervention strategies as well as the specific, change-enhancing tactics that these strategies suggest.

INTERVENTION STRATEGIES

Intervention Goals

Intervention efforts will optimally aspire to serve both preventive and rehabilitative purposes. I agree with Martin, Sechrest, and Redner (1981), who view prevention and rehabilitation as part of a continuum rather than as discrete entities. The commonly used distinction among primary, secondary, and tertiary prevention (Bolman, 1969) is relevant here. Primary prevention efforts typically are broadly applied interventions designed to reduce the incidence of a particular disorder or class of behaviors. Secondary prevention interventions are usually targeted toward especially at-risk populations showing early signs of the condition in question. Tertiary prevention interventions, equivalent to rehabilitation, are efforts to reduce the recurrence of or impairment from conditions that have already set in. All three levels—primary, secondary, and tertiary (rehabilitation)—are relevant to the successful management of low-level aggression. We collectively should aspire, for example, to substantially reduce the incidence of bullying in our schools; to devote particular effort at doing so in classrooms and with youths likely to be bully prone; and also to intervene energetically at the community, school, class, and individual levels when it is clear that bullying has in fact taken place. Primary, secondary, tertiary.

Beyond the combined preventive and remedial thrusts, I would urge as a primary goal of intervention efforts an earnest zero-tolerance strategy. As I noted earlier, we are a society that has downsized deviance. Our heightened attention—in schools, for example—to fights, assaults, weapons, and drugs has been accompanied by lessened attention to disruptiveness, cursing, threats, bullying, and other incarnations of low-level aggression. So, too, in other venues: The delinquent youth who receives a series of mere cautions from the family court judge and no negative consequences until several infractions have occurred is being taught that deviance is downsized. The acting-up child whose aggression at home is ignored until it approaches peak intensity, the spray-painting vandal who has tagged much of his neighborhood and received only peer admiration for his efforts, the adult jaywalker, the driver accustomed to rolling stops at stop signs, the neighbor ignoring dog leash laws, and other perpetrators of minor and typically unpunished infractions have each learned a similar downsizing lesson. Zero tolerance of deviant behavior is in effect in U. S. schools, but only for such high-level disruptiveness as bringing weapons or drugs into the schoolhouse. I urge in the strongest possible terms that both the spirit and the concrete tactics of zero tolerance be extended down the ladder to the several low-level aggressive infractions that have been the focus of this book. This philosophical and tactical shift in perspective, it should be noted, is as relevant for the parent, counselor, employer, youth care worker, or other change agent as it is for the classroom teacher.

Prescriptive Programming

Consistently effective rehabilitative and preventive interventions are, in my view, likely to be treatments developed, implemented, and evaluated according to the spirit and methodology of *prescriptive programming* (Goldstein & Stein, 1976). Simple to define in general terms but quite difficult to implement effectively, prescriptive programming recognizes that different individuals will be responsive to different change methods. The central question in prescriptive programming is "Which types of persons meeting with which types of change agents for which types of interventions will yield optimal outcomes?" This view runs counter to the prevailing one-true-light assumption, the antithesis of a prescriptive viewpoint, which is that specific interventions are sufficiently powerful to override substantial individual differences and aid heterogeneous groups of people.

The spirit and substance of the alternative many-true-lights, prescriptive programming approach have many roots. In work with emotionally disturbed adults and children, for example, there is Kiesler's (1969) grid model, matching treaters, treatments, and clients; Magaro's (1969) individualization of the psychotherapy offered and the psychotherapist offering it as a function of patient social class and premorbid personality; and our own factorial, tridifferential research schema for enhancing the development of prescriptive matches (Goldstein, 1978; Goldstein & Stein, 1976). In elementary and secondary education contexts, examples of prescriptive programming include Keller's (1966) personalized instruction; Cronbach and Snow's (1977) aptitude-treatment interactions; Hunt's (1972) matching of student conceptual level and teacher instructional style; and Klausmeier, Rossmiller, and Sailey's (1977) individually guided education model.

As I have suggested in another, related context:

> While it seems but a truism to assert that "different youth benefit from different programs," program implementors often act otherwise and employ but one program or type of program with many diverse types of youth. [We] strongly recommend a prescriptive orientation to program development and implementation in which the unique needs of culturally diverse youth are significantly taken into account and responded to in the form of different programs, different program combinations and sequences, and different program implementors depending upon program-relevant youth characteristics, as well as characteristics of their peers, family, community, and the program-providing agency. (New York State Taskforce on Juvenile Gangs, 1990, pp. 43–44)

Appreciative Programming

Who shall write our intervention prescriptions? I urge a joint collaboration between the expert-by-credential (psychologist, teacher, counselor, probation officer) and the expert-by-experience, that is, the perpetrator of low-level aggression.

I am not proposing that change agents give up the reins, only that they loosen them, now and then allowing recipients of their services to place their hands on the reins next to their own. The beneficial consequences of such appreciative program selection and development are not merely hoped-for outcomes. I and others have clearly demonstrated such consequences with gang-attracted youth in school settings (Goldstein & McGinnis, 1997) and with long-term gang members in community contexts (Goldstein et al., 1994). In both settings, we have provided Aggression Replacement Training (Goldstein, Glick, & Gibbs, 1998), one major component of which seeks to teach youths an extended curriculum of social skills for use in challenging everyday situations (i.e., Skillstreaming). In implementing such social skills instruction, we have employed a process we describe as "negotiating the curriculum":

> Many of the youths for whom Skillstreaming is appropriate chronically ascribe responsibility for their antisocial acts to others. They externalize; rarely is something their fault. . . . A teacher or parent may have indicated on the Skillstreaming Checklist that the youngster seldom or almost never uses two or three dozen of the prosocial skills listed. Yet the youth checks but a few of the skills as deficient! However inaccurate and inadequate such a self-picture may be, knowledge by the trainer of those few, self-admitted trainee deficiencies is golden. Teaching these skills (in addition to those that are trainer selected) has proven to be an especially positive facilitator of trainee motivation. In what might be called a "consumer model," we give the "customer" what he or she feels is needed. The customer then much more eagerly returns to our store. Thus, as frequently as every other Skillstreaming session for any given group, we begin the meeting not by announcing and enacting a modeling display for a skill chosen by the trainers but, instead, with "How is it going?" or "What's been happening to you all since our last meeting?" Out of the brief discussion such openings engender often comes information about difficulties at home, in school, on the street, or elsewhere—difficulties that

can be ameliorated or resolved by the Skillstreaming skill the trainers and trainees then jointly select and portray. The earlier in the group's life such negotiation of the curriculum commences the better. In fact, in the group's very first session, when open discussion of life difficulties by trainees may still be uncomfortable, the trainer can initiate such negotiation by tallying on a chalkboard the skills checked on the Skillstreaming Checklist by all the members of the group, without revealing who checked which ones, and then by teaching the one or ones checked most often. (Goldstein & McGinnis, 1997, pp. 25–26)

I urge change agents in school, agency, community, and other settings to seek other means of enacting both the spirit and substance of a collaborative, appreciative perspective.

Comprehensive Programming

In the earlier examinations of bullying, harassment, vandalism, and shoplifting, I sought to illustrate the need to view intervention as a total-push effort, one planned and implemented at several levels simultaneously.

Every act of aggression grows from a complex set of sources and thus has several causes. I frequently give a lecture on why corporal punishment is an ineffective means for changing behavior, a means that helps teach the lesson that might makes right and thus increases the chances that the youth being punished will become more, not less aggressive. On several occasions, a member of the audience has challenged my recommendation against such punishment, saying, "I got hit, and I turned out OK." I'm sure most such claims are true because 90% of American children are hit by their parents to varying degrees as they grow up, and most turn out not to be overly aggressive. But such protestations miss the point. Aggression grows from a complex of causes. One's own punishment history is but one such source. Alone, its contribution may not be enough to yield aggression; in combination with other sources, it may well do so.

So when Johnny curses Billy, the reasons are usually several and diverse. Some indeed are "in" Johnny: his personality, temperament, self-control, tolerance for frustration, and skills for dealing with provocation, and the "scripts" he carries with him for interpreting the behavior of others. However, much of the source of Johnny's aggression may be external, often in the sheer presence and behavior of others: coercive behavior by his parents, aggression by the peer group he hangs out with, his heavy diet of television violence. Each of these adds fuel to the potential fire. The presence of weapons and provocation by a possible victim are other external influences upon potential impulses toward aggression. Complex problems demand complex solutions. Aggression is a complex problem. We will best succeed in controlling it when we deal both with the perpetrator and with as many of its "outside" sources as we can.

My own research for many years has focused on evaluating a method that we have developed for teaching seriously delinquent youths alternative constructive skills for dealing with frustration and provocation as well as steps for directly controlling their anger. I call the method Aggression Replacement Training (Goldstein et al., 1998). In the studies that I and others have done on this method, our success in teaching such skills, as well as in keeping the youngsters from getting back into trouble and being returned to prison, has always been greater when we used the training both with the youths themselves and with the important others in their lives—family, peers, fellow gang members—who often play such major roles in supporting and encouraging the youths' aggression. Aggression will not be reduced by simple and sometimes simple-minded solutions. Needed, instead, are solutions that match, in their comprehensiveness, the complexity of aggression's roots itself.

INTERVENTION TACTICS

A strategy is one's plan, philosophy, schema, or orientation. Tactics are the concrete steps one follows to carry out one's plan. This section concerns a number of specific tactical recommendations for the prevention and remediation of low-level aggression, offered here to supplement the several such intervention approaches described earlier in the book.

Behavior Modification

The behavior modification movement is now decades old, and I will not seek to review at any length its many well-established methods for making positive impact on behaviors such as low-level aggression. I refer the reader to such sources as Goldstein and Keller (1987), Kazdin (1975), Martin and Pear (1983), and H. M. Walker (1995). One set of such tactical means, however, does deserve special comment because its research base demonstrating effectiveness is both long and deep. I speak here of the *consistent offer of positive reinforcement for behaviors that are desirable alternatives to low-level aggression coupled with consistent consequating with nonviolent punishment of all instances of behaviors that are low-level aggression.* In elaboration of this recommendation, I offer three points.

First, zero tolerance of low-level aggression requires that every instance of its occurrence be followed by a punitive consequence. Much of our contemporary use of punishment, however, whether at school, at home, or elsewhere, is in my view much too severe and embodies the very types of aggression that promote rather than inhibit aggression by the target person. Research on punishment makes clear that its swiftness and certainty are at least as important in determining its effectiveness as is its severity (Axelrod & Apsche, 1982; Van Houten, 1982). Thus, I strongly recommend that the behavior modification tactic of punitively consequating all instances of low-level aggression be implemented by means of extinction, time-out, response cost, overcorrection, contingency contracting, and other similarly nonviolent punishers.

Second, "catch them being good" is one of the oft-repeated but seldom implemented truisms of behavior modification. Despite its demonstrated effectiveness in accelerating positive behaviors, as shown by literally hundreds of studies of positive reinforcement, in actual practice we as parents, teachers, and employers have been very generous in offering criticism, reprimands, and cautions but very slow to praise, approve, or reward on-task, nonviolent, or other desirable behaviors. Doing so will prove to be an especially potent means for promoting nondeviant, prosocial, positive alternatives to low-level aggression. Further, if delivered publicly, within earshot of other students, siblings, or fellow employees who themselves would appreciate such appreciation, positive reinforcement can have good effects on their behaviors also:

> Steven, do you remember last week when Larry took
> your pencil, and the things you called him? Remember?
> We had to not only punish him, but you too because of
> what you said. Now I see he did it again, and I'll take
> care of him in a moment. But you didn't curse him this
> time, and I want to just let you know I think it's great that
> you didn't, and that you controlled your temper so well.
> Really nice job!

Throughout this book the major theme has been that effective consequating of low-level aggression has marked potential for inhibiting both its continuance and its escalation. In the spirit of "catch them being good" and in a manner consistent with behavior modification's use of shaping, it is worth noting a parallel process—and outcome: The consistent rewarding of low-level *prosocial* behavior is likely to promote its continuance and escalation. I speak here, for example, of the value of heightened positive attention (praise, approval) by teachers, parents, and others to simple kindness, low-level empathy, minimal sharing or caring, tentative cooperativeness, and other prosocial beginnings. My recommendation, in other words, is to "catch them being even a little good."

Third, and finally, my behavior modification tactical recommendation also strongly stresses consistency. Note my emphasis on the need for *all* positive behaviors to be followed by positive consequences and *all* negative behaviors to be followed by (nonviolent) negative consequences. Such consistency can, of course, at best only be approximated (and should be changed to intermittent consequences when positive response by the target is well established). I urge it so strongly, however, because occasional praise or punishment is in some ways worse than none at all. It is vital not only that the teacher, parent, employer, or other intervenor be consistent in consequence delivery (trying to reward/punish *every* time it is appropriate), but also that the teachers and other staff within a school, the parents within a home, and the employers within a firm be consistent with one another. In a sense, one may highlight the need for consistency by suggesting that each person involved in the act of low-level aggression holds a self-proclaimed task. For the acting-up youth perpetrating the aggression, the task is a testing of limits—How much can I get away with? For the intervening teacher or parent, the task is a limit-setting use of praise (for desirable behaviors) and punishment (for undesirable behaviors). I am urging, then, that such limit-setting, praise, and punishment consequating be conducted in as consistent a manner as possible.

Intervention Integrity

Intervention integrity is the degree to which the intervention as conducted follows the intervention as planned. Most interventions chronically suffer from substantial plan-implementation discrepancy. Even in those rather exceptional instances in which the intervention strategy is concretized in a systematic manner and in which the intervenor is well trained in its implementation, the actual application of procedures will often depart substantially from the underlying plan. A wide and usually unpredictable variety of "emergencies," "exigencies," "realities," and the like may arise. Class sizes or caseloads may expand. Workers may grow tired, lazy, or overburdened. Planned supervision and tracking may only partially materialize. Even if appropriately described, detailed, and exemplified in an intervention procedures manual, the intervention plan may fail to anticipate an array of crucial circumstances. Whatever the bases for diminished intervention integrity, program efficacy is likely to suffer. Interventions cannot, nor should they be, automated or implemented unswervingly and unresponsively in a manner dictated by program manuals, and I am not championing such literalness of application here. However, well-thought-out interventions, adequately reflected in detailed intervention procedures, deserve implementation in a manner consistent with their planning.

Intervention Intensity

Inadequacy of amount, level, or dosage characterizes many interventions directed at altering or preventing low-level aggression. True, different perpetrators will require differing amounts of intervention for reliable change to occur. However, we typically suffer from an insufficiency rather than an excess of change-oriented activity. Along with ensuring consistency among intervenors, I urge providing a heavy, rich, or substantial "dose" of the interventions offered—be it the reward/punishment sequence noted earlier; the comprehensive, multilevel school-home-community type of programming for bullying, harassment, vandalism, and shoplifting also noted earlier; or other "full-spectrum" means. It is clear that aggression is typically a firmly rooted, well-supported behavior that frequently will yield only to equally intense antiaggression intervention.

INTERVENTION EVALUATION

I do not aim here to provide either a primer or a complete discussion of guidelines for conducting rigorous intervention evaluations. For such guidelines, the reader is referred to Barlow, Hayes, and Nelson (1984); Bellack and Hersen (1984); and Krathwohl (1985). My purpose here, in a manner complementary to such basic material, is to highlight those aspects of the intervention evaluation process that appear especially central to evaluation of attempts to prevent or remediate low-level aggressive behavior.

Rigor-Relevance Balance

Ogden Lindsley (personal communication, June 6, 1965) spoke of three orientations to experimentation on intervention effectiveness. The Rigorless Magician orientation is reflected in the shoot-from-the-hip, impressions-count-for-everything stance of the individual who eschews objective measurement of effect and relies totally on clinical judgment. At the opposite extreme is the Rigor Mortician, so fixated on objective measurement that he or she sacrifices the richness, uniqueness, and individuality of the very phenomena being studied in the effort to obtain standardized measurement information. An intermediate position, and to be recommended, is that of the Rigorous Clinician. Here, the goal is to balance the rigor of experimental design and measurement with relevance to the real world of those being studied. Rigor of the evaluation is facilitated by use of the several design and measurement characteristics recommended in the sources already cited. Relevance of the intervention and its evaluation to the real world of perpetrators—that is, its external, ecological, or social validity—is to be promoted throughout the intervention evaluation process.

Evaluation Design

A wide variety of evaluation designs have been employed in the study of intervention effectiveness, broadly defined. Some are experimental designs, examining efficacy via between-group, within-group, or intrasubject comparisons. In carrying out such an examination, the evaluator may compare the full intervention with the full intervention minus one or more of its components in order to determine which components are active (the dismantling evaluation strategy). Or the evaluator, building incrementally, may begin with a narrow or circumscribed intervention and add components, making stepwise comparison with each addition (the constructive evaluation strategy). Alternatively, two or more different full interventions or intervention packages may be compared (the comparative evaluation strategy). The evaluator's ability or inability to control nonintervention aspects of the intervention context and to employ randomization of selection of participants and their assignment to intervention conditions, along with related operational considerations, will determine whether the evaluation conducted is an experiment, a quasi-experiment, a correlational evaluation, or a case study.

Case studies can serve as valuable sources of new interventions and provide useful clues (but not conclusions) about how, when, and with whom such interventions are likely to be effective. However, case history–based impressions of intervention effectiveness may be seriously biased (Kazdin, 1980). They may serve as excellent sources for hypothesis generation but poor sources for hypothesis testing. The intervention methods pioneered and reported in the contexts of such case studies must be evaluated for their efficacy in a less impressionistic, more objective manner—usually requiring an evaluation experiment. Stated more broadly, in attempts to better understand the intervention process and to improve the effectiveness of interventions, a combination of diverse qualitative and quantitative evaluation designs will be required.

Measurement of effect in such evaluations will optimally be similarly diverse. First, it will be multisource. No one concerned with the impact of an intervention—evaluator, perpetrator, target—perceives the "truth." All report from their own idiosyncratic, subjective perspectives. Truth can best be construed as information conjointly reflecting diverse subjective viewpoints, whether they converge or diverge.

Such measurement will also ideally be multimethod. It has been demonstrated that responses to a measuring instrument are in part a function of the form of that measure and thus can contribute to error variance. Use of diverse types of measures (self-report, other report, behavioral, archival, etc.) may largely compensate for this source of error variance.

Both proximal and distal effectiveness criteria will optimally be included in the evaluation's dependent variable measurement. Proximal measures seek to reflect changes in youths' behaviors and attitudes that are the direct target of the intervention. Distal measures seek to capture derivative changes (i.e., changes that in turn are potentiated if direct target changes first occur). Thus, if such proximal changes as enhanced social skills, anger control, and problem-solving ability first occur, then such distal outcomes as better school performance, employment, and reduction in low-level aggressive behaviors become more possible.

Both proximal and distal effectiveness criterion measurement will optimally take place on both an immediate postintervention and an extended follow-up basis. Interventions rarely serve as inoculations. Even when an intervention is immediately effective, the gain often fails to be durable. Nor should we expect it to endure, both because existing interventions are seldom that potent and because the real-life environment often pushes the perpetrators in a direction quite opposite from that targeted by the intervention. Thus, in order to discern whether and to what degree an intervention employed is powerful enough to reverse this common failure of generalization and yield proximal and/or distal effects that do endure, long-term follow-up measurement of intervention outcome is crucial.

I have highlighted in this section the major features of high-quality research designed to evaluate rigorously the efficacy of intervention efforts. As the chapters in this book make clear, interventions exist. The task of determining their effectiveness for reliably reducing low-level aggression still looms large before us.

Conclusion: Intervention Obstacles and Opportunities

This book has been a journey through the major domains of low-level aggression, including several forms of verbal, physical, criminal, and minimal maltreatment. I have also sketched a series of useful strategies and tactics for seeking to reduce such harmful behavior and thwart its escalation. My own decades-long involvement in such intervention efforts leaves me neither optimistic nor pessimistic regarding their likely success. Instead, I characterize my expectations as realistic, consisting of a history, demonstrated by me and many others engaged in such intervention work, of success in collecting "small wins," that is, a modest but far from inconsequential number of successes. Aggression is, after all, not an easy behavior to change.

For a growing number of American children and adolescents, for example, aggressive behavior is overlearned, consistently successful, and generously supported by the important people in their lives. Parents, teachers, delinquency workers, and others seeking to change such behavior continue to have difficulty doing so with many youngsters. Their first obstacle is the sheer frequency with which the lesson "aggression works" is taught to many youth in our society during their developing years.

Many young people grow up with parents who settle their own disputes aggressively and who frequently employ hitting as a major means of discipline with the youngsters themselves, as well as with the youngsters' siblings. Young people play for long periods with aggressive toys used in aggressive games with aggressive peers; they spend thousands of hours playing aggressive video games and viewing televised violence; they may attend a school that uses corporal punishment. Perhaps they join an aggressive gang or other peer group.

At home, on the street, at school, in front of the tube, their lives are awash in aggression, which not only is frequent but which also embodies many of the lesson qualities that promote rapid and lasting learning. It is arousing, it is seen in specific "how-to" detail, it is often carried out by persons the youth admires, and most important, it very often succeeds. As childhood continues and gives way to adolescence, the youths' well-learned lessons often become more and more evident in their own behavior. The aggression they have so often seen work for others becomes their own frequent way of responding.

Aggressive lessons learned well and used successfully will persist only if the important people in the youth's life support such behavior. Unfortunately, such encouragement of the notion "might makes right" is very common—from family, from peers, and from others. In a recent survey comparing chronic fighters with nonfighters in one large U.S. city's secondary schools, 80% of the fighters but less than half of the nonfighters said that their families wanted them to hit if provoked (Goldstein & Conoley, 1997).

Many youths will, in fact, be severely punished and humiliated if they don't use force when parents or others think they should. Similar demands for aggressive action, and praise for its use, are an equally common feature of peer group pressure for many youngsters. Such pressure is increasingly apparent for both gang and nongang adolescents, boys and girls alike, and at younger and younger ages. Having learned well how to be aggressive, found aggression to be consistently successful, and received generous encouragement and support from important others to keep using it, chronically aggressive youngsters have other qualities that keep the nasty behavior going. One, stated simply, is that they don't know what to do instead. The positive, nonviolent, constructive alternatives to aggression that such youngsters might use instead of fists or guns are alternatives that they have seen too seldom, tried too seldom, and at times been punished for using if they did so. Cursing, bullying, or hitting the adversary is the means chosen because negotiating, walking away, getting help from an uninvolved adult, making light of the disagreement, and other nonviolent solutions are alternatives rarely seen or attempted by the youths and rarely supported by the other people who are significant in their lives.

Aggression so often is hard to change because it is taught early, taught often, and taught well; is supported and encouraged by important others; and seems to be the best and often the only alternative for children and adolescents who never really learned otherwise.

Once aggression is well learned and well supported by important others, the likelihood of its perpetuation and even escalation is furthered both by a series of aggression-promoting misperceptions or misinterpretations of the surrounding world that are characteristic of frequently aggressive persons and by a series of self-deceptive rationalizations that such persons employ to avoid experiencing guilt about harming others.

Aggression-Perpetuating Misperceptions

Thoughts lead to actions. Most people, most of the time, choose not to behave aggressively because they think such actions are immoral, antisocial, and just plain wrong. Persons who are frequently angry and aggressive act differently than most of us. Do they think differently also? The answer from researchers studying the thought processes of such persons clearly seems to be yes (Gibbs, Potter, & Goldstein, 1995). How do they think? What are their thoughts?

First, their thinking is typically *self-centered.* "When I get mad, I don't care who gets hurt." "If I see something I like, I take it." "If I want to do something, I don't care if it's legal or not." Their view of their world is "me first."

In a misperception that accompanies this egocentric way of seeing things, persons who are frequently aggressive often *view others as being hostile* toward them even when they are not. They misinterpret neutral behavior by others, seeing it, instead, as aggression directed toward them. This is why so many youths interpret being looked at (a neutral act) as a challenge, a threat, or a put-down (a hostile act). Similarly, if they are accidentally bumped in a crowded school hallway between classes, they are prone to believe the bumping is intentional.

Self-centered thinking and seeing hostility from others even when it is not there, in the thinking of people who are frequently aggressive, call for a response. The first response is often a *mislabeling* of what must be done, such as "I have to defend myself" or "Hitting him will knock some sense into him" or "No way I can let him get away with it."

Mislabeling often combines with two other common thinking distortions to make aggression almost inevitable. One is called *assuming the worst* ("If I don't smack him I'll look like a punk"). The other is called *externalizing* or *blaming others* ("It's his fault, he's asking for it, I'll smack him").

Added to this are yet two more distorted ways of thinking about the world, and again both make aggression more likely. One is called *false consensus:* the belief that other people think and act as I do, that there is nothing unusual about me. *Anchoring,* the final thinking mode common in chronic aggressors, is a resistance to changing one's thinking, even when new evidence supporting the opposite comes along.

Self-centeredness, seeing hostility not there, mislabeling, assuming the worst, blaming others, false consensus, and anchoring: These are the thinking distortions commonly made by chronically aggressive children, adolescents, and adults. Thoughts *do* lead to actions. It is clear, then, that in trying to reduce low-level aggressive behavior in our society, a good first step is to work on changing the kinds of thinking likely to lead to such behavior.

Guilt-Inhibiting Rationalizations

How can people behave aggressively toward others, especially at high levels but even at low levels, without condemning themselves for doing so? According to Bandura (1973), several self-deceptive rationalizing processes may take place.

Minimization of one's own aggression in which it is compared with worse behavior by others. "OK, I punched him and kicked him in the head, but at least I used my own fists and feet, not a knife or gun like some guys do."

Justification of one's own aggression in terms of higher moral principles. Perhaps the best example of this type of self-vindication and denial of responsibility is the frequent recourse taken by nations at war to the claim that "God is on our side" and the companion notion that theirs is a righteous, holy battle.

Displacement of responsibility. Here the individual avoids ownership of his or her own aggressive behavior by shifting responsibility for it to others—for example, "He made me do it"; "They made me do it"; "Everyone was doing it."

Diffusion of responsibility. Aggression, especially on a large scale, may require for its enactment the services of many different people, each contributing his or her small part to the large effort. It is often possible under such circumstances to make each contribution seem and feel relatively harmless, especially if the persons involved are kept (by others or themselves) relatively ignorant of the overall aggressive effort. The Nazi concentration camp death machine, a product composed of many individual contributions, well illustrates such diffusion of responsibility.

Dehumanization of victims. It appears to be the case that the greater the empathy we feel for other people, the more we perceive their world and humanness, the less able we are to hurt them. The opposite also apparently is true. The more we are able to view someone as something less than human, or even as of another species, the more readily we can commit aggression toward that person. Racial or religious stereotyping, the view of the enemy in wartime, or even our attitude toward fans of the other team at a heated sports contest are each good examples of our tendency to give such persons a demeaning label or name, see the others as "them" and unlike "us," and via such dehumanizing enable ourselves to hurt them.

Deindividuation. As noted earlier, this is a guilt-reducing, aggression-promoting phenomenon that often occurs in riots, mob or crowd violence, and other forms of group aggression. Each person, in a sense, temporarily loses his or her individual identity to become part of a larger collective. Rather than a spreading out, sharing, or diffusion of responsibility as we have described, deindividuation instead serves as a denial of responsibility. The highly emotional, aggressive collective violence by large groups of fans at soccer, football, or other athletic matches illustrates this quality well.

Attribution of blame to victims. A related but different type of denial of responsibility for one's own aggressive behavior is holding its target responsible. As Bandura (1973) puts it, here "aggressors see themselves as essentially persons of good will who are forced into punitive actions by villainous opponents" (p. 214). Victims, it is held, bring it on themselves. Not uncommonly, youths who are chronically delinquent or adults who are career criminals are adept at trying to explain away their antisocial behaviors with detailed descriptions of how the victims' stupidity, resistance, hesitancy, or other qualities "made me do it."

Graduated desensitization. Repeated performances of unpleasant behavior, especially when taken in small steps, can progressively decrease its unpleasantness and increase its perpetrator's tolerance for and acceptance of both the behavior itself and his or her own perception of self as an individual capable of doing such things. In this manner, the level of aggression can gradually increase, as we have noted several times throughout this book, until eventually the perpetrator can carry out cruel and violent acts with little discomfort.

Hygienic positioning. Here the aggressor assumes a position distant from the impact or consequences of his or her own violent behavior in order to deny it. Sometimes this distancing is literally true, as when a soldier fires a missile or a large artillery piece at a distant target or a bombardier drops bombs from an altitude of many miles. At other times, the distancing is figurative, such as when one uses verbal deniers to describe one's own aggressive acts; for example, the victim was "offed" or "wasted," not "killed" or "murdered," or, as in concentration camp terminology, "Units were processed" rather than "Human beings were slaughtered."

Aggression is often taught well, strongly rewarded, enhanced by misperceptions of one's own and the other's behavior, and freed further by the use of a series of guilt-inhibiting rationalizations. Yet, in spite of these several diverse and powerful obstacles, aggression intervention efforts are often successful and have led to a growing accumulation of small wins by the practitioner and researcher community. This book is offered as but one additional contribution to this effort.

References

Agnew, R. (1998). The causes of animal abuse: A social-psychological analysis. *Theoretical Criminology, 2,* 177–209.

Ahmad, Y., & Smith, P. (1994). Bullying in schools and the issue of sex differences. In J. Archer (Ed.), *Male violence.* London: Routledge.

Allcorn, S. (1994). *Anger in the workplace.* Westport, CT: Quorum Books.

American Association of University Women. (1993). *The AAUW survey on sexual harassment in America's schools.* Washington, DC: Author.

Anderson, J. (1977). *Vandalism in the Unified School District of Los Angeles County.* Unpublished doctoral dissertation, University of Southern California, Los Angeles.

Arnett, J. J. (1996). Sensation seeking, aggressiveness, and adolescent reckless behavior. *Personality and Individual Differences, 20,* 693–702.

Arora, C. M. J. (1994). Is there any point in trying to reduce bullying in secondary schools? *Educational Psychology in Practice, 10,* 155–162.

Ascione, F. R. (1992, September). *Cruelty to animals in childhood and adolescence.* Paper presented at the American Humane Association Conference, Herdon, VA.

Ascione, F. R. (1993). Children who are cruel to animals and later aggression against people. *Anthrozoös, 6,* 226–246.

Ascione, F. R., Thompson, T. M., & Black, T. (1997). Childhood cruelty to animals: Assessing dimensions and motivations. *Anthrozoös, 10,* 390–398.

Asher, S. R., & Coie, J. D. (Eds.). (1990). *Peer rejection in childhood.* New York: Cambridge University Press.

Athens, L. (1985). Character contests and violent criminal conduct: A critique. *Sociological Quarterly, 26,* 419–431.

Axelrod, S., & Apsche, J. (Eds.). (1982). *The effects and side effects of punishment on human behavior.* New York: Academic.

Baenninger, R. (Ed.). (1991). *Targets of violence and aggression.* Amsterdam: North Holland.

Baier, J. L., & Williams, P. (1983). Fraternity hazing revisited: Current alumni and active member attitudes toward hazing. *Journal of College Student Personnel, 24,* 300–305.

Bandura, A. (1973). *Aggression: A social learning analysis.* Englewood Cliffs, NJ: Prentice Hall.

Barlow, D., Hayes, S. C., & Nelson, R. O. (1984). *The scientist practitioner.* New York: Pergamon.

Barner-Barry, C. (1986). Rob: Children's tacit use of peer ostracism to control aggressive behavior. *Ethology and Sociobiology, 7,* 281–293.

Bath, H. I. (1994). Temper tantrums in group care. *Child and Youth Care Forum, 12,* 5–27.

Batsche, G., & Knoff, H. M. (1994). Bullies and their victims: Understanding a pervasive problem in the schools. *School Psychology Review, 23,* 165–174.

Baumer, T. L., & Rosenbaum, D. P. (1984). *Combatting retail theft: Programs and strategies.* Boston: Butterworth.

Bayh, B. (1978). School discipline, violence and vandalism: Implications for teacher preparation. *Action in Teacher Education, 1,* 3–10.

Beirne, P. (1998). *For a non-speciesist criminology: Animal abuse as an object of study.* Unpublished manuscript.

Bellack, A. S., & Hersen, M. (1984). *Research methods in clinical psychology.* New York: Pergamon.

Benoit, P. J. (1983). The use of threats in children's discourse. *Language and Speech, 26,* 305–329.

Bentham, J. (1781). *An introduction to the principles of morals and legislation.* Oxford: Clarendon.

Bentley, K. M., & Li, A. K. (1994). Bully and victim problems in elementary schools and students' beliefs about aggression. *Canadian Journal of School Psychology, 11,* 153–165.

Berkowitz, L., Lepinski, J. P., & Angulo, E. J. (1969). Awareness of own anger level and subsequent aggression. *Journal of Personality and Social Psychology, 11,* 293–300.

Bernstein, J. Y., & Watson, M. W. (1997). Children who are targets of bullying: A victim pattern. *Journal of Interpersonal Violence, 12,* 483–498.

Besag, V. (1997). The playground. In M. Elliott (Ed.), *Bullying: A practical guide to coping for schools.* London: Pitman.

Bickman, L., & Green, S. K. (1977). Situational cues and crime reporting: Do signs make a difference? *Journal of Applied Social Psychology, 7,* 1–18.

Bies, R. J., Tripp, T. M., & Kramer, R.M. (1997). At the breaking point: Cognitive and social dynamics of revenge in organizations. In R. A. Giacalone & J. Greenberg (Eds.), *Antisocial behavior in organizations.* Thousand Oaks, CA: Sage.

Bjorkqvist, K. L., Lagerspetz, K. M. J., & Kaukiainen, A. (1992). Do girls manipulate and boys fight? *Aggressive Behavior, 18,* 117–127.

Blauvelt, P. D. (1980). School security doesn't have to break the bank. *Independent School, 40,* 47–50.

Blurton Jones, N. (1972). Categories of child-child interaction. In N. Blurton Jones (Ed.), *Ethological studies of child behavior.* London: Cambridge University Press.

Bolman, W. M. (1969). Toward realizing the prevention of mental illness. In L. Bellack & H. Barten (Eds.), *Progress in community mental health.* New York: Grune & Stratton.

Borden, R. J. (1975). Witnessed aggression: Influence of an observer's sex and values on aggressive responding. *Journal of Personality and Social Psychology, 31,* 567–573.

Boulton, M. J. (1991). A comparison of structural and contextual features of middle school children's playful and aggressive fighting. *Ethology and Sociobiology, 12,* 119–145.

Boulton, M. J. (1992). Rough physical play in adolescents: Does it serve a dominance function? *Early Education and Development, 3,* 312–333.

Boulton, M. J. (1993). Children's abilities to distinguish between playful and aggressive fighting: A developmental perspective. *British Journal of Developmental Psychology, 11,* 249–263.

Boulton, M. J. (1994). The relationship between playful and aggressive fighting in children, adolescents and adults. In J. Archer (Ed.), *Male violence.* London: Routledge.

Boulton, M. J. (1996). A comparison of 8- and 11-year-old girls' and boys' participation in specific types of rough-and-tumble play and aggressive fighting: Implications for functional hypotheses. *Aggressive Behavior, 22,* 271–287.

Boulton, M. J., & Smith, P. K. (1994). Bully/victim problems in middle school children: Stability, self-perceived competence, peer perceptions, and peer acceptance. *British Journal of Developmental Psychology, 12,* 315–329.

Boulton, M. J., & Underwood, K. (1992). Bully/victim problems among middle school children. *British Journal of Educational Psychology, 62,* 73–87.

Brantingham, P. J., & Brantingham, P. L. (1991). *Environmental criminology.* Newbury Park, CA: Sage.

Brown, G. (1997). *Sabotage.* Nottingham, UK: Spokesman Books.

Bryan, W. A. (1987). Contemporary fraternity and sorority issues. In R. B. Winston, Jr., W. R. Nettles III & J. H. Opper, Jr. (Eds.), *Fraternities and sororities on the contemporary college campus.* San Francisco: Jossey-Bass.

Buchanan, E. T., Shanley, M., Correnti, R., & Hammond, E. (1982). Hazing: Collective stupidity, insensitivity and irresponsibility. *NASPA Journal, 20,* 56–68.

Buss, A. H. (1961). *The psychology of aggression.* New York: Wiley.

Buss, D. M., Gomes, M., Higgins, D. S., & Lauterbach, K. (1987). Tactics of manipulation. *Journal of Personality and Social Psychology, 52,* 1219–1229.

Cairns, R. B., & Cairns, B. D. (1991). Social cognition and social networks: A developmental perspective. In D. J. Pepler & K. H. Rubin (Eds.), *The development and treatment of childhood aggression.* Hillsdale, NJ: Erlbaum.

Cameron, M. O. (1964). *The booster and the snitch: Department store shoplifting.* New York: Free Press.

Cameron, P. (1969). Frequency and kinds of words in various social settings, or what the hell is going on? *Pacific Sociological Review, 12,* 101–104.

Carroll, J., & Weaver, F. (1986). Shoplifters' perceptions of crime opportunities: A process-tracing study. In D. B. Cornish & R. V. Clarke (Eds.), *The reasoning criminal.* New York: Springer-Verlag.

Carter, S. L. (1998). *Civility: Manners, morals, and the etiquette of democracy.* New York: Basic.

Cash, T. F. (1995). Developmental teasing about physical appearance: Retrospective descriptions and relationships with body image. *Social Behavior and Personality, 23,* 123–130.

Caspi, A., Elder, G. H., & Bem, D. J. (1987). Moving against the world: Life-course patterns of explosive children. *Developmental Psychology, 23,* 308–313.

Casserly, M. D., Bass, S. A., & Garrett, J. R. (1980). *School vandalism: Strategies for prevention.* Lexington, MA: Lexington.

Chandler, M., Greenspan, S., & Barenboim, C. (1974). Assessment and training of role-taking and referential communication skills in institutionalized emotionally disturbed children. *Developmental Psychology, 10,* 546–553.

Christensen, H. H., Mabery, K., McAllister, M. E., McCormick, D. P. (1988). *Cultural resource protection.* Denver: Rocky Mountain Forest and Range Experiment Station.

Clarke, R. V. (1990). Deterring obscene phone callers: Preliminary results from the New Jersey experience. *Security Journal, 1,* 143–148.

Clarke, R. V. (Ed.). (1992). *Situational crime prevention: Successful case studies.* New York: Harrow & Heston.

Clayman, S. E. (1993). Booing: The anatomy of a disaffiliative response. *American Sociological Review, 58,* 110–130.

Clement, C. E., Hyg, M. S., & Ervin, M. D. (1972). Historical data in the evaluation of violent subjects. *Archives of General Psychiatry, 27,* 621–624.

Cohen, D., Nisbett, R. E., Bowdle, B. F., & Schwarz, N. (1996). Insult, aggression, and the Southern culture of honor. *Journal of Personality and Social Psychology, 70,* 945–960.

Cohen, S. (1973). Campaigning against vandalism. In C. Ward (Ed.), *Vandalism.* London: Architectural Press.

Cohen, S. (1974). Breaking out, smashing up and the social context of aspiration. *Working Papers in Cultural Studies, 5,* 37–63.

Coie, J. D., & Dodge, K. A. (1983). Continuities and changes in children's sociometric status: A five-year longitudinal study. *Merrill-Palmer Quarterly, 29,* 261–282.

Coie, J. D., Dodge, K A., Terry, R., & Wright, V. (1991). The role of aggression in peer relations: An analysis of aggressive episodes in boys' play groups. *Child Development, 62,* 812–826.

Costabile, A., Smith, P. K., Matheson, L., Aston, J., Hunter, T., & Boulton, M. J. (1991). Cross-national comparison of how children distinguish serious and playful fighting. *Developmental Psychology, 27,* 881–887.

Cox, D., Cox, A. D., & Moschis, G. P. (1990). When consumer behavior goes bad: An investigation of adolescent shoplifting. *Journal of Consumer Research, 17,* 149–159.

Craighead, W. E., Kimball, W. H., & Rehak, P. J. (1979). Mood changes, physiological responses, and self-statements during social rejection imagery. *Journal of Consulting and Clinical Psychology, 47,* 385–396.

Cratty, B. J. (1981). *Social psychology in athletics.* Englewood Cliffs, NJ: Prentice-Hall.

Crick, N. R. (1995). Relational aggression: The role of intent attributions, feelings of distress, and provocation type. *Development and Psychopathology, 7,* 313–322.

Crino, M. D. (1994). Employee sabotage: A random or preventible phenomenon? *Journal of Managerial Issues, 6,* 311–330.

Cron, T. (1998). *Driving me crazy: School transportation and student discipline.* Santa Fe, NM: Goin' Mobile.

Cronbach, L. J., & Snow, R. E. (1977). *Aptitudes and instructional messages.* New York: Irvington.

Csikszentmihalyi, M., & Larsen, R. (1978). *Intrinsic rewards in school crime.* Hackensack, NJ: National Council on Crime and Delinquency.

Cullen, F. T., Clark, G. A., & Polanzi, C. (1982). The seriousness of crime revisited. *Criminology, 2,* 83–102.

Cunningham, M. R., Barbee, A. P., & Cruen, P. B. (1997). Social allergens and the reactions they produce: Escalation of annoyance and disgust in love and work. In R. M. Kowalski (Ed.), *Aversive interpersonal behaviors.* New York: Plenum.

Dale-Green, P. (1963). *Cult of the cat.* Boston: Riverside Press.

Dansky, B. S., & Kilpatrick, D. G. (1997). Effects of sexual harassment. In W. O'Donohue (Ed.), *Sexual harassment: Theory, research, and treatment.* Boston: Allyn & Bacon.

Dawe, H. C. (1934). An analysis of two hundred quarrels of preschool children. *Child Development, 5,* 139–157.

DeAngelis, T. (1998). Ostracism. *American Psychological Association Monitor, 29,* 17–18.

DeBunza, C. (1974). *A study of school vandalism: Causes and prevention measures currently found in selected secondary schools throughout Alabama.* Unpublished doctoral dissertation, University of Alabama, Montgomery.

Decalmer, P., & Glendenning, F. (1997). What is elder abuse and neglect? In P. Decalmer, P., & F. Glendenning (Eds.), *The mistreatment of elderly people.* London: Sage.

deCharms, R. (1968). *Personal causation.* New York: Academic.

deCharms, R. (1976). *Enhancing motivation: Change in the classroom.* New York: Irvington.

Deci, E. L. (1975). *Intrinsic motivation.* New York: Plenum.

Deffenbacher, J. L., Oetting, E. R., & Lynch, R. S. (1994). Development of a driving anger scale. *Psychological Reports, 74,* 83–91.

Destke, M. C., Penner, L. A., & Ulrich, K. (1974). Observers reporting of shoplifting as a function of thief's race and sex. *Journal of Social Psychology, 94,* 213–221.

DiBattista, R. A. (1991). Creating new approaches to recognize and deter sabotage. *Public Personnel Management, 20,* 347–352.

DiPietro, J. A. (1981). Rough and tumble: A function of gender. *Developmental Psychology, 17,* 50–58.

Dobash, R., & Dobash, R. (1977–1978). Wives: The appropriate victims of marital violence. *Victimology, 2*, 426–442.

Dodge, K. A., & Coie, J. D. (1987). Social-information processing factors in reactive and proactive aggression in children's peer groups. *Journal of Personality and Social Psychology, 53*, 1146–1158.

Dodge, K. A., & Frame, C. L. (1982). Social cognitive biases and deficits in aggressive boys. *Child Development, 53*, 620–635.

Doob, A. N., & Gross, A.E. (1968). Status of frustrator as an inhibitor of horn-honking responses. *Journal of Social Psychology, 76*, 213–218.

Driscoll, J. M. (1981). Aggressiveness and frequency-of-aggressive-use ratings for pejorative epithets by Americans. *Journal of Social Psychology, 104*, 111–126.

Dubois, P. (1979). *Sabotage in industry.* Harmondsworth, UK: Pelican.

Ducey, M. (1976). *Vandalism in high schools: An exploratory discussion.* Chicago: Institute for Juvenile Research.

Duffalo, D. C. (1976). Convenience stores, armed robbery and physical environmental features. *American Behavioral Scientist, 20*, 227–246.

Dunayer, J. (1995). Sexist words, speciesist roots. In C. J. Adams & J. Donovan (Eds.), *Animals and women.* Durham, NC: Duke University Press.

Einon, D., & Potegal, M. (1994). Temper tantrums in young children. In M. Potegal & J. F. Knutson (Eds.), *The dynamics of aggression.* Hillsdale, NJ: Erlbaum.

Elliott, D. S. (1994). Serious violent offenders: Onset, developmental course, and termination. *Criminology, 32*, 1–21.

Elliott, M. (1997a). A whole-school approach to bullying. In M. Elliott (Ed.), *Bullying: A practical guide to coping for schools.* London: Pitman.

Elliott, M. (1997b). Bullies and victims. In M. Elliott (Ed.), *Bullying: A practical guide to coping for schools.* London: Pitman.

Elliott, M. (1997c). Bullying and the under fives. In M. Elliott (Ed.), *Bullying: A practical guide to coping for schools.* London: Pitman.

Elliott, M., & Kilpatrick, J. (1994). *How to stop bullying: A kidscape training guide.* London: Kidscape.

Ellison, P. A., Govern, J. M., Petri, H. L., & Figler, M. H. (1995). Anonymity and aggressive driving behavior: A field study. *Journal of Social Behavior and Personality, 10*, 265–272.

Emler, N. (1994). Gossip, reputation, and social adaptation. In R. F. Goodman & A. Ben-Ze'ev (Eds.), *Good gossip.* Lawrence: University Press of Kansas.

Epstein, M. H., Repp, A. C., & Cullinan, D. (1978). Decreasing "obscene" language of behaviorally disordered children through the use of a DRL schedule. *Psychology in the Schools, 15*, 419–423.

Epstein, N., & Krakower, S. (1974). A measure of verbal aggression. *Perceptual and Motor Skills, 39*, 215–223.

Eron, L. D., Huesmann, R., Dubow, E., Romanoff, R., & Yarmel, P. W. (1987). Aggression and its correlates over 22 years. In D. H. Crowell, I. M. Evans, & C. P. O'Connell (Eds.), *Childhood aggression and violence.* New York: Plenum.

Evans, C., & Eder, D. (1993). "No exit": Processes of social isolation in the middle school. *Journal of Contemporary Ethnography, 22,* 139–170.

Fabian, L. J., & Thompson, J. K. (1989). Body image and eating disturbance in young females. *International Journal of Eating Disorders, 8,* 63–74.

Fagan, J., & Wilkinson, D. L. (1998). Social contexts and functions of adolescent violence. In D. S. Elliott, B. A. Hamburg, & K. R. Williams (Eds.), *Violence in American schools.* Cambridge, England: Cambridge University Press.

Farrington, D. P. (1991). Childhood aggression and adult violence: Early precursors and later-life outcomes. In D. J. Pepler & K. H. Rubin (Eds.), *The development and treatment of childhood aggression.* Hillsdale, NJ: Erlbaum.

Favre, D., & Tsang, V. (1998). The development of anti-cruelty laws during the 1800s. In R. Lockwood & F. R. Ascione (Eds.), *Cruelty to animals and interpersonal violence.* West Lafayette, IN: Purdue University Press.

Federal Bureau of Investigation. (1978). *Crime in the United States.* Washington, DC: U.S. Government Printing Office.

Fedler, F., & Pryor, B. (1984). An equity theory explanation of bystanders' reactions to shoplifting. *Psychological Reports, 54,* 746.

Felson, R. B. (1978). Aggression as impression management. *Social Psychology, 41,* 205–213.

Felson, R. B. (1992). "Kick em when they're down": Explanations of the relationship between stress and interpersonal aggression and violence. *The Sociological Quarterly, 33,* 1–16.

Felson, R. B., Baccaglini, W., & Gmelch, G. (1986). Bar-room brawls: Aggression and violence in Irish and American bars. In A. Campbell & J. J. Gibbs (Eds.), *Violent transactions: The limits of personality.* Oxford, UK: Blackwell.

Felthous, A. R. (1980). Childhood antecedents of aggressive behaviors in male psychiatric patients. *Bulletin of the American Academy of Psychiatry and Law, 8,* 104–110.

Felthous, A. R. (1981). Childhood cruelty to cats, dogs and other animals. *Bulletin of the American Academy of Psychiatry and the Law, 9,* 48–53.

Felthous, A. R., & Bernard, H. (1979). Enuresis, firesetting, and cruelty to animals: The significance of two-thirds of this triad. *Journal of Forensic Science, 24,* 240–246.

Felthous, A. R., & Kellert, S. R. (1987). Psychosocial aspects of selecting animal species for physical abuse. *Journal of Forensic Sciences, 32,* 1713–1723.

Feshbach, N. D. (1978). Studies of empathic behavior in children. In B. A. Maher (Ed.), *Progress in experimental personality research* (Vol. 8). New York: Academic.

Festinger, L., Pepitone, A., & Newcombe, T. (1952). Some consequences of deindividuation in a group. *Journal of Abnormal and Social Psychology, 47,* 382–389.

Figlio, R. M. (1975). The seriousness of offenses: An evaluation by offenders and nonoffenders. *The Journal of Criminal Laws and Criminology, 66,* 189–200.

Fine, G. (1989). *Study of problem calls.* Unpublished survey, Hartsdale, NY.

Fine, G. A. (1977). Social components of children's gossip. *Journal of Communication, 27,* 181–185.

Fine, G. A., & Rosnow, R. L. (1978). Gossip, gossipers, gossiping. *Personality and Social Psychology Bulletin, 4,* 161–169.

Fitzgerald, L. F., Gold, Y., & Brock, K. (1990). Responses to victimization: Validation of an objective policy. *Journal of College Student Personnel, 27,* 34–39.

Fitzgerald, L. F., & Shullman, S. (1993). Sexual harassment: A research analysis and agenda for the 90s. *Journal of Vocational Behavior, 42,* 5–29.

Fitzgerald, L. F., Swan, S., & Magley, V. J. (1997). But was it really sexual harassment? In W. O'Donohue (Ed.), *Sexual harassment: Theory, research, and treatment.* Boston: Allyn & Bacon.

Floyd, N. M. (1985). "Pick on somebody your own size": Controlling victimization. *The Pointer, 29,* 9–17.

Follingstad, D. R., Rutledge, L. L., Berg, B. J., Hause, E. S., & Polek, D. S. (1990). The role of emotional abuse in physically abusive relationships. *Journal of Family Violence, 5,* 107–120.

Foote, R., & Woodward, J. (1973). A preliminary investigation of obscene language. *Journal of Psychology, 83,* 263–275.

Ford, C. V. (1996). *Lies! Lies! Lies! The psychology of deceit.* Washington, DC: American Psychiatric Press.

Forgas, J. P., Brown, L. B., & Menyhart, J. (1980). Dimensions of aggression: The perception of aggressive episodes. *British Journal of Social and Clinical Psychology, 19,* 215–227.

Franken, R. E., & Brown, D. J. (1995). Why do people like competition? *Personality and Individual Differences, 19,* 175–184.

Freedman, J. L., & Fraser, C. C. (1966). Compliance without pressure: The foot-in-the-door technique. *Journal of Personality and Social Psychology, 4,* 195–202.

Frey, C., & Graff, H. (1994). Serious and playful aggression in Brazilian girls and boys. *Sex Roles, 30,* 249–268.

Fry, D. (1990). Play aggression among Zapotec children: Implications for the practice hypothesis. *Aggressive Behavior, 16,* 321–340.

Fumento, M. (1998, August). "Road rage" versus reality. *The Atlantic Monthly,* pp. 12–17.

Garbarino, J. (1978). *The human ecology of school crime.* Hackensack, NJ: National Council on Crime and Delinquency.

Garbarino, J., & Vondra, J. (1987). Psychological maltreatment: Issues and perspectives. In M. Brassard, R. Germain, & S. N. Hart (Eds.), *Psychological maltreatment of children and youth.* New York: Pergamon.

Garrity, C., Jens, K., Porter, W., Sager, N., & Short-Camilli, C. (1994). *Bully-proofing your school.* Longmont, CO: Sopris West.

Gates, L., & Rohe, W. (1987). Fear and reactions to crime. *Urban Affairs, 22,* 425–453.

Gauthier, J., & Pellerin, D. (1982). Management of compulsive shoplifting through covert sensitization. *Journal of Behavior Therapy and Experimental Psychiatry, 13,* 73–75.

Geason, S., & Wilson, P. R. (1990). *Preventing graffiti and vandalism.* Canberra: Australian Institute of Criminology.

Gelfand, D. M., Hartmann, D. P., Walder, P., & Page, B. (1973). Who reports shoplifters? A field-experimental study. *Journal of Personality and Social Psychology, 25,* 276–285.

Geller, D. M., Goodstein, L., Silver, M., & Sternberg, W. C. (1974). On being ignored: The effects of violation of implicit rules of social interaction. *Sociometry, 37,* 541–556.

Gelles, R. J. (1972). "It takes two": The roles of victim and offender. In R. J. Gelles (Ed.), *The violent home: A study of physical aggression between husband and wives.* Thousand Oaks, CA: Sage.

Gergen, M. (1990). Beyond the evil empire: Horseplay and aggression. *Aggressive Behavior, 16,* 381–398.

Giacalone, R. A. (1990, July). Employee sabotage: The enemy within. *Supervisory Management,* pp. 6–7.

Giacalone, R. A., & Knouse, S. B. (1990). Justifying wrongful employee behavior: The role of personality in organizational sabotage. *Journal of Business Ethics, 9,* 55–61.

Gibbs, J. C., Potter, G. B., Goldstein, A. P. (1995). *The EQUIP program: Teaching youth to think and act responsibly through a peer-helping approach* . Champaign, IL: Research Press.

Gilbert, S. J. (1981). Another look at the Milgram obedience studies: The role of the graduated series of shock. *Personality and Social Psychology Bulletin, 7,* 690–695.

Gilliam, J., Stough, L., & Fad, K. (1991). Interventions for swearing. In G. Stoner, M. R. Shinn, & H. M. Walker (Eds.), *Interventions for achievement and behavior problems.* Silver Spring, MD: National Association of School Psychologists.

Glendenning, F. (1997). What is elder abuse and neglect? In P. Decalmer & F. Glendenning (Eds.), *The mistreatment of elderly people.* London: Sage.

Goffman, E. (1971). *Relations in public places.* New York: Basic.

Goldman, N. (1961). A socio-psychological study of school vandalism. *Crime and Delinquency, 7,* 221–230.

Goldstein, A. P. (Ed.). (1978). *Prescriptions for child mental health and education.* New York: Pergamon.

Goldstein, A. P. (1988). *The Prepare Curriculum: Teaching prosocial competencies.* Champaign, IL: Research Press.

Goldstein, A. P. (1992, May 4). *School violence: Its community context and potential solutions.* Testimony presented to the Subcommittee on Elementary, Secondary and Vocational Education, Committee on Education and Labor, U.S. House of Representatives, Washington, DC.

Goldstein, A. P. (1994). *The ecology of aggression.* New York: Plenum.

Goldstein, A. P. (1996a). *The psychology of vandalism.* New York: Plenum.

Goldstein, A. P. (1996b). *Violence in America.* Palo Alto: Davies-Black.

Goldstein, A. P., & Conoley, J. C. (1997). *School violence intervention: A practical handbook.* New York: Guilford.

Goldstein, A. P., Glick, B., & Gibbs, J. C. (1998). *Aggression Replacement Training: A comprehensive intervention for aggressive youth* (rev. ed.). Champaign, IL: Research Press.

Goldstein, A. P., Harootunian, B., & Conoley, J. C. (1994). *Student aggression: Prevention, control, replacement.* New York: Guilford.

Goldstein, A. P., & Keller, H. (1987). *Aggressive behavior: Assessment and intervention.* New York: Pergamon.

Goldstein, A. P., & McGinnis, E. (1997). *Skillstreaming the adolescent: New strategies and perspectives for teaching prosocial skills* (rev. ed.). Champaign, IL: Research Press.

Goldstein, A. P., Palumbo, J., Striepling, S. , & Voutsinas, A. M. (1995). *Break it up: A Teacher's Guide to Managing Student Aggression.* Champaign, IL: Research Press.

Goldstein, A. P., & Rosenbaum, A. (1982). *Aggress-less.* Englewood Cliffs, NJ: Prentice Hall.

Goldstein, A. P., & Stein, N. (1976). *Prescriptive psychotherapies.* New York: Pergamon.

Goldstein, J. H., Davis, R. W., & Herman, D. (1975). Escalation of aggression: Experimental studies. *Journal of Personality and Social Psychology, 31,* 162–170.

Goldstein, J. H., Davis, R. W., Kernis, M., & Cohn, E. S. (1981). Retarding the escalation of aggression. *Social Behaviors and Personality, 9,* 65–70.

Gottfredson, S. D., Young, K. L., & Laufer, W. S. (1980). Additivity and interactions in offense seriousness scales. *Journal of Research in Crime and Delinquency, 17,* 26–41.

Gottman, J. M. (1982). Emotional responsiveness in mental conversations. *Journal of Communication, 32,* 108–120.

Graziano, A. M. (1989). *The disinhibition hypothesis and the escalation of violence: Learning to be a monster.* Paper presented at a conference on the Law and the Legitimation of Violence, State University of New York at Buffalo.

Graziano, A. M. (1994). Why we should study subabusive violence against children. *Journal of Interpersonal Violence, 9,* 412–419.

Greenbaum, S. (1988). *School bully and victimization* (Resource Paper). Malibu, CA: National School Safety Center.

Greenbaum, S., Turner, B., & Stephens, R. D. (1989). *Set straight on bullies.* Malibu, CA: National School Safety Center.

Greenberg, B. S. (1969). *School vandalism: A national dilemma.* Menlo Park, CA: Stanford Research Institute.

Greenberg, B. S. (1976). The effects of language intensity modification on perceived verbal aggressiveness. *Communication Monographs, 45,* 130–139.

Greer, D. L. (1983). Spectator booing and the home advantage: A study of social influence in the basketball arena. *Social Psychology Quarterly, 46,* 252–261.

Griffiths, R., & Shapland, J. M. (1979). The vandal's perspective: Meanings and motives. In P. Bural (Ed.), *Designing against vandalism.* New York: Van Nostrand Reinhold.

Grossman, C. D. (1995). *On killing.* Boston: Little, Brown.

Gruber, J. E. (1992). A typology of personal and environmental sexual harassment: Research and policy implications for the 1990's. *Sex Roles, 26,* 447–464.

Gruber, J. E. (1997). An epidemiology of sexual harassment: Evidence from North America and Europe. In W. O'Donohue (Ed.), *Sexual harassment: Theory, research, and treatment.* Boston: Allyn & Bacon.

Gutek, B. A. (1985). *Sex and the workplace: The impact of sexual behavior and harassment on women, men, and organizations.* San Francisco: Jossey-Bass.

Hall, D. M. (1998). The victims of stalking. In J. R. Meloy (Ed.), *The psychology of stalking.* San Diego: Academic.

Halperin, J. M., Newcorn, J. H., Matier, K., Bedi, S., Hall, S., & Sherma, V. (1995). Impulsivity and the initiation of fights in children with disruptive behavior disorders. *Journal of Child Psychology and Psychiatry, 36,* 1199–1211.

Hamalainen, M., & Pulkkinen, L. (1996). Problem behavior as a precursor of male criminality. *Development and Psychopathology, 8,* 443–455.

Hammond, E. H. (1981). *Fraternity hazing: Impact and implication.* Unpublished manuscript, University of Louisville, Kentucky.

Hannerz, U. (1967). Gossip, networks, and culture in the Black American ghetto. *Ethos, 32,* 35–60.

Harmon, R., Rosner, R., & Owens, H. (1995). Obsessional harassment and erotomania in a criminal court population. *Journal of Forensic Sciences, 40,* 188–196.

Harootunian, B. (1986). School violence and vandalism. In S. J. Apter & A. P. Goldstein (Eds.), *Youth violence: Programs and prospects.* New York: Pergamon.

Harris, L., Gergen, K. J., & Lannamann, J. W. (1986). Aggression rituals. *Communications Monographs, 53,* 252–265.

Hauber, A. R. (1980). The social psychology of driving behavior and the traffic environment: Research on aggressive behaviour in traffic. *International Review of Applied Psychology, 29,* 461–474.

Hauber, A. R. (1989). Influencing juvenile offenders by way of alternative sanctions in community settings. In H. Wegener (Ed.), *Criminal behavior and the justice system.* New York: Springer-Verlag.

Heller, K., Price, R. H., Reinharz, S., Riger, S., Wandersman, A., & D'Aunno, T. A. (1984). *Psychology and community change.* Homewood, IL: Dorsey.

Heller, M. C., & White, M. A. (1975). Rates of teacher approval and disapproval to higher and lower ability classes. *Journal of Educational Psychology, 67,* 796-800.

Hellman, D. S., & Blackman, N. (1966). Enuresis, firesetting and cruelty to animals: A triad predictive of adult crime. *American Journal of Psychiatry, 122,* 1431–1435.

Henderson, J. Q. (1981). A behavioral approach to stealing: A proposal for treatment based on ten cases. *Journal of Behavioral Therapy and Experimental Psychiatry, 12,* 231–236.

Hendrick, C., & Murfin, M. (1974). Project library ripoff: A study of periodical mutilation in a university library. *College and Research Libraries, 35,* 402–411.

Hiew, C. C. (1981). Prevention of shoplifting: A community action approach. *Canadian Journal of Criminology, 23,* 57–68.

Higgins, C. (1994). Improving the school ground environment as an anti-bullying intervention. In P. Smith & S. Sharp (Eds.), *School bullying: Insights and perspectives.* London: Routledge.

Hoffman, P. (1984). Psychological abuse of women by spouses and live-in lovers. *Women and Therapy, 3,* 37–47.

Hold-Cavell, B. C. (1985). Showing-off and aggression in young children. *Aggressive Behavior, 11,* 303–314.

Hoover, J. H., & Hazler, R. J. (1991). Bullies and victims. *Elementary School Guidance and Counseling, 25,* 212–219.

Hoover, J. H., & Juul, K. (1993). Bullying in Europe and the United States. *Journal of Emotional and Behavior Problems, 2,* 25–29.

Howard, J. L. (1978). Factors in school vandalism. *Journal of Research and Development in Education, 11,* 13–18.

Humphreys, A., & Smith, P. K. (1987). Rough-and-tumble play, friendship, and dominance in school children: Evidence for continuity and change with age. *Child Development, 58,* 210–212.

Hunt, D. E. (1972). Matching models for teacher training. In B. R. Joyce & M. Weil (Eds.), *Perspectives for reform in teacher education.* Englewood Cliffs, NJ: Prentice Hall.

Hunter, J. (1978, October). Defensible space in practice. *The Architect's Journal,* pp. 675–677.

Ianni, F. A. J. (1979). The social organization of the high school: School-specific aspects of school crime. In E. Wenk & N. Harlow (Eds.), *School crime and disruption.* Davis, CA: Responsible Action.

Idisis, Y. (1996). *Meta moral judgment among preschool children.* Unpublished master's thesis, Bar-Illan University, Ramat Gan, Israel.

Infante, D. A., Riddle, B. L., Horwath, C. L., & Tumlin, S. A. (1992). Verbal aggressiveness: Messages and reasons. *Communication Quarterly, 40,* 116–126.

Infante, D. A., Sabourin, T. C., Rudd, J. E., & Shannon, E. A. (1990). Verbal aggression in violent and nonviolent marital disputes. *Communication Quarterly, 38,* 361–371.

Infante, D. A., & Wigley, C. J. (1986). Verbal aggressiveness: An interpersonal model and measure. *Communication Monographs, 53,* 61–69.

Irwin, J. R. (1976). Vandalism: Its prevention and control. *National Association of Secondary School Principals Bulletin, 60,* 55–59.

Jackson, J. (1990). An investigation into theft from shops among juveniles. *Practice, 4,* 16–42.

Jaeger, M. E., Skleder, B. R., & Rosnow, R L. (1994). Gossip, gossipers, gossipees. In R. F. Goodman & A. Ben-Ze'ev (Eds.), *Good gossip.* Lawrence: University Press of Kansas.

Jaffe, Y., Shapir, N., & Yinon, Y. (1981). Aggression and its escalation. *Journal of Cross-Cultural Psychology, 12,* 21–36.

Jaffe, Y., & Yinon, Y. (1979). Retaliatory aggression in individuals and groups. *European Journal of Social Psychology, 9,* 177–186.

Jamieson, B. (1987). Public telephone vandalism. In D. Challinger (Ed.), *Preventing property crime.* Canberra: Australian Institute of Criminology.

Janowitz, M. (1975). Sociological theory and social control. *American Journal of Sociology, 81,* 82–108.

Jay, T. B. (1977). Doing research with dirty words. *Maledicta, 1,* 234–256.

Jay, T. B. (1992). *Cursing in America.* Philadelphia: John Benjamins Publishing.

Kashani, J. H., Burbach, D. J., & Rosenberg, T. K. (1988). Perception of family conflict resolution and depressive symptomatology in adolescents. *Journal of the American Academy of Child and Adolescent Psychiatry, 27,* 42–48.

Katz, J. E. (1990). Caller-ID, privacy and social processes. *Telecommunications Policy, 14,* 372–411.

Katz, J. E. (1994). Empirical and theoretical dimensions of obscene phone calls to women in the United States. *Human Communication Research, 21,* 155–182.

Kazdin, A. E. (1975). *Behavior modification in applied settings.* Homewood, IL: Dorsey.

Kazdin, A. E. (1980). *Research design in clinical psychology.* New York: Harper & Row.

Kellam, A. M. P. (1969). Shoplifting treated by aversion to a film. *Behaviour Research and Therapy, 7,* 125–127.

Keller, F. S. (1966). A personal course in psychology. In R. Ubrich, T. Stachnik, & J. Mabry (Eds.), *Control of human behavior.* Glenview, IL: Scott, Foresman.

Kellert, S. R. (1983). Affective, cognitive, and evaluative perceptions of animals. In I. Altman & J. F. Wohlwill (Eds.), *Behavior and the natural environment.* New York: Plenum.

Kellert, S. R., & Berry, J. K. (1980). *Knowledge, affection and basic attitudes toward animals in American society.* Springfield, VA: National Technical Information Services.

Kellert, S. R., & Felthous, A. R. (1985). Childhood cruelty toward animals among criminals and noncriminals. *Human Relations, 38,* 1113–1129.

Kelling, G. L., & Coles, C. M. (1996). *Fixing broken windows: Restoring order and reducing crime in our communities.* New York: Free Press.

Kelly, E., & Cohn, T. (1988). *Racism in schools—New research evidence.* Stoke-on-Trent, UK: Trentham Books.

Kenrick, D. T., & MacFarlane, S. W. (1986). Ambient temperature and horn-honking: A field study of the heat/aggression relationship. *Environment and Behavior, 18,* 179–181.

Kernis, M., Granneman, B. D., & Barclay, L. C. (1989). Stability and level of self-esteem as predictors of anger arousal and hostility. *Journal of Personality and Social Psychology, 56,* 1013–1022.

Keutzer, C. S. (1972). Kleptomania: A direct approach to treatment. *British Journal of Medical Psychology, 45,* 159–163.

Kienlen, K. K. (1998). Developmental and social antecedents of stalking. In J. R. Meloy (Ed.), *The psychology of stalking.* San Diego: Academic.

Kiesler, D. J. (1969). A grid model for theory and research. In L. D. Eron & R. Callahan (Eds.), *The relation of theory to practice in psychotherapy.* Chicago: Aldine.

Kingston, A. J., & Gentry, H. W. (1977). Discipline problems: Then and now. *National Association of Secondary School Principals Bulletin, 61,* 94–99.

Kingston, L., & Prior, M. (1995). The development of patterns of stable, transient, and school-age onset aggressive behavior in young children. *Journal of the American Academy of Child and Adolescent Psychiatry, 34,* 348–358.

Kinney, D. A. (1994). "Everybody knows your business": Gossip and friendship patterns among African American adolescents in an urban high school. *Sociological Abstracts, 42,* 42.

Kinney, T. A. (1994). An inductively derived typology of verbal aggression and its association to distress. *Human Communication Research, 21,* 183–222.

Klausmeier, H. J., Rossmiller, R. A., & Sailey, M. (1977). *Individually guided elementary education.* New York: Academic.

Klemke, L. W. (1992). *The sociology of shoplifting.* Westport, CT: Praeger.

Koch, E. L. (1975). School vandalism and strategies of social control. *Urban Education, 10,* 54–72.

Kowalski, R. M., & Erickson, J. R. (1997). Complaining: What's all the fuss about? In R. M. Kowalski (Ed.), *Aversive interpersonal behavior.* New York: Plenum.

Krasner, L. (1980). *Environmental design and human behavior.* New York: Pergamon.

Krathwohl, D. R. (1985). *Social and behavioral science research.* San Francisco: Jossey-Bass.

Kraut, R. E. (1976). Deterrent and definitional influences on shoplifting. *Social Problems, 25,* 358–368.

Kulka, R. A. (1978). School crime as a function of person-environment fit. *Theoretical Perspectives on School Crime, 1,* 17–24.

Labig, C. E. (1995). *Preventing violence in the workplace.* New York: American Management Association.

Labrell, F. (1994). A typical interaction behavior between fathers and toddlers: Teasing. *Early Development and Parenting, 3,* 125–130.

LaForge, A. E. (1996). *Tantrums: Secrets to calming the storm.* New York: Pocket Books.

Lagerspetz, K. M., Bjorkqvist, K. L., & Peltonen, T. (1988). Is indirect aggression typical of females? *Aggressive Behavior, 14,* 403–414.

LaGrange, R. L., Ferraro, K. R., & Supanic, M. (1992). Perceived risk and fear of crime: Role of social and physical incivilities. *Journal of Research in Crime and Delinquency, 29,* 311–334.

Lane, D. A. (1989). Bullying in school: The need for an integrated approach. *School Psychology International, 10,* 211–215.

Leather, P., & Lawrence, C. (1995). Perceiving pub violence: The symbolic influence of social and environmental factors. *British Journal of Social Psychology, 34,* 395–407.

LeBlanc, M. (1990). Two processes of the development of persistent offending: Activation and escalation. In L. Robins & M. Rutter (Eds.), *Straight and devious pathways from childhood to adulthood.* New York: Cambridge University Press.

LeBlanc, M. (1996). Changing patterns in the perpetration of offences over time: Trajectories from early adolescence to the early 30's. *Studies on Crime and Crime Prevention, 5,* 151–165.

Lee, V. E., Croninger, R. G., Linn, E., & Chen, X. (1996). The culture of sexual harassment in secondary schools. *American Educational Research Journal, 33,* 383–417.

Leftwich, D. (1977). *A study of vandalism in selected public schools in Alabama.* Unpublished doctoral dissertation, University of Alabama, Birmingham.

Lerner, M. J. (1980). *Belief in a just world: A fundamental delusion.* New York: Plenum.

Levi, M., & Jones, S. (1985). Public and police perception of crime seriousness in England and Wales. *British Journal of Criminology, 25,* 234–250.

Levin, J., & Arluke, A. (1987). *Gossip: The inside scoop.* New York: Plenum.

Levin, J., & Kimmel, A. J. (1977). Gossip columns: Media small talk. *Journal of Communication, 27,* 169–175.

Levy-Leboyer, C. (Ed.). (1984). *Vandalism: Behavior and motivations.* Amsterdam: North Holland.

Lewis, D. A., & Salem, G. (1986). Community crime prevention: An analysis of a developing perspective. *Crime and Delinquency, 27,* 405–421.

Linstead, S. (1985). Breaking "the purity" rule: Industrial sabotage and the symbolic process. *Personnel Review, 15,* 12–19.

Lloyd-Goldstein, R. (1998). De-Clerambault on-line: A survey of erotomania and stalking from the old world to the World Wide Web. In J. R. Meloy (Ed.), *The psychology of stalking.* San Diego: Academic.

Lo, L. (1994). Exploring teenage shoplifting behavior: A choice and constraint approach. *Environment and Behavior, 26,* 613–639.

Lockwood, R., & Hodge, G. R. (1986, September). The tangled web of animal abuse: The links between cruelty to animals and human violence. *The Humane Society News,* pp. 1–6.

Loeber, R., & Hay, D. F. (1994). Developmental approaches to aggression and conduct problems. In M. Rutter & D. F. Hay (Eds.), *Development through life: A handbook for clinicians.* Malden, MA: Blackwell Scientific.

Loeber, R., & Stouthamer-Loeber, M. (1998). Development of juvenile aggression and violence: Some common misconceptions and controversies. *American Psychologist, 53,* 242–259.

Loeber, R., Wung, P., Keenan, K., Giroux, B., Stouthamer-Loeber, M., Van Kammen, W. B., & Maughan, B. (1993). Developmental pathways in disruptive child behavior. *Development and Psychopathology, 5,* 103–133.

Lubel, S., Wolf, Y., & Krausz, E. (1992). Inter-ethnic differences in the judgment of filmed violence. *International Journal of Group Tensions, 23,* 314–319.

Luckenbill, D. F. (1977). Criminal homicides as a situated transaction. *Social Problems, 25,* 176–186.

Lumley, F. E. (1925). *Means of social control.* New York: Century.

Mac Devitt, J. W., & Kedzierzawski, G. D. (1988). A structural group format for first offense shoplifters. *International Journal of Offender Therapy and Comparative Criminology, 32,* 155–164.

Macdonald, J. M. (1961). *The murderer and his victim.* Springfield, IL: Charles C Thomas.

Maclean, N. (1993). *Young men and fire.* University of Chicago Press.

Macmillan, J. (1975). *Deviant drivers.* Westmead, UK: Saxon House, D. C. Heath.

Magaro, P. A. (1969). A prescriptive treatment model based upon social class and premorbid adjustment. *Psychotherapy: Theory, Research and Practice, 6,* 57–70.

Mann, L. (1981). The baiting crowd in episodes of threatened suicides. *Journal of Personality and Social Psychology, 41,* 703–709.

Manning, M., Heron, J., & Marshall, T. (1978). Styles of hostility and of social interactions at nursery, at school and at home. An extended study of children. In L. A. Hersov & M. Berger (Eds.), *Aggression and anti-social behavior in childhood and adolescence.* Oxford, UK: Pergamon.

Marsh, P., & Collett, P. (1986). *Driving passion: The psychology of the car.* Boston: Faber & Faber.

Marsh, P., Rosser, E., & Harre, R. (1978). *The rules of disorder.* London: Routledge.

Marshall, L. (1994). Physical and psychological abuse. In W. R. Cupach & B. H. Spitzberg (Eds.), *The dark side of interpersonal communication.* Hillsdale, NJ: Erlbaum.

Martin, G., & Pear, J. (1983). *Behavior modification: What it is and how to do it.* Englewood Cliffs, NJ: Prentice Hall.

Martin, P. (1980). The consequences of being abused and neglected: How the child fares. In C. H. Kempe & R. E. Helfer (Eds.), *The battered child.* University of Chicago Press.

Martin, S. E., Sechrest, L., & Redner, R. (1981). *New directions in the rehabilitation of criminal offenders.* Washington, DC: National Academy Press.

Marzagao, L. R. (1972). Systematic desensitization treatment of kleptomania. *Journal of Behavior Therapy and Experimental Psychiatry, 3,* 327–328.

Mason, D. L. (1979). *Fine art of art security—protecting public and private collections against theft, fire, and vandalism.* New York: Van Nostrand Reinhold.

Massucci, J. (1984). School vandalism: A plan of action. *National Association of Secondary School Principals Bulletin, 68,* 18–20.

Matek, O. (1988). Obscene phone callers. *Journal of Social Work and Human Sexuality, 7,* 113–130.

Mathie, J. P., & Schmidt, R. E. (1977). Rehabilitation and one type of arsonist. *Fire and Arson Investigator, 28,* 53–56.

Mayer, G. R., & Butterworth, T. W. (1979). A preventive approach to school violence and vandalism: An experimental study. *Personnel and Guidance Journal, 57,* 436–441.

Mayer, G. R., Butterworth, T., Nafpaktitis, M., & Sulzer-Azaroff, B. (1983). Preventing school vandalism and improving discipline: A three-year study. *Journal of Applied Behavior Analysis, 16,* 355–369.

Mayer, G. R., Nafpaktitis, M., Butterworth, T., & Hollingsworth, P. (1987). A search for the elusive setting events of school vandalism: A correlational study. *Education and Treatment of Children, 10,* 259–270.

Mayer, G. R., & Sulzer-Azaroff, B. (1991). Intervention for vandalism. In G. Stoner, M. R. Shinn, & H. M. Walker (Eds.), *Interventions for achievement and behavior problems.* Silver Spring, MD: National Association of School Psychologists.

McCarthy, B. (1994). Warrior values: A socio-historical survey. In J. Archer (Ed.), *Male violence.* London: Routledge.

McCarthy, J. D. (1991). In C. McPhail (Ed.), *The myth of the madding crowd.* New York: Aldine de Gruyter.

McCown, W. G., Johnson, J. L., & Shure, M. B. (Eds.). (1993). *The impulsive client: Theory, research, and treatment.* Washington, DC: American Psychological Association.

McGuire, J. (1997). "Irrational" shoplifting and models of addiction. In J. E. Hodge, M. McMurran, & C. R. Hollin (Eds.), *Addicted to crime?* West Sussex, UK: Wiley.

McPherson, M., & Carpenter, J. (1981). *Rural youth vandalism in four Minnesota counties.* Minneapolis: Minnesota Crime Prevention Center.

McShane, F. J., & Noonan, B. A. (1993). Classification of shoplifters by cluster analysis. *International Journal of Offender Therapy and Comparative Criminology, 37,* 29–40.

Mead, B. T. (1975). Coping with obscene phone calls. *Medical Aspects of Human Sexuality, 9,* 127–128.

Meloy, J. R. (1992). *Violent attachments.* Northvale, NJ: Jason Aronson.

Meloy, J. R. (1996). Stalking (obsessional following): A review of some preliminary studies. *Aggression and Violent Behavior, 1,* 147–162.

Meloy, J. R. (1998). *The psychology of stalking.* San Diego: Academic Press.

Michalowski, R. J. (1975). Violence in the road: The crime of vehicular homicide. *Journal of Research in Crime and Delinquency, 12,* 30–43.

Miedzian, M. (1992). *Boys will be boys: Breaking the link between masculinity and violence.* New York: Doubleday.

Milgram, S. (1963). Behavioral study of obedience. *Journal of Abnormal and Social Psychology, 67*, 371–378

Miller, P. A., & Eisenberg, N. (1988). The relation of empathy to aggressive and externalizing/antisocial behavior. *Psychological Bulletin, 103*, 324–344.

Miller, W. I. (1993). *Humiliation*. Ithaca, NY: Cornell University Press.

Mitchell, S., & Rosa, P. (1979). Boyhood behavior problems as precursors of criminality: A fifteen-year follow-up study. *Journal of Child Psychology and Psychiatry, 22*, 19–33.

Mills, N. (1997). *The triumph of meanness*. Boston: Houghton Mifflin.

Moffitt, T. E. (1993). Adolescence-limited and life-course-persistent antisocial behavior: A developmental taxonomy. *Psychological Review, 100*, 674–701.

Mooney, A., Creeser, R., & Blatchford, P. (1991). Children's views on teasing and fighting in junior high schools. *Educational Research, 33*, 103–112.

Moore, R. H. (1984). Shoplifting in middle America: Patterns and motivational correlates. *International Journal of Offender Therapy and Comparative Criminology, 28*, 53–64.

Moos, R. H., & Insel, P. M. (1974). *Issues in social ecology*. Palo Alto: National Press Books.

Morreall, J. (1994). Gossip and humor. In R. F. Goodman & A. Ben-Ze'ev (Eds.), *Good gossip*. Lawrence: University Press of Kansas.

Mosher, D. L., & Proenza, L. M. (1969). Intensity of attack, displacement and verbal aggression. *Psychonomic Science, 12*, 359–360.

Munday, R. (1986, February 14). Who are the shoplifters? *New Society*, pp. 274-276.

Nagin, D. S., Farrington, D. P., & Moffitt, T. E. (1995). Life-course trajectories of different types of offenders. *Criminology, 33*, 111–139.

National Institute of Justice. (1997, October). *Research in brief*. Washington, DC: Author.

Neill, S. R. St. J. (1976). Aggressive and non-aggressive fighting in twelve- to thirteen-year-old pre-adolescent boys. *Journal of Child Psychiatry, 17*, 213-220.

Neill, S. R. St. J. (1986). Rough-and-tumble and aggression in school children: Serious play? *Animal Behavior, 33*, 1380–1381.

Nevo, O., Nevo, B., & Derech-Zehavi, A. (1994). The tendency to gossip as a psychological disposition: Constructing a measure and validating it. In R. F. Goodman & A. Ben-Ze'ev (Eds.), *Good gossip*. Lawrence: University Press of Kansas.

New York State Taskforce on Juvenile Gangs. (1990). *Reaffirming prevention*. Albany, NY: Author.

Novaco, R. W. (1991). Aggression on roadways. In R. Baenninger (Ed.), *Targets of violence and aggression*. New York: Elsevier.

Novaco, R. W., Stokols, D. S., & Milanesi, L. (1990). Objective and subjective dimensions of travel impedance as determinants of commuting stress. *American Journal of Community Psychology, 18*, 231–257.

Novelli, J. (1993, July/August). Better behavior for better learning. *Instructor*, pp. 74–79.

Nowakowski, R. (1966). *Vandals and vandalism in the schools: An analysis of vandalism in large school systems and a description of 93 vandals in Dade County schools.* Unpublished doctoral dissertation, University of Miami.

O'Connell, M., & Whelan, A. (1996). Taking wrongs seriously. *British Journal of Criminology, 36*, 299–318.

O'Donnell, J., Hawkins, J. D., & Abbott, R. D. (1995). Predicting serious delinquency and substance use among aggressive boys. *Journal of Consulting and Clinical Psychology, 63*, 529–537.

O'Donohue, W. (1997). Sample lesson plans. In W. O'Donohue (Ed.), *Sexual harassment: Theory, research, and treatment.* Boston: Allyn & Bacon.

Office of Juvenile Justice and Delinquency Prevention. (1997, October). *Juvenile Justice Bulletin.* Washington, DC : Author.

O'Hair, H. D., & Cody, M. J. (1994). Deception. In W. R. Cupach & B. H. Spitzberg (Eds.), *The dark side of interpersonal communication.* Hillsdale, NJ: Erlbaum.

Oldfield, M. (1956). *The cat in the mysteries of magic and religion.* New York: Castle Books.

Olweus, D. (1978). *Aggression in the schools: Bullies and whipping boys.* New York: Wiley.

Olweus, D. (1984). Aggressors and their victims: Bullying at school. In N. Frude & H. Gault (Eds.), *Disruptive behavior in schools.* New York: Wiley.

Olweus, D. (1987). Bully/victim problems among school children. In J. P. Myklebust & R. Ommundsen (Eds.), *Psykologprofesjonen mot ar 2000.* Oslo: Universitetsforlget.

Olweus, D. (1989). Prevalence and incidence in the study of anti-social behavior: Definitions and measurements. In M. Klein (Ed.), *Cross-national research in self-reported crime and delinquency.* Dordrecht, The Netherlands: Kluwer.

Olweus, D. (1991). Bully/victim problems among school children: Basic facts and effects of a school-based intervention program. In D. Pepler & K. H. Rubin (Eds.), *The development and treatment of childhood aggression.* Hillsdale, NJ: Erlbaum.

Olweus, D. (1993). *Bullying at school: What we know and what we can do.* Oxford, UK: Blackwell.

O'Moore, A. M. (1997). What do teachers need to know? In M. Elliott (Ed.), *Bullying: A practical guide to coping for schools.* London: Pitman.

Pablant, P., & Baxter, J. C. (1975). Environmental correlates of school vandalism. *Journal of the American Institute of Planners, 41*, 270–279.

Palmer, C. J. (1996). Violence and other forms of victimization in residence halls: Perspectives of resident assistants. *Journal of College Student Development, 37*, 268–277.

Paludi, M. A. (1997). Sexual harassment in schools. In W. O'Donohue (Ed.), *Sexual harassment: Theory, research, and treatment.* Boston: Allyn & Bacon.

Panko, W. L. (1978). *Taxonomy of school vandalism.* Unpublished doctoral dissertation, University of Pittsburgh.

Parry, M. (1968). *Aggression on the road.* London: Tavistock.

Patterson, G. R. (1992). Developmental changes in antisocial behavior. In R. De V. Peters, R. J. McMahon, & V. L. Quinsey (Eds.), *Aggression and violence throughout the lifespan.* Thousand Oaks, CA: Sage.

Pearce, J. (1997). What can be done about the bully? In M. Elliott (Ed.), *Bullying: A practical guide to coping for schools.* London: Pitman.

Pellegrini, A. D. (1988). Elementary-school children's rough-and-tumble play and social competence. *Developmental Psychology, 24,* 802–806.

Pellegrini, A. D. (1994). The rough play of adolescent boys of differing sociometric status. *International Journal of Behavioural Development, 17,* 525–540.

Pellegrini, A. D. (1995). A longitudinal study of boys' rough-and-tumble play and dominance during early adolescence. *Journal of Applied Developmental Psychology, 16,* 77–93.

Pepler, D. J., Craig, W. M., Ziegler, S., & Charach, A. (1994). An evaluation of an anti-bullying intervention in Toronto schools. *Canadian Journal of Community Mental Health, 13,* 95–110.

Pernanen, K. (1991). *Alcohol in human violence.* New York: Guilford.

Perry, D. G., Williard, J. C., & Perry, L. C. (1990). Peers' perceptions of the consequences that victimized children provide aggressors. *Child Development, 61,* 1310–1325.

Plas, J. M. (1986). *Systems psychology in the schools.* New York: Pergamon.

Plous, S. (1993). Psychological mechanisms in the human use of animals. *Journal of Social Issues, 49,* 11–52.

Porter, G. V. (1980). *The control of vandalism in urban recreation facilities: A revision of the defensible space model.* Unpublished doctoral dissertation, Boston University.

Potegal, M., & Davidson, R. J. (1997). Young children's post tantrum affiliation with their parents. *Aggressive Behavior, 23,* 329–341.

Prentky, R. A., & Carter, D. L. (1984). The predictive value of the triad for sex offenders. *Behavioral Science and the Law, 2,* 341–354.

Rainwater, L. (1966). *Behind ghetto walls: Black families in a Federal slum.* Chicago: Aldine.

Ramey, D. T. (1981). *Group climate, campus image and attitudes of fraternity men regarding pledge hazing.* Unpublished doctoral dissertation, Indiana University, Bloomington.

Raush, H. L. (1965). Interaction sequences. *Journal of Personality and Social Psychology, 2,* 487–499.

Rautaheimo, J. (1989). The making of an arsonist. *Fire Prevention, 223,* 30–35.

Ray, J. (1987, April). Every twelfth shopper: Who shoplifts and why? *Social Caseworker,* pp. 234–239.

Reed, N. H. (1981). *Psychopathic delinquency, empathy, and helping behavior.* Unpublished doctoral dissertation, Loyola University, Chicago.

Reiss, A. J. (1985). *Policing a city's central district: The Oakland story.* Washington, DC: U. S. Department of Justice.

Reit, S. V. (1985). *Sibling rivalry.* New York: Ballantine.

Richards, P. (1976). *Patterns of middle class vandalism: A case study of suburban adolescence.* Unpublished doctoral dissertation, Northwestern University, Evanston, IL.

Richardson, D. R. (1999). What is indirect aggression? Discriminating between direct and indirect aggression. *Aggressive Behavior, 25,* 30.

Richmond, D. R. (1987). Putting an end to fraternity hazing. *NASPA Journal, 24,* 48–52.

Rigby, K., & Cox, I. (1996). The contribution of bullying at school and low self-esteem to acts of delinquency among Australian teenagers. *Personality and Individual Differences, 2,* 609–612.

Rigby, K., & O'Brien, M. (1992). *The influence of family factors on bully/victim behaviour.* Unpublished manuscript, Sydney, Australia.

Rivers, I., & Smith, P. K. (1994). Types of bullying behaviors and their correlates. *Aggressive Behavior, 20,* 359–368.

Roff, J.D., & Wirt, R. D. (1984). Childhood aggression and social adjustments as antecedents of delinquency. *Journal of Abnormal Child Psychology, 12,* 111–126.

Rohe, W. M., & Burby, R. J. (1988). Fear of crime in public housing. *Environment and Behavior, 20,* 700–720.

Rohner, R. P., & Rohner, R. P. (1980). Antecedents and consequences of parental rejection: A theory of emotional abuse. *Child Abuse and Neglect, 4,* 189–198.

Roland, E. (1989). A system oriented strategy against bullying. In E. Roland & E. Munthe (Eds.), *Bullying: An international perspective.* London: Fulton.

Roland, E. (1993). Bullying: A developing tradition of research and management. In D. Tattum (Ed.), *Understanding and managing bullying.* Oxford, England: Heinemann Educational.

Roscoe, B., Strause, J. S., & Goodwin, M. P. (1992). Sexual harassment: Early adolescents' self-reports of experiences and acceptance. *Adolescence, 29,* 515–522.

Rose, A. M., & Prell, A. E. (1955). Does the punishment fit the crime? A study in social valuation. *American Journal of Sociology, 61,* 247–259.

Rosow, J. M. (1975). *The worker and the job.* Englewood Cliffs, NJ: Prentice Hall.

Ross, D. M. (1996). *Childhood bullying and teasing: What school personnel, other professionals, and parents can do.* Alexandria, VA: American Counseling Association.

Rossi, P. H., Waite, E., Bose, C. E., & Berk, R. E. (1974). The seriousness of crimes: Normative structure and individual differences. *American Sociological Review, 39,* 224–237.

Rubel, R. J. (1977). *Unruly schools: Disorders, disruptions, and crimes.* Lexington, MA: D. C. Health.

Russell, D. H. (1973). Emotional aspects of shoplifting. *Psychiatric Annals, 3,* 77–79.

Sabella, R. A., & Myrick, R. D. (1995). Peer facilitators confront sexual harassment. *The Peer Facilitator Quarterly, 13,* 17–23.

Sacco, V. F. (1985). Shoplifting prevention: The role of communication-based intervention strategies. *Canadian Journal of Criminology, 27,* 15–29.

Salisbury, J., & Jackson, D. (1996). *Challenging macho values: Practical ways of working with adolescent boys.* London: Falmer Press.

Salmivalli, C., Karhunen, J., & Lagerspetz, K. M. (1996). How do the victims respond to bullying? *Aggressive Behavior, 22,* 99–109.

Salmivalli, C., Lagerspetz, K. M., Bjorkqvist, K. L., Osterman, K., & Kaukiainen, A. (1996). Bullying as a group process: Participant roles and their relationship to social status in the group. *Aggressive Behavior, 22,* 1–15.

Sampson, R. J., & Laub, J. H. (1993). *Crime in the making.* Cambridge: Harvard University Press.

Sandler, B., & Paludi, M. (1993). *Educator's guide to controlling sexual harassment.* Washington, DC: Thompson.

Sartin, P. (1970). *L'homme au travail, forçat du temps?* Paris: Gamma.

Saunders, D. G., Lynch, A. B., Grayson, M., & Linz, D. (1987). The inventory of beliefs about wife beating. *Violence and Victims, 2,* 39–57.

Savitz, L. (1986). Obscene phone calls. In T. F. Hartnagel & R. A. Silverman (Eds.), *Critique and explanation: Essays in humor of Gwynne Nettler.* New Brunswick, NJ: Transaction Books.

Schafer, M., & Smith, P. K. (1996). Teachers' perceptions of play fighting and real fighting in primary school. *Educational Research, 38,* 173–181.

Schwartz, S., & Wood, H. V. (1991). Clinical assessment and intervention with shoplifters. *Social Work, 36,* 234–238.

Scrimger, G. C., & Elder, R. (1981). *Alternative to vandalism—"Cooperation or wreakreation."* Sacramento: California Office of the Attorney General School Safety Center.

Sechrest, D. K. (1969). Comparison of inmates' and staff's judgments of the severity of offenses. *Journal of Research in Crime and Delinquency, 6,* 41–55.

Sellin, T., & Wolfgang, M. R. (1964). *The measurement of delinquency.* New York: Wiley.

Selman, R. L. (1980). *The growth of interpersonal understanding: Developmental and clinical analyses.* New York: Academic.

Shapiro, J. P., Baumeister, R. F., & Kessler, J. W. (1991). A three-component model of children's teasing: Aggression, humor, and ambiguity. *Journal of Social and Clinical Psychology, 10,* 459–472.

Sharkey, W. F. (1997). Why would anyone want to intentionally embarrass me? In R. M. Kowalski (Ed.), *Aversive interpersonal behavior.* New York: Plenum.

Shaw, W. (1973). Vandalism is not senseless. *Law and Order, 12,* 14–19.

Sheffield, C. J. (1989). The invisible intruder: Women's experience of obscene phone calls. *Gender and Society, 3,* 483–488.

Skogan, W. G. (1990). *Disorder and decline.* Berkeley: University of California Press.

Skogan, W. G., & Maxfield, M. G. (1981). *Coping with crime: Individual and neighborhood reactions.* Newbury Park, CA: Sage.

Skolnick, J., & Bailey, D. (1986). *The new blue line.* New York: Free Press.

Slee, P. T. (1993). Bullying: A preliminary investigation of its nature and the effects of social cognition. *Early Child Development and Care, 87,* 47–57.

Smith, M. D., & Morra, N. N. (1994). Obscene and threatening telephone calls to women: Data from a Canadian national survey. *Gender and Society, 8,* 584–596.

Smith, P. K., & Levan, S. (1995). Perceptions and experiences of bullying in younger pupils. *British Journal of Educational Psychology, 65,* 489–500.

Smith, P. K., & Lewis, K. (1985). Rough-and-tumble play, fighting and chasing in nursery school children. *Ethology and Sociobiology, 6,* 175–181.

Smith, P. K., & Sharp, S. (1994a). The problem of school bullying. In P. K. Smith & S. Sharp (Eds.), *School bullying: Insights and perspectives.* London: Routledge.

Smith, P. K., & Sharp, S. (1994b). *School bullying: Insights and perspectives.* London: Routledge.

Smith, R. P., & Taylor, C. M. (1985). Irritability: Definition, assessment and associated factors. *British Journal of Psychiatry, 147,* 127–136.

Soloman, G. S., & Ray, J. B. (1984). Irrational beliefs of shoplifters. *Journal of Clinical Psychology, 40,* 1075–1077.

Sommer, K. L., & Baumeister, R. F. (1997). Making someone feel guilty: Causes, strategies, and consequences. In R. M. Kowalski (Ed.), *Aversive interpersonal behavior.* New York: Plenum.

Sparks, R., Genn, H., & Dodd, D. (1977). *Surveying victims.* London: Wiley.

Stattin, H., & Magnusson, D. (1989). The role of early aggressive behavior in the frequency, seriousness, and types of later crimes. *Journal of Consulting and Clinical Psychology, 57,* 710–718.

Stefanko, M. S. (1989). *Rates of secondary school vandalism and violence: Trends, demographic differences, and the effects of the attitudes and behaviors of principals.* Unpublished doctoral dissertation: Claremont College, Claremont, CA.

Steffensmeier, D. J., & Terry, R.M. (1973). Deviance and respectability: An observational study of reactions to shoplifting. *Social Forces, 51,* 417–426.

Stein, N. (1995). Sexual harassment in school: The public performances of gendered violence. *Harvard Educational Review, 65,* 145–162.

Stephenson, P., & Smith, D. (1997). Why some schools don't have bullies. In M. Elliott (Ed.), *Bullying: A practical guide to coping for schools.* London: Pitman.

Stets, J. E. (1990). Verbal and physical aggression in marriage. *Journal of Marriage and the Family, 52,* 501–514.

Stinchcombe, A. L., Adams, R., Heimer, C., Scheppele, K., Smith, T., & Taylor, D. G. (1980). *Crime and punishment in public opinion.* San Francisco: Jossey-Bass.

Stoner, G., Shinn, M. R., & Walker, H. M. (Eds.). (1991). *Intervention for achievement and behavior problems.* Silver Spring, MD: National Association of School Psychologists.

Stover, D. (1990, November). How to be safe and secure against school vandalism. *The Executive Educator,* pp. 20–30.

Straus, M. A. (1974). Leveling, civility, and violence in the family. *Journal of Marriage and the Family, 35,* 13–29.

Straus, M. A., & Sweet, S. (1992). Verbal/symbolic aggression in couples: Incidence rates and relationships to personal characteristics. *Journal of Marriage and the Family, 54,* 346–357.

Strauss, S. (1994). Sexual harassment at an early age. *Principal, 74*(1), 26–30.

Suedfeld, P. (1990). *Psychology and torture.* New York: Hemisphere.

Sutton, J., & Smith, P. K. (1999). Bullying as a group process: An adaptation to the participant role approach. *Aggressive Behavior, 25,* 97–111.

Suls, J. M. (1977). Gossip as social comparison, *Journal of Communication, 27,* 164–168.

Szwed, J. F. (1966). Gossip, drinking, and social control: Consensus and communication in a Newfoundland parish. *Ethnology, 5,* 434–441.

Tannen, D. (1998). *The argument culture.* New York: Random House.

Taylor, G. (1994). Gossip as moral talk. In R. F. Goodman & A. Ben-Ze'ev (Eds.), *Good gossip.* Lawrence: University Press of Kansas.

Taylor, R. B., & Gottfredson, S. (1986). Environmental design, crime, and prevention: An examination of community dynamics. In A. J. Reiss & M. Tonry (Eds.), *Communities and crime.* University of Chicago Press.

Taylor, R. B., & Hall, M. M. (1986). Testing alternative models of fear of crime. *Journal of Criminology and Criminal Law, 77,* 151–189.

Taylor, S. P., Shuntich, R. J., & Greenberg, A. (1979). The effects of repeated aggressive encounters on subsequent aggressive behavior. *The Journal of Social Psychology, 107,* 199–208.

Thomas, C. W., & Bilchik, S. (1985). Prosecuting juveniles in criminal courts: A legal and empirical analysis. *Journal of Criminal Law and Criminology, 76,* 439–479.

Thompson, J. K., Fabian, L. J., Moulton, D. O., Dunn, M. E., & Altabe, M. N. (1991). Development and validation of the physical appearance related teasing scale. *Journal of Personality Assessment, 56,* 513–521.

Thurstone, L. (1927). The method of paired comparisons for social values. *Journal of Abnormal and Social Psychology, 21,* 384–400.

Till, F. (1980). *Sexual harassment: A report on the sexual harassment of students.* Washington, DC: National Advisory Council on Women's Education.

Tizard, B., Blatchford, P., Burke, J., Farquahar, C., & Plewis, I. (1988). *Young children at school in the inner city.* London: Erlbaum.

Tjaden, P., & Thoennes, N. (1998, April). Stalking in America: Findings from the national violence against women survey. *Research in Brief.* Washington, DC: National Institute of Justice.

Toch, H. (1986). True to you, darling, in my fashion: The notion of contingent consistency. In A. Campbell & J. J. Gibbs (Eds.), *Violent transactions: The limits of personality.* Oxford: Basil Blackwell.

Treschman, A. E. (1969). Understanding the stages of a typical temper tantrum. In A. E. Treschman, J. K. Whittaker, & L. K. Brendtro (Eds.), *The other 23 hours.* New York: Aldine.

Tuppern, C. J. S., & Gaitan, A. (1989). Constructing accounts of aggressive episodes. *Social Behavior, 4,* 127–143.

Turner, C. B., & Cashdan, S. (1988). Perception of college students' motives for shoplifting. *Psychological Reports, 62,* 855–862.

Tygert, C. (1988). Public school vandalism: Toward a synthesis of theories and transition to paradigm analysis. *Adolescence, 23,* 187–199.

U. S. Merit Systems Protection Board. (1981). *Sexual harassment in the federal workplace: Is it a problem?* Washington, DC: U. S. Government Printing Office.

Vangelisti, A. L. (1994). Messages that hurt. In W. R. Cupach & B. H. Spitzberg (Eds.), *The dark side of interpersonal communication.* Hillsdale, NJ: Erlbaum.

Van Houten, R. (1982). Punishment: From the animal laboratory to the applied setting. In S. Axelrod & J. Apsche (Eds.), *The effects and side effects of punishment on human behavior.* New York: Academic.

Vermeulen, H., & Odendaal, J. J. (1993). Proposed typology of companion animal abuse. *Anthrozoös, 6,* 248–257.

Vestermark, S. D., & Blauvelt, P. D. (1978). *Controlling crime in the school: A complete security handbook for administrators.* West Nyack, NY: Parker.

Vetter, H. J. (1969). *Language behavior and communication: An introduction.* Itasca, IL: Peacock.

Viemero, V. (1996). Factors in childhood that predict later criminal behavior. *Aggressive Behavior, 22,* 87–97.

Vissing, Y. M., Straus, M. A., Gelles, R. J., & Harrop, J. W. (1991). Verbal aggression by parents and psychological problems of children. *Child Abuse and Neglect, 15,* 223–238.

Walker, H. M. (1995). *The acting-out child.* Longmont, CO: Sopris West.

Walker, L. (1979). *The battered women.* New York: Harper & Row.

Walker, L. (1983). The battered woman syndrome study. In D. Finkelhor, R. Gelles, G. Hotaling, & M. Straus (Eds.), *The dark side of families.* Thousand Oaks, CA: Sage.

Walker, L., & Meloy, J. R. (1998). Stalking and domestic violence. In J. R. Meloy (Ed.), *The psychology of stalking.* San Diego: Academic.

Walker, M. A. (1978). Measuring the seriousness of crimes. *British Journal of Criminology, 18,* 348–364.

Walker, W. D., Rowes, R. C., & Quinsey, V. L. (1993). Authoritarianism and sexual aggression. *Journal of Personality and Social Psychology, 65,* 1036–1045.

Walsh, D. P. (1978). *Shoplifting: Controlling a major crime.* New York: Holmes & Meier.

Ward, C. (Ed.). (1973). *Vandalism.* London: Architectural Press.

Warm, T. R. (1997). The role of teasing in development and vice versa. *Developmental and Behavioral Pediatrics, 18,* 97–101.

Warner, P. K. (1988). Aural assault: Obscene telephone calls. *Qualitative Sociology, 11,* 302–318.

Warr, M. (1989). What is the perceived seriousness of crime? *Criminology, 27,* 795–819.

Weeks, S. (1976). Security against vandalism: It takes facts, feelings and facilities. *American School and University, 48,* 36–46.

Wehby, J. H., Symons, F. J., & Shores, R. E. (1995). A descriptive analysis of aggressive behavior in classrooms for children with emotional and behavioral disorders. *Behavioral Disorders, 20,* 87–105.

Weinmayer, V. M. (1969). Vandalism by design: A critique. *Landscape Architecture, 59,* 286.

Weisfeld, G. (1994). Aggression and dominance in the social world of boys. In J. Archer (Ed.), *Male violence.* London: Routledge.

White, G. L., & Mullen, P. D. (1989). *Jealousy: Theory, research, and clinical strategies.* New York: Guilford.

White, J., & Fallis, A. (1980). *Vandalism prevention programs used in Ontario schools.* Toronto: Ontario Ministry of Education.

Whitlock, F. A. (1971). *Death on the road: A study in social violence.* London: Tavistock.

Wiesenthal, D. L. (1990). Psychological aspects of vandalism. In P. J. D. Drenth, J. A. Sergeant, & R. J. Takens (Eds.), *European perspectives in psychology* (Vol. 3). New York: Wiley.

Williams, D. E., & Schaller, K. A. (1993). Peer persuasions: A study of children's dominance strategies. *Early Child Development and Care, 88,* 31–41.

Williams, K. D. (1997). Social ostracism. In R. M. Kowalski (Ed.), *Aversive interpersonal behaviors.* New York: Plenum.

Williams, K. D., Sherman-Williams, B., & Faulkner, S. (1996). [A survey of a representative U. S. sample on the incidence of using the silent treatment]. Unpublished raw data.

Williams, K. D., & Sommer, K. L. (1997). Social ostracism by co-workers: Does rejection lead to loafing or competition? *Personality and Social Psychology Bulletin, 23,* 693–706.

Wilmot, W. W. (1987). *Dyadic communication.* New York: Random House.

Wilson, J. Q. (1986). The urban unease: Community versus the city. *The Public Interest, 12,* 25–39.

Wilson, J. Q., & Kelling, G. L. (1982, March). Broken windows: The police and neighborhood safety. *Atlantic,* pp. 29–38.

Wilson, J. Q., & Petersilia, J. (1995). *Crime.* San Francisco: Institute for Contemporary Studies Press.

Wilson, R. (1977). Vandalism and design. *The Architect's Journal, 166,* 795–798.

Wilson, S. (1979). Observations on the nature of vandalism. In P. Bural (Ed.), *Designing against vandalism.* New York: Van Nostrand Reinhold.

Wise, J. (1982, September). A gentle deterrent to vandalism. *Psychology Today,* pp. 28–31.

Woffordt, S., Mihalic, D. E., & Menard, S. (1994). Continuities in marital violence. *Journal of Family Violence, 9,* 195–225.

Wolf, Y., Moav, Y., & Silfen, P. (1991). Judgments of verbal and physical aggression: An integrative perspective. *Crime and Social Deviance, 18,* 39–62.

Wolfgang, M., Figlio, R., Tracy, P., & Singer, S. (1985). *The national surveys of crime severity.* Washington, DC: U. S. Department of Justice.

Wood, D. (1991). In defense of indefensible space. In P. J. Brantingham & P. L. Brantingham (Eds.), *Environmental criminology.* Prospect Heights, IL: Waveland.

Yaffe, E. (1995, November). Expensive, illegal, and wrong: Sexual harassment in our schools. *Phi Delta Kappan,* pp. 1–15.

Yambert, P. A., & Donow, C. F. (1984). Are we ready for ecological commandments? *Journal of Environmental Education, 3,* 13–16.

Yankelovich, D. (1975, April). How students control their drug crisis. *Psychology Today,* pp. 39–42.

Yates, E. (1986). The influence of psycho-social factors on non-sensical shoplifting. *International Journal of Offender Therapy and Comparative Criminology, 30,* 203–211.

Zimbardo, P. G. (1969). The human choice: Individuation, reason and order versus deindividuation, impulse and chaos. In W. J. Arnold & D. Levine (Eds.), *Nebraska symposium on motivation.* Lincoln: University of Nebraska Press.

Zimbardo, P. G. (1973). A field experiment in auto-stripping. In C.Ward (Ed.), *Vandalism.* London: Architectural Press.

Zona, M. A., Palarea, R. E., & Lane, J. C., Jr. (1998). Psychiatric diagnosis and the offender-victim typology of stalking. In J. R. Meloy (Ed.), *The psychology of stalking.* San Diego: Academic.

Zweig, A., & Ducey, M. H. (1978). *A paradigmatic field: A review of research on school vandalism.* Hackensack, NJ: National Council on Crime and Delinquency.

Zwier, G., & Vaughn, G. M. (1984). Three ideological orientations in school vandalism research. *Review of Educational Research, 54,* 263–292.

Name Index

Subject Index

About the Author

Arnold P. Goldstein joined the clinical psychology section of Syracuse University's Psychology Department in 1963 and both taught there and directed its Psychotherapy Center until 1980. In 1981, he founded the Center for Research on Aggression, which he currently directs. He joined Syracuse University's Division of Special Education in 1985 and in 1990 helped organize and codirect the New York State Taskforce on Juvenile Gangs. Dr. Goldstein has a career-long interest, as both researcher and practitioner, in difficult-to-reach clients. Since 1980, his main research and psychoeducational focus has been youth violence. Dr. Goldstein's many books include, among others, *Delinquents on Delinquency; The Gang Intervention Handbook; Break It Up: A Teacher's Guide to Managing Student Aggression;* and the recently revised editions of *Skillstreaming the Adolescent: New Strategies and Perspectives for Teaching Prosocial Skills; Aggression Replacement Training: A Comprehensive Intervention for Aggressive Youth;* and *The Prepare Curriculum: Teaching Prosocial Competencies.*